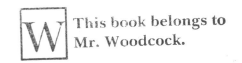
This book belongs to
Mr. Woodcock.

MORE
MONTANA
CAMPFIRE
TALES

fifteen historical na

D0873491

Dave Walter

FARCOUNTRY
PRESS

Helena, Montana

For Amanda and Emily:

Recipients of the torch;

protectors of the land.

This book may not be reproduced in whole or in part by any means
(with the exception of short quotes for the purpose of review)
without the permission of the publisher.
For more information on our books write:
Farcountry Press, P.O. Box 5630, Helena, MT 59601
or call: (800) 654-1105 or visit farcountrypress.com
Created, produced, and designed in the United States of America.
Printed in United States of America.

ISBN 1-56037-236-2

CONTENTS

INTRODUCTION

The introduction to *Montana Campfire Tales* (1997) suggests that Montana history is like a complex mosaic. The larger pieces represent major events/themes like the Battle of the Little Big Horn and the homesteading boom/bust. The smaller shards provide less-well-known stories, but are packed with color, detail, context, warmth, and humor.

By that simile, *More Montana Campfire Tales* adds to the field mass of smaller shards. Bertie Miller's cross-dressing exploits provide insights into the social realities of 1890s Montana life. The story of the Blackfeet's "Ceded Strip" offers background to what remains a most contentious issue in the twenty-first century. The Plentywood radicals amaze and confound—and remind the reader of complexities his seventh-grade Montana-history class ignored. These fifteen tales are renderings of lesser-known, but no less important, Montana happenings. They are investigations into the intriguing and the remarkable.

In May of 1931, "Tertius" Clark—the wealthy 29-year-old grandson of "Copper King" William Andrews Clark—produced and directed a month-long pack trip into primitive country that would become the Bob Marshall Wilderness and the Scapegoat Wilderness. The trip recalled similar mountain treks in which members of the Clark family had engaged since the turn of the century. Tertius sought

> ...to photograph, in natural colors, the scenic beauty and the wild game of the primitive country we had in the past covered by trail. And, perhaps more important, to lead a life in the wilderness with all of the "populous solitude" of the darkness and isolation that yawned on every side.

Tertius engaged an outfitter and a camp-tender and arranged for lavish amounts of supplies to be trucked to the Seeley Lake trailhead by the Missoula Mercantile Company. In addition to several still cameras, Tertius packed two 16-mm. Kodacolor cameras for motion-picture work.

For a month, the Clark party trailed through the headwaters of the South Fork of the Flathead, over the Chinese Wall, and into the Sun River Valley, before returning to the Clearwater. They climbed mountains, fished, shot exquisite photographs and movies, and explored hidden fastnesses.

Nightly the men gathered around the campfire, ate sumptuous meals, played cards, and told stories. They very well could have recounted Paul Boyton's river exploits, or the Great Grey Cliff Train Robbery, or the Overland Westerners epic trek, or the killing of Tom Manning. Whatever the tales they told, their camaraderie grew and deepened over their evening fires and conversations.

Tertius died in a spectacular airplane crash in Arizona a year later. Between the 1931 party's joyful emergence at Holland Lake Lodge and his 1932 death, Clark edited his journal from the Montana pack trip into a typescript entitled "Our Last Frontier"—five copies of which survive.

Tertius' title alone prompts scores of questions. Whether named from thoughtful insight or arrogance, "Our Last Frontier" provides yet another amazing Montana campfire tale. And those tales are vital to the larger story of Montana history. They are our stories.

They are full of adventure and recognizable detail. They occur just close enough to home that we can see ourselves in the settings, in the tragedies, in the questions, and in the issues. They enliven the evenings around our own campfires—however remote or urban. Enjoy some *More Montana Campfire Tales*.

One incurs a legion of debts in the course of assembling this type of reader. Most of these pieces appeared first in the bimonthly *Montana Magazine*. To two long-suffering editors at the magazine I owe much: Carolyn Cunningham and Beverly Magley. In instance after instance, they made me a better writer with their involvement and advice and concern. Immense thanks to you both.

An equally overwhelming debt I owe to an institution. The Montana Historical Society has employed me for more than two decades, providing me with the materials and the opportunity to pursue my love of Montana history. Society colleagues and patrons have proven a consistent source of research ideas, sound advice, and caring comment. Thank you all.

Throughout my writing career, I have had the privilege of working with excellent editors. None exceeds the technical skill, the historical knowledge, and the perception of Barbara Fifer. I am grateful for her expertise, for her enthusiasm, and particularly for her friendship. Thank you so much, Barbara.

Every writer owes much to his family, from whom he steals time to pursue his craft. My daughters, Emily and Amanda, are quickest to remind me of this theft! Nevertheless the psychological damage they have suffered appears, at this point, to be minimal. I am very grateful to them for their humor and support. Similarly my wife, Marcella, remains my most honest and, therefore, my most valuable critic. None of this work would have been possible without her encouragement, forbearance, and review. Thank you, dear, once again.

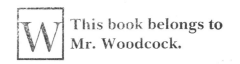

CHAPTER ONE

"WHAT I DID WITH MY SUMMER VACATION"
EMMA COWAN IN YELLOWSTONE NATIONAL PARK, 1877

The National Park, or Geyser Land, is a tract of land 55 by 65 miles in extent, situated at the sources of the Madison and Yellowstone Rivers. It is in the northwestern part of Wyoming Territory, about 300 miles southeast of Helena, the Capital of Montana Territory.

Owing to its many wonders, Congress has set it aside from pre-emption, and reserved it as a park for the Nation. It is of late becoming prominent as an object of interest to tourists.

Frank D. Carpenter, Adventures in Geyser Land, *1878*

Emma Carpenter Cowan's spirits soared as she packed provisions into the spring wagon. Although it was only early August, the summer of 1877 already had become interminably hot and dry. Moreover, the Cowans and everyone else in the small mining town of Radersburg—nestled in the Elkhorn Mountains, nine miles west of Toston—were suffering a horrendous grasshopper plague. So, when Emma's brother Frank Carpenter suggested a trip to the new Yellowstone National Park, the young housewife could not leave her sweltering, sealed-up home quickly enough.

The Yellowstone "Wonderland" always had fascinated 24-year-old Emma. When the Carpenter family had settled in Virginia City in 1864, they befriended an old trapper. The mountain man told miraculous stories of boiling rivers, exploding geysers, bubbling pools of colored mud, exquisite terrace formations, and an omnipresent pall of sulphur that challenged their imaginations.

Emma had never forgotten those tales. And she had made her first trip to explore Yellowstone's dazzling marvels in 1873—the year after Congress created the nation's (and the world's) first national park.

Emma Cowan anticipated her second trip to the "Wonderland" even more because she could share it with George, her husband of almost two years. This 35-year-old Civil War veteran had arrived in Helena in 1865 and passed the Montana bar in 1872. In 1877 he was successfully practicing law in Boulder, Radersburg, and Helena.

Nine adventurers trailed out of Radersburg on August 5, including Emma and George Cowan; Emma's 27-year-old bother Frank, a mining developer from Helena; and Emma's 13-year-old sister Ida, who served as Emma's female companion.

In addition, Frank brought along three of his young Helena friends: A. J. Arnold, a mining speculator; William Dingee, who owned the Pony Saloon; and Albert Oldham, a gunsmith and music teacher.

Two residents of Radersburg completed the party: Charles Mann, the Jefferson County district-court clerk, an accomplished artist, and a Cowan family friend; Henry Myers, a middle-aged teamster and handyman, hired as a cook for the excursion.

The vacationers had planned on almost a month in the national park, plus about a week's travel each way. So they packed foodstuffs, tents, camping equipment, fishing tackle, guns, musical instruments, and clothing in a two-horse spring wagon and in a double-seated carriage. Four saddle horses—including "Bird," Emma's pony that she rode side-saddle—and George Cowan's dog, Dido, complemented the troupe.

In the hot, dry weather, the tourists averaged 30 miles a day. Their route ran from Radersburg to the Three Forks of the Missouri, then up the Jefferson River, and across the divide into the Madison Valley.

At Sterling, the party heard rumors of Indian trouble—a Nez Perce uprising in Idaho Territory. Yet, as Emma recalled

Emma and George Cowan in later years.
Photos courtesy of Montana Historical Society, Helena

("Reminiscences of Pioneer Life," *Contributions to the Historical Society of Montana,* Vol. 4, 1903, 161):

> Although some advised us not to go farther, we did not think it anything more than an old-time Indian scare. And when morning came, bright and beautiful, we decided to go on our way.

The decision seemed reasonable. Since the defeat of George Armstrong Custer's men at the Battle of the Little Big Horn the preceding summer, federal troops had inundated the country. Most native bands had been forced onto reservations or had been chased by the Army into Canada.

Where the Madison River turns east, the party left the riverside road and followed dimmer ruts south, through the Raynolds Pass defile, to Henry's Lake in Idaho Territory. For three days the vacationers amused themselves spearing fish, hunting birds and deer, and exploring. On August 13 they left Henry's Lake, crossed over Targhee Pass, entered Yellowstone Park through its present-day West Entrance, and rejoined the Madison River.

That evening the party met two grizzled mountain prospectors, Wood and Hicks. This pair had just traveled through the geyser basins with U.S. Army General William T. Sherman and his sightseeing party of twelve. At that time, the general's detail was leaving the Park via the Yellowstone River to Fort Ellis, near Bozeman.

By mid-August, the "Radersburg Nine" had established a base camp in the Lower Geyser Basin, along the Firehole River, near Fountain Geyser. Emma recounted (*Contributions,* 163-164):

> We were in fine health and enjoying the outdoor life to the utmost. We seemed to be in a world of our own....Neither mail nor news of any sort had reached us since leaving the ranches on the Madison....One can scarcely realize the intense solitude which then pervaded this land, fresh from the Maker's hand as it were....We had at last reached Wonderland.

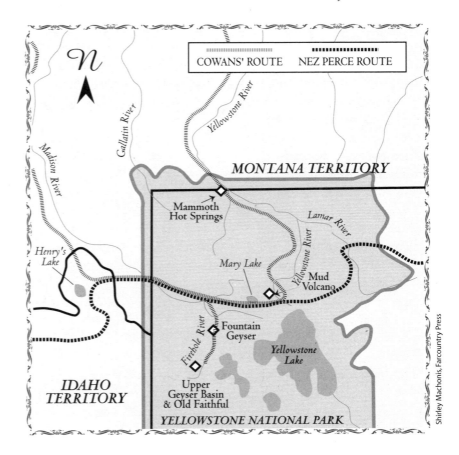

COWANS' ROUTE   NEZ PERCE ROUTE

Gallatin River

Yellowstone River

Madison River

MONTANA TERRITORY

Mammoth
Hot Springs

Lamar River

Henry's
Lake

Mary Lake

Yellowstone River

Mud
Volcano

Firehole River

Fountain
Geyser

Yellowstone
Lake

IDAHO
TERRITORY

Upper
Geyser Basin
& Old Faithful

YELLOWSTONE NATIONAL PARK

Shirley Machonis, Farcountry Press

On August 17 the party left their baggage wagon and trailed into the Upper Geyser Basin. The Bear Gulch miner George Huston accompanied the party on this side trip, serving as guide. The carefree group quickly settled into camp near Castle Geyser, just north of Old Faithful.

The preceding week Huston also had met the Sherman party, from whom he had learned of the Big Hole Battle on August 9. In that predawn Army attack on the sleeping Nez Perce encampment, 87 natives were killed, 33 of them warriors. Sherman's people did not know where the remaining 700 tribesmen—driving nearly 2,000 head of stock—had gone.

But Huston was not worried. To his Radersburg charges he passed on General Sherman's assurance that the Indians would not enter the area, because "their superstitious minds associate [it] with hell, by reason of its geysers and hot-springs."

For three days, under Huston's leadership, Emma and her friends visited the dazzling sensations of the Upper Geyser Basin, each one more amazing than the last. Others in the group ventured to see Yellowstone Lake and Falls. On August 23 the Cowans and their friends reunited beside Fountain Geyser—including Dido, who had never left the baggage wagon. That evening the tourists discussed whether they should extend their 10-day stay in "Wonderland." However, Emma noted (*Contributions*, 166):

> Home seemed a very desirable place just at this particular time, and we decided with one accord to break camp in the morning, with a view of reaching it as soon as possible.

Her brother Frank added (*Adventures in Geyser Land,* 89):

> This being our last night in the Basin, we instituted a grand jollification. The guitar and violin are produced and music, singing, and dancing follow. [Charles] Mann makes a sketch of the camp, with [Albert] Oldham conspicuous in his Indian costume, in which we have dressed him for the occasion.
>
> We finish the evening's entertainment with a "pigeon wing" from [William] Dingee, a "double shuffle" from [A. J.] Arnold, and a song in full chorus entitled "Flitting Away."

The camp roused at dawn on August 24. The Radersburg crew planned to spend the Cowans's second wedding anniversary retracing its route—out of the Lower Geyser Basin, to the upper Madison River, west over Targhee Pass, to Henry's Lake.

Those plans change drastically, though, when Dingee trudged down to Tangled Creek and filled the coffee pot. He looked up to discover three mounted natives across the stream. The warriors followed the frightened saloon-keeper back to camp. Soon 30 other horsemen filed in. As Emma said, "The woods seemed full of them!" By this time, all of the whites were huddling together around the fire.

The Radersburg vacationers had encountered the 21-year-old Nez Perce scout Yellow Wolf and his advance party, searching for a safe route through the national park. After the devastating encounter at the Big Hole two weeks earlier, the Nez Perces straggled east—with each band driving its large horse herd before it. General Oliver O. Howard and 600 men trailed the Indians in a delayed, but persistent, pursuit.

Every Nez Perce man, woman, and child had suffered incredible personal loss in the Big Hole massacre. Scores of additional wounded died during the subsequent forced march, and their bodies had to be abandoned along the route by the survivors. Most families had fled the battlefield leaving their household goods and supplies. Their prized horses already were weary from the 800-mile flight.

For the retreat to the Great Plains, the Nez Perces did not rely on a single overall commander. Rather, the leaders of the half-dozen individual New Perce bands met in council to decide tactics and strategy. Nevertheless, small, virtually autonomous parties of young warriors ran lightning-swift scouting sorties into the countryside.

The Big Hole massacre had incensed these young men, and they became the greatest potential threat to whites. The "Radersburg Nine" easily could have been annihilated that August morning. But Yellow Wolf honored the council's admonition that the U.S. soldier—not the white civilian—was the enemy of the Nez Perces. Emma described the scene (*Contributions*, 167):

After some consultation, the men decided to break camp at once and attempt to move out, as though nothing unusual was at hand....Some little time was required to pull down tents, load the wagons, harness and saddle the horses, and make ready for travel....

While Mr. Cowan was engaged elsewhere, one of the men—Mr. [A. J.] Arnold, I think—began dealing out sugar and flour to the Indians on their demand. My husband soon observed this and peremptorily ordered the Indians away, not very mildly either. Naturally they resented it, and I think this materially lessened our chances of escape.

Finally the tourist caravan brazenly pushed north. In this attempt to leave the Lower Geyser Basin, however, the Cowan party was escorted by about 40 of Yellow Wolf's heavily armed scouts. Soon they passed the women and children of the leader Joseph's band—the "women's camp"—who were turning east to ascend Nez Perce Creek. Within an hour, the Cowan procession encountered another contingent of 60 warriors, who ordered the whites to backtrack and fall in behind the retreating "women's camp."

The party—still accompanied by Yellow Wolf's scouts—rode a couple of miles up the creek toward Mary Lake, until fallen timber blocked the carriage and the wagon. Unhitching the horses, Emma and her friends grabbed some clothing from the wagon and abandoned the vehicles and their contents to the warriors.

It gave us no pleasure to see our wagon over-hauled, ransacked, and destroyed. Spokes were cut from the buggy wheels and used as whip handles....One young chap dashed past us with several yards of pink mosquito bar tied to his horse's tail.

(Contributions, 168)

Seven miles farther, in a clearing near Mary Lake, the column overtook the "women's camp," which had stopped for lunch. Here Hohoto (Lean Elk or Poker Joe), who guided the Nez Perces east from the Big Hole, spoke to the captives directly in English. He said that the tourists would be released if they agreed to "trade" their horses, saddles, firearms, and ammunition for a few exhausted Indian ponies, a beat-up Indian saddle, and a mule with a bullet wound in his shoulder.

George Cowan and his companions grudgingly agreed. In the confusion of the exchange, William Dingee and A. J. Arnold slipped into the dense timber and escaped, heading west. Hohoto told the remaining seven vacationers to mount up and head toward the Lower Geyser Basin as quickly as possible—to avoid the hot-headed young marauders whom no leader could control.

The frightened group had covered only half a mile when a phalanx of 25 young warriors overtook them, turned them around, and escorted them back up the trail, again east toward Mary Lake. Just after passing the noon-camp clearing, Emma felt the tension snap (*Contributions, 170-171*):

> Suddenly, without warning, shots rang out. Two Indians came dashing down the trail in front of us. My husband was getting off his horse. I wondered for what reason. I soon knew, for he fell as soon as he reached the ground—fell headlong down the hill. Shots followed and Indian yells, and all was confusion.
>
> In less time than it takes me to tell it, I was off my horse and by my husband's side, where he lay against a fallen pine tree. I heard my sister's screams and called to her. She came and crouched by me, as I knelt by his side. I saw he was wounded in the leg above the knee and, by the way the blood spurted out, I feared an artery had been severed....

Still, the rogue Nez Perces persisted.

> Looking back and up over my shoulder, I saw an Indian with an immense navy pistol trying to get a shot at my husband's head. Wrenching my arm from his grasp, I leaned over my husband, only to be roughly drawn aside.
>
> Another Indian stepped up, a pistol shot rang out, my husband's head

fell back, and a red stream trickled down his face from beneath his hat. The warm sunshine, the smell of blood, the horror of it all, a faint remembrance of seeing rocks thrown at his head, my sister's screams, a sick faint feeling, and all was blank.

In the confusion of the attack on the Cowans, two more of the party—Charles Mann and Henry Myers—successfully escaped into the brush. Albert Oldham was shot in the left cheek; the ball knocked out two teeth and sliced his tongue at the base before exiting through his jaw. The musician crumpled against the trunk of a tree. Frank Carpenter saw the shooting of George Cowan, but he could not reach his sisters.

The warriors left Oldham and George Cowan for dead. They mounted a shrieking Ida behind one rider, lashed a still-unconscious Emma behind another, and ordered Frank into line. Under the protection of Hohoto—who had been sent by the leader Looking Glass to protect the whites—the survivors reached the safety of the Nez Perce evening camp in the Hayden Valley, just west of the Yellowstone River. Clearly the council leaders had not authorized the attack on the Cowans.

That night Emma and Frank slept in Joseph's camp, while Hohoto protected Ida. Emma mused (*Contributions,* 173):

> My brother and I sat out a weary vigil by the dying embers of the campfire, sadly wondering what the coming day would bring forth....Near morning, rain began falling. A squaw arose, replenished the fire, and then came and spread a piece of canvas over my shoulders to keep off the dampness.

On August 25 the Nez Perce bands moved through the Hayden Valley and forded the Yellowstone River near Mud Volcano. There the leaders held an afternoon council and determined to free Emma, Frank, and Ida. Led by Hohoto, the captives recrossed the Yellowstone River and worked their way into the woods.

The Nez Perces provided two weary ponies for the women to ride, but left Frank afoot. Supplying some clothing, bedding, bread, and matches, Hohoto pointed to a trail that paralleled the Yellowstone River, admonishing (*Adventures*, 163-164).

> You go down river, way down. No stop. Go all night. No stop. You go three days, get'm Bozeman. You go all night….[If] you no get'm Bozeman [in] three days, bad Injuns catch'm you….Go quick now. Go quick!

For safety, the fugitives traveled only in the woods during daylight. Even at night they carefully skirted clearings and avoided silhouetted ridge lines. Once they passed the Falls of the Yellowstone, Emma recognized the country from her 1873 visit.

Finally, late in the afternoon of August 26, near Tower Junction, the trio stumbled onto a squad of soldiers under the command of Lieutenant Charles Schofield. This scouting detachment had been detailed from Fort Ellis to find the Nez Perces. After supper, the entire group mounted Army stock for a fast trip to McCartney's small hotel at Mammoth Hot Springs, arriving about midnight. From the Springs, Frank penned a message to be telegraphed to his brother in Helena (*Adventures*, 186):

> Emma, Ida and myself alive; Cowan and Oldham killed. Saw Cowan and Oldham shot. Balance missing. I think all are killed, but don't know. Will send particulars when I reach Bozeman.

At noon on August 28, more than three weeks after leaving Radersburg, Emma Cowan's trip into Yellowstone National Park ended in Bozeman. Convinced that they were the expedition's only three survivors, Emma and Ida removed to their parents' ranch near present-day Townsend. Frank organized a party of Bozeman residents and, on August 29, returned to the "Wonderland" to recover the bodies of his friends.

Astonishingly, no such bodies existed! Charles Mann and Henry Myers were rescued after only one day in the wilds. Although the two had separated, General Howard's advance scouts found them both near Madison Junction on the afternoon of August 25. A bullet hole through the brim of Mann's hat punctuated his story.

The first two escapees—William Dingee and A. J. Arnold—spent four days working their way northwest through the timber to Gibbon River, down the Madison, around Targhee Pass, and into General Howard's camp on Henry's Lake. Without blankets or coats, surviving on four small fish, the pair had bushwhacked 40 miles overland to safety.

On August 29 Howard's full command moved into the national park and discovered Albert Oldham along the Madison River road. The musician, shot through the face, had lain in the brush for 36 hours before beginning his 20-mile flight, traveling mostly after dark. When Oldham was found by Howard's soldiers, his infected tongue had become so swollen that he barely could swallow or breathe.

Most remarkably, George Cowan also survived. He had been shot first through the right thigh. Then the soft ball from the close-range pistol explosion had flattened against his forehead and still protruded directly above his nose. Left for dead, Cowan regained consciousness several hours later and pulled himself to his feet—only to be shot again above the left hip by a lone warrior driving several horses up the trail.

Once again left for dead, Cowan found that he could drag himself on his elbows through the brush. By midnight he crossed Nez Perce Creek and started downstream. Three days after the attack, the wounded attorney dragged himself into the site where the Radersburg tourists had abandoned their wagon and carriage. He had crawled nine miles in 63 hours and was rewarded by finding Dido under the wagon box, awaiting his return.

The two worked their way farther down the creek, to the party's old campsite in the Lower Geyser Basin. Here Cowan scavenged 12 matches, a tin can, and a handful of coffee beans among the camp remains. The hot coffee was his first meal in four days.

The next morning, August 29, Cowan dragged himself again through Nez Perce Creek to the edge of the Firehole River, before he collapsed. There an advance scout for Howard's command discovered him. Shot three times, his legs paralyzed, and without food, George Cowan had crawled 14 miles in five days to be rescued.

Attended by his friends Albert Oldham and A. J. Arnold, Cowan slowly regained strength. The survivors, secure in an Army ambulance, accompanied Howard's plodding troops to the Yellowstone River and then joined the supply train that the general released to return to Fort Ellis. On September 14, three weeks after his rescue along the Firehole River, Cowan reached the Bottler Ranch near Emigrant.

On September 7, Emma—already dressed in the traditional black raiments of mourning—received a startling news report (*Helena Daily Independent* extra, September 6, 1877):

COWAN ALIVE

HE IS WITH GENERAL HOWARD'S COMMAND

Bozeman, Sept. 5—Two scouts just in from Howard's command say that Cowan is with Howard and is doing well and will recover. He is shot through the thigh and in the side and wounded in the head....This news is reliable.—Langhorne.

Still, Emma awaited confirmation. An agonizing 10 days passed. Finally, on September 18, she received a telegram from a Bozeman friend: "Mr. Cowan will be here tomorrow. Getting along all right."

Emma dashed to Bozeman, only to find that George's strength had failed again, and he remained at the Bottler Ranch. The young wife hired a double-seated carriage and pushed the additional 40 miles from Bozeman into the Paradise Valley. She finally reached her husband's bedside on September 21, and her brother Frank later wrote (*Adventures*, 227):

> The meeting of Cowan and his wife can be better imagined than described. Their joy was too sacred for public perusal.

Miraculously, the 700 Nez Perces pushed their enormous horse herds through Yellowstone Park, continued to evade General Howard, and emerged on the Montana plains. Not until the Bear's Paw Battle (September 30–October 5, south of Chinook) did the U.S. Army catch the retreating natives.

On October 5—the day that Chief Joseph surrendered to General Howard and Colonel Nelson A. Miles—Emma and George Cowan finally returned to their home in Radersburg. Here Emma would supervise his complete recovery. Exactly two months had elapsed since the "Radersburg Nine" had departed for Yellowstone. The grasshopper scourge was over.

SOURCES

Bits and pieces of the Cowan story can be found in the scores of newspaper accounts, diary entries, government reports, and historical narratives covering the Nez Perce retreat through Montana in 1877. Most notable of these sources are: Mark H. Brown, *The Flight of the Nez Perce: A History of the Nez Perce War* (New York: G. P. Putnam's Sons, 1967); Brown, "Yellowstone Tourists and the Nez Perce," *Montana: The Magazine of Western History,* 16, #3 (Summer, 1966), 30-43; Merrill D. Beal, *"I Will Fight No More Forever": Chief Joseph and the Nez Perce War* (Seattle: University of Washington, 1963); Rex C. Myers, "The Settlers and the Nez Perce," *Montana: The Magazine of Western History,* 27, #4 (Autumn, 1977), 20-29.

The Nez Perce perspective on the retreat and the Yellowstone incidents is given equitable treatment in: Lucullus V. McWhorter, *Hear Me My Chiefs! Nez Perce History and Legend* (Caldwell, Idaho: Caxton Printers, 1942); McWhorter, *Yellow Wolf: His Own Story* (Caldwell, Idaho: Caxton Printers, 1940); Allen P. Slickpoo, *Nonn Nee-Me-Poo: The Culture and History of the Nez Perces* (Lapwai, Idaho: Nez

Perce Tribe, 1973); Bruce Hampton, *Children of Grace: The Nez Perce War of 1877* (New York: Henry Holt and Company, 1994); Aubrey L. Haines, *An Elusive Victory: The Battle of the Big Hole* (West Glacier: Glacier Natural History Association, 1991); William L. Lang, "Where Did the Nez Perces Go in Yellowstone in 1877?", *Montana: The Magazine of Western History,* 40, #1 (Winter, 1990), 14-29.

In addition to the Cowan party, other white tourists and adventurers encountered the Nez Perces in Yellowstone. These variations can be followed in Montana newspapers. Contemporary journalistic accounts run from August through November, 1877, and can be found in: the (Bozeman) *Avant Courier;* the *Bozeman Times;* the (Deer Lodge) *New North West;* the *Helena Daily Herald;* the *Helena Independent;* the (Missoula) *Weekly Missoulian;* the (Virginia City) *Madisonian;* and the *Butte Miner.*

The official military aspects of the Nez Perce flight can be tracked in: U.S. Congress, "Report of the Secretary of War, 1876-1877," in U.S. 45th Congress, 2nd Session, House of Representatives Executive Document 1, Part 2, Vol. I.

And an excellent companion to tracing the Cowan party's movements on the ground is: Cheryl Wilfong, *Following the Nez Perce Trail: A Guide to the Nee-Me-Poo National Historic Trail, with Eyewitness Accounts* (Corvallis: Oregon State University, 1990).

In 1878 Frank D. Carpenter published his account of the Yellowstone vacation as *The Wonders of Geyser Land* (Black Earth, Wisc.: Burnett and Son, Printers, 1878). This volume was reprinted in 1935 as: Heister D. Guie and Lucullus V. McWhorter, eds., *Adventures in Geyser Land* (Caldwell, Idaho: Caxton Printers, 1935). Although Emma Cowan published her versions of the Yellowstone adventure in several places, the most complete is: Mrs. George F. Cowan, "Reminiscences of Pioneer Life," *Contributions to the Historical Society of Montana,* Vol. IV (Helena: Independent Publishers, 1903), 156-187.

CHAPTER TWO

ROUGHING IT IN RUBBER

WHEREIN DAREDEVIL PAUL BOYTON NAVIGATES 1,675 MILES
OF THE YELLOWSTONE RIVER AND THE MISSOURI RIVER IN 1881,
BRAVING ALL NATURE OF TRIALS AND TRIBULATIONS, WHILE MOSTLY
LYING FLAT ON HIS BACK, ATTIRED IN AN INDIA-RUBBER SUIT;
OR, "THE STORY OF THE INCREDIBLE FLOATING MAN"

On that sunny, crisp, mid-September morning in 1881, several dozen residents of the frontier settlement of Glendive, Montana Territory, stood on the bank of the Yellowstone River in absolute disbelief. They could conceive of nothing more bizarre than what they were witnessing. Who would ever believe their stories? No one with a firm grasp on reality!

The focus of the crowd's attention was a 5-feet 10-inch, 180-pound, mustachioed young man, clad from head to toe in a pliant, gray-brown rubber suit, standing at river's edge. While a small U.S. Army band from nearby Camp Porter played military airs, their commander, Colonel Wesley Merritt, signaled a cannon to fire its salute. Merritt's daughter then presented the peculiar water creature with a miniature American flag, and he plodded out into the shallow flow. In his wake he dragged a shiny new cockleshell named *Baby Mine*.

Knee-deep in the current, the 32-year-old daredevil raised his bugle and blew a shrill cavalry charge. Ever the showman, Boyton next lit a small cigar and clenched it in his teeth. He then stretched out in the Yellowstone's flow, grasped his double-bladed paddle, and slipped feet-first down the river. A bit hesitantly, the crowd cheered—for whatever it was that they had just witnessed!

With little doubt, Paul Boyton's departure from Glendive on

Boyton in 1870, wearing medals awarded during the Franco-Prussian War.
Photo courtesy of Murphy Library, University of Wisconsin-La Crosse

September 17, 1881, marked the most bizarre event in the fledgling town's history. What an unbelievable place this Montana frontier was! Buffalo hunters were scouring the Yellowstone Valley to slaughter the last bison; cattlemen were replacing them on the open range with huge herds of Texas-based longhorns. Only five years earlier, George Armstrong Custer had been vanquished at the Battle of the Little Bighorn. Just two months ago the Northern Pacific Railroad's first steam engine had arrived in town, igniting a flurry of construction. And already a world-renown adventurer—"the

Incredible Floating Man"—had chosen Glendive to begin his 1,675-mile voyage to St. Louis, Missouri!

Much of this local amazement depended on Boyton's peculiar outfit—both his inflatable India-rubber body suit and his unique support craft *Baby Mine*. The 35-pound waterproof suit was the 1872 patented invention of Iowan Clark S. Merriman. It enveloped Boyton—leaving only his face and hands exposed—in five chambers, each with its own blow-up tube. When all five compartments were inflated, "the Floating Wonder" could descend a river prone, feet-first, with his head elevated to pick his way among oncoming obstacles.

Once afloat, Boyton positioned on his chest the bugle and a small hatchet, each attached by a cord to his suit. He clutched an 8-foot, double-bladed paddle, which he used to steer and to fend off snags, rocks, and brush. He normally stroked at 100 beats per minute—but he could improve that speed with a small sail, erected on a mast held in a socket between his ankles. A cord attached to the peak of Paul's inflated hood connected the swimmer with his supply boat, so he could drag it behind him.

Baby Mine was Boyton's own creation: a watertight, soldered-copper, oval cockleshell 3 feet long, 16 inches wide, and 22 inches deep. The original *Baby* had been crafted in France in 1873, but it had taken a severe beating through the years. Paul had contracted a St. Paul, Minnesota, coppersmith to create a new cockleshell for his Yellowstone-Missouri expedition. This second version had the legend *Baby Mine of St. Paul* painted on its bow.

The new *Baby Mine* carried all of Boyton's necessities, either firmly attached to its flat-topped, lipped lid or tightly packed inside. Paul kept a compass, a clock, a thermometer, and a candle headlight on the lid. Two pockets within the craft held his maps, stationery, pens and ink, mirror, brush, and comb.

Packed tightly in the body of *Baby Mine* were a barometer, another hatchet, a revolver, a short-stock rifle, boxes of ammunition, a hunting knife, field glasses, signal rockets, matches, shaving supplies, a small oil stove, and a bottle of oil for fuel. In addition, the cache included Boyton's dry clothes, silverware, soap, towels, extra candles, rubber cement and patches, a well-stocked medicine chest, and his indispensable cigars, tobacco, and pipe.

Paul also carried food for about ten days—dried meat and fruits, milk, coffee, crackers, and cake—although he seldom lacked fresh fish or small game for dinner. The copper craft carried no liquor, as Paul long had declared himself a teetotaler. On dry land, fully loaded, *Baby Mine* weighed about 150 pounds.

As strange as "the Incredible Floating Man" seemed to the rough-and-tumble residents of Glendive, they saw that he had perfected this form of derring-do. In fact, by 1881, the amazing Paul Boyton already had navigated more than 25,000 miles of rivers, lakes, and oceans around the world. He planned this epic, 1,675-mile float of the Yellowstone-Missouri to be his triumphant, culminating tour de force.

As Paul paddled beyond the mouth of Glendive Creek, he may have reflected how he always had sought adventure and how he had gained both fame and fortune from his courage. In an era long before radio, satellite television, and "X-treme Sports Games," Boyton captivated thousands of spectators with his thrilling exploits. Although challenged in popular-press headlines by long-distance walkers, bridge jumpers, and Niagara Falls barrel dare devils, his fame had spread quickly as he piled one death-defying act upon another.

Paul Boyton was born in Dublin, Ireland, in 1849, and raised in Pittsburgh, Pennsylvania. At a very young age, he learned to swim in the Allegheny River, and he became known as a boy who would take any "dare." In 1864, at the age of 15, he joined the Union Navy in search of adventure. Released a year later, he traveled to the Caribbean, hunting marine curiosities for his father's import business. After a short stint with some Mexican revolutionaries, he signed on with a French contingent in 1870 to battle the Prussians.

Back in New York City, the young man became a mercenary in a plot to free Cuba from Spanish rule and then a prospector for diamonds in South America and for gold in California. After sailing around the world in a square-rigger, he took a job as the head lifeguard at Atlantic City, New Jersey. In two summers' work there, he saved 71 distressed swimmers. And then, at Atlantic City, he met Clark Merriman.

Merriman had patented his "Life-Preserving Dress" in 1872 and was looking for "a daring young man" to perform some stunts to boost its sales. Boyton accepted the challenge and devised a scheme to stow away on the oceanliner *Queen*, bound for England. Two days from Liverpool and 30 miles off the southwest Irish coast, Paul dropped overboard into the sea. A storm pounded him into Trefaska Bight, near Skibbereen, where he dodged an almost-sure death and received a hero's welcome. Boyton then took to the Dublin stage to regale a paying audience that idolized him. Thanks to Mr. Merriman's India-rubber suit, Paul Boyton became an international showman.

For the next five years, "the Perilous Paddler" challenged every major river in Europe and captivated audiences with his tales. He floated the Severn, the Thames, the Dee, and the Trent rivers in England, whereupon he received a gold chronometer from Queen Victoria. His theater appearances in London alone earned him $1,750 a week. He then swam the English Channel, from France to Dover—a trip of 23 hours and 6 cigars.

Boyton performed exhibitions across the Continent—in Paris, Rome, Berlin, Madrid, Brussels—and he floated the Elbe, the Loire, the Rhine, the Rhone, the Danube, the Tagus, the Seine, and the Tiber rivers. After Paul's 83-hour trip down the Po River, King Victor Emmanuel awarded him the Cross of the Order of the Crown of Italy. Not to be outdone, Mercedes, the young Queen of Spain, knighted Boyton. In his lagoon performances at the Paris Exposition in 1878, "the Incredible Floating Man" fired signal flares, built a raft, caught fish, released pigeons, and sank a mock ship—to the delight of thousands.

Boyton returned to the United States in 1879 as an international celebrity. With his brother Michael as business manager and press agent, Paul swam the Monongahela, the Delaware, and the Allegheny rivers. His evening opera-house performances earned more than $2,000 a week. When he plied the Connecticut River, Michael sent a rider down the riverside trail ahead of Paul, shouting, "Here comes that pesky swimmer 'round the bend, and he's a-comin' like forty!"

Boyton then proceeded to take Washington, D.C., by storm. After a special performance at the federal Naval Yards, the halls of Congress rang with Boyton's praises. And newspapers across the country featured Boyton when President Rutherford B. Hayes hosted "the agile swimmer" at the White House.

In 1881 Paul rode the Ohio River and several portions of the Mississippi. Then Michael conceived the ultimate float: from the wilderness of Montana Territory, high in the Missouri River drainage, more than 1,675 miles to St. Louis. It would be the consummate challenge for the world's acknowledged "river desperado." And so, Paul Boyton arrived in the frontier town of Glendive late in the season: the farthest west that he could ride the train and still find water deep enough to paddle downriver.

On the first day out of Glendive, Paul spent most of his time searching for deep water, sparring off rocks, and paddling frantically. That night, while Boyton stopped beside the Yellowstone, a startled elk charged through the campsite. Paul fired on the intruder, wounded him, and chased him in the dark—but to no avail. When he returned to camp, he found that one end of his double-bitted paddle had burned in the campfire, so he spent much of the night fashioning a replacement.

During the next two days, Boyton met no one. He amused himself by bugling at wildlife and watching them run. At one point, near present-day Sidney, a snag ripped his suit, which quickly filled with water. After some riverside patching work, however, he con-

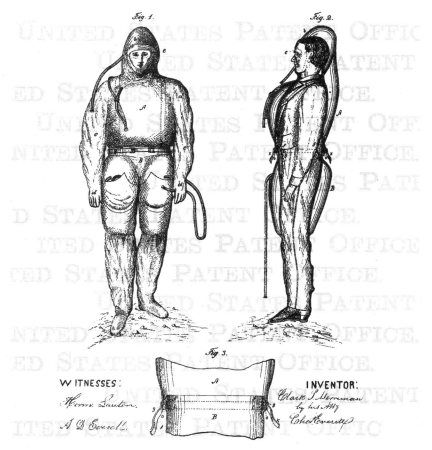

The drawings that Merriman used to register his patent of the "Life-Preserving Dress."
Photo courtesy of Murphy Library, University of Wisconsin-La Crosse

tinued the float. Then, before he reached the mouth of the Yellowstone, an immense bison herd forced Paul to shore, to wait for almost an hour while it crossed the river.

A warm reception at Fort Buford, on the Montana-Dakota border, enticed Boyton to lay over for a day to replace his oar. Local Mandans who watched this oddity test his new paddle in the Missouri dubbed him "the Beaver with Two Tails." When "Beaver Boyton" resumed his trip, he determined to swim long days. One afternoon, a bankside Indian shot at the strange floating object, but Boyton sent the surprised hunter running with a blast from his bugle.

Below Fort Buford, Boyton enjoyed deeper water that allowed him to run longer days. At Buford, Paul had learned of the death of President James A. Garfield—shot in Washington, D.C., in July. So, "the Frog Man" swept up to the levee at Fort Stevenson "with the flag on *Baby* at half mast."

One evening on the upper Missouri, Boyton camped with a bunch of cowhands who provided him a hot beefsteak meal and stories around the fire. Only later did Paul learn that they were rustlers whom a local sheriff captured the next day. After another long stretch on the river, Paul met the steamboat *Eclipse* and learned that he was still 100 miles above Fort Berthold.

Boyton later spoke candidly about how the Missouri stacked up against the other great rivers that he had tackled (*St. Joseph Gazette*, November 7, 1881):

> It is alone in its characteristics. I couldn't name a stream in the world that compares with it. Every other river has a channel, and I can tell it by the lay of the land, if by nothing else. But the Missouri—well, it's a conundrum. As a party up the river remarked, "The good Lord made the Missouri, but he hasn't located it yet."

On Paul's eighth day out of Glendive, a trapper shot at the adventurer—thinking him "a bear on a log." Boyton responded with a bugle blast, and then he cooked lunch for the fur man on his oil stove. "The Perilous Paddler" reached Fort Berthold on September 25 and announced his arrival by firing two signal rockets high over the landing. A large crowd at the fort feted him and listened to his amazing tales long into the night. Here, incredulous local natives christened the phenom *Minnewachatcha*—"Mysterious Water Sprite."

Boyton's characterization of his Missouri River experience in Dakota Territory was not inspiring (*St. Joseph Gazette*, November 7, 1881):

> You can't imagine the feeling of utter loneliness that came over me at the sight of those long, sterile wastes that stretched away for miles without number on either hand, with nothing to talk to except Baby. These were places where a notch in a tree made by an axe would have been a welcome sign.
>
> And all around you is silence, except for the gurgling sound of the water and the hideous cackling of flocks of wild geese. The scene now and then is relieved only by high sand bluffs that rise straight from the water's edge, or by stretches of forests with an occasional glimpse of a wild deer bounding away at the top of its speed.

On September 28 Boyton climbed out of the Missouri at Bismarck, Dakota Territory, after surviving two days of strong winds, driving rain, and thunderstorms. He laid over a day and lectured that evening at the Bismarck Opera House to a standing-room-only crowd. The *Bismarck Tribune* recounted (September 30, 1881):

> He described his adventures from the famous landing on the stormy coast of Ireland to his knight-hood by Mercedes, the beautiful young queen of Spain; his fight with sharks in the Straits of Messina [between Sicily and Italy]; roughing it in rubber on the rivers Rhine, Po, Danube, Tagus, Seine, Nile, and in the Straits of Gibraltar. He exhibited his celebrated little boat Baby Mine, and showed the audience how he could camp out, build a raft, cook a meal, and hunt and fish without ever leaving the water.

While in Bismarck the celebrity was approached by 21-year-old James Creelman, a New York City newspaper correspondent. Creelman had come west as a stringer for the *New York Herald* to write about Indians, but he found "Beaver Boyton's" quest of the Missouri a much more compelling story.

The two men purchased a rowboat for the reporter, so he could accompany "the Incredible Floating Man" to St. Louis. Creelman ultimately combined his two assignments at Fort Yates, where he met and interviewed the Sioux leaders Rain-in-the-Face, Low Dog, and Long Soldier.

Through October and into November, the two men pushed from before dawn until after dark, trying to beat the descending winter weather. From stops en route, Creelman filed his columns by telegraph with the *Herald* in New York City. An example of the correspondent's flowery prose (*New York Herald*, October 23, 1881):

> Pierre, Dakota Territory—October 11, 1881.
>
> In the midst of a hurricane, Captain Paul Boyton arrived here early this morning in an exhausted condition after one of the roughest night's voyaging he has ever experienced. Twenty-five days ago he started from Glendive, and up to the present time the Captain has lost 40 pounds in weight, but nothing in spirits.
>
> This deterioration in physique is due to the terrible exposure and hard work which he has undergone. Although the most experienced boatmen declare that Boyton cannot possibly survive the journey, he has announced that he will not stop until he has paddled through the mouth of the Missouri River into the "Father of Waters" beyond.
>
> In order to free the task from some of the greatest dangers which surround it, General [Alfred] Terry has issued a general order to the various forts along the Missouri, directing the officers to inform the Indians of the Captain's approach and to warn them that he must not be molested. Still, several bands of Sioux started on a buffalo hunt before the order was promulgated, and the Captain runs considerable risk of being shot by mistake....

At Fort Randall, the pair met the heroic Sioux Sitting Bull, who recently had returned from his Canadian exile and surrendered to the U.S. Army. Sitting Bull watched Boyton's antics in the swirling river and concluded that he could float so well "because he was hollow inside." When the swimmer and the boater reached Sioux City, Iowa, more than 1,000 thrilled townsmen pulled Boyton from the water and carried him on their shoulders in an impromptu parade through the community.

Then, just days later at Omaha, Nebraska, tragedy struck. Paul was demonstrating his skills at the levee to an appreciative crowd, estimated at over 5,000. Suddenly a local lad shouted that he could swim even better, plunged into the current, and drowned before Boyton could rescue him. A sobered Paul canceled his evening theater performance and departed the next day, by river.

Paddling long days in decreasing light, Boyton and Creelman pushed into the lower Missouri Valley. Local newspapers marked their progress and speculated about their chances of reaching St. Louis before winter weather caught them. For days the pair fought icy rains, gusty headwinds, and an occasional Great Plains blizzard. However, they frequently spent their nights beside bonfires built by riverbank farmers, and ate sumptuous meals prepared by those farmers' admiring wives.

Reaching St. Joseph, Missouri, early in November, Boyton and Creelman stayed for three days, enjoying the comforts of a complimentary hotel room. Civic leaders enticed Paul to speak at the Tootle Opera House (admission: 50¢) on his second night in town. The international showman's elan was demonstrated in his departure from St. Joe on November 8 (*St. Joseph Gazette*, November 9, 1881):

> Captain Boyton got to work inflating the air chambers of his suit and placed his little craft, Baby Mine, upon the dancing wavelets that glistened in the sunshine. Then he shook hands with many of those gathered on the banks, and thanked all who had received him so kindly. He borrowed a light from Major Fred Smith, flopped over on his back and was soon out in the current, paddling off down the stream.
>
> The Captain then took two rockets from Baby Mine. When he was about 200 yards from the shore, he touched them to his cigar and fired them off in quick succession. This was greeted with three hearty cheers from the crowd, and Boyton was gone.

No one can appreciate how utterly lonely a man can become when floating through these immense solitudes. Sometimes I would sing my paddling songs to keep up my spirits, but the echoes which the hills and ravines sent back were so weird and unearthly that I preferred to hear the cackling of the wild geese or the whistling of the wind through the trees.

Paul Boyton to James Creelman,
near Fort Yates, Dakota Territory, October 1, 1881;
New York Herald, *October 22, 1881*

Finally, on November 19, Paul and his rowboat escort reached St. Charles, just above the mouth of the Missouri. A special dispatch to the *St. Louis Globe Democrat* announced (November 20, 1881):

> St. Charles.—Captain Boyton arrived here at 12:30 today. The river was rolling high on account of strong wind, and the current was very swift. His face and suit were coated with ice. He ate his dinner off the Baby Mine and started for the mouth of the Big Muddy at 3:00 p.m. He will camp at the mouth of the river and will start for St. Louis tomorrow. He expects to arrive there about 2:00 p.m.

Despite this notice, when "Beaver Boyton" and James Creelman reached the St. Louis waterfront, no large crowds braved the frigid weather to greet them. The *Globe Democrat* commented (November 21, 1881):

> "The Paddler of His Own Canoe" has returned from his perilous voyage down the Missouri. When he arrived yesterday at 4 o'clock, no one seemed to expect his arrival and, when he came ashore at the foot of Carr Street, he met only the usual loungers found in that locality. There was no stir of any kind, and the termination of the voyage was rather an inglorious end for "the climax of a lifetime," which is how the Captain has billed the trip.
>
> The cold wave which wafted down over this region several days ago

subjected Captain Boyton to all the rigors of a wintry climate, and his natatory experience towards the close was none too pleasant.

In fact, the animated floater presented a closer resemblance to an attenuated section of an iceberg than any other form of creation. As the waves lapped the sides of his rubber suit and dashed over his face, they immediately congealed, rendering his suit cumbersome and unwieldy.

Notwithstanding this disappointing welcome, the fact remained that Paul Boyton–"the Incredible Floating Man"—had challenged the Yellowstone and the Missouri rivers, in low water and wintry weather, and survived. On his back, he had covered the 1,675 miles between Glendive and St. Louis in 64 days, and he had made respectable money lecturing along the way. Further, he had supplied Creelman with sensational material for his serialized reports in the *New York Herald*. By anyone's standards, Paul Boyton's last river float added a major accomplishment to his list of exploits.

A second St. Louis paper, the *Post-Dispatch*, treated "the Perilous Paddler" with greater respect (November 21, 1881):

> So far as human pluck and endurance are concerned, Mr. Paul Boyton, the back-sliding navigator, is certainly as remarkable a man as this century has produced....
>
> A moment's thought given to the weary hours, the dreary nights, the dangers by currents, the monotonous paddling, the awful snags, the numbing cold, and all of the vicissitudes incident to such a trip will give one a bare idea of the stupendous character of this feat.

Boyton and Creelman stayed a week in St. Louis—the guests of hoteliers and restaurateurs—and enjoyed their fame as "the toast of the town." While recovering from his ordeal, Paul delivered several lectures to packed houses. Nevertheless, the *Post-Dispatch* jabbed away at the popular hero—referring to him as "the Frog Man" (November 21, 1881):

It may be regretted that such splendid courage and indomitable will are not directed to more valuable and instructive purposes, but it must be admired all the same. It is understood that Boyton ends his career as a man-fish here and that he is to settle down now to rheumatism and the writing of thrilling books of adventure.

Paul Boyton's miraculous triumph over the Yellowstone-Missouri did prove his final river gamble. During the next decade, the adventurer restricted himself to tamer swims among Lake Michigan ice floes and to gentler night floats in the Great Salt Lake. In 1892 he created "Paul Boyton's Water Circus" and toured the show for several years. Then, in 1895, he settled at Sea Lion Park in Brooklyn and developed the famous "Shoot the Chutes" thrill ride that became a mainstay at the Coney Island amusement park.

By the turn of the century, "Beaver Boyton"—then in his fifties— had retired to his comfortable home at Sheepshead Bay, Ireland. Here, indeed, he wrote an autobiographical adventure book entitled *The Story of Paul Boyton: Voyages on All the Great Rivers of the World, Paddling over 25,000 Miles in a Rubber Dress—a Rare Tale of Travel and Adventure.* For the next two decades, he concentrated on trips to the Caribbean to collect rare tropical birds. On one such trip in 1925, Boyton contracted pneumonia and, at the age of 76, he died in Ireland.

"When I finish this voyage, I will break my paddle and go ashore forever," said Captain Paul Boyton to me two hours after we landed here this morning. "Yes," he added, "the old Missouri is the hardest river I ever paddled down, and it has altered my ideas about aquatic travel so much that although I have navigated rivers in my dress for over ten years, I feel more ignorant than when I commenced, in the face of this winding, muddy water problem."

James Creelman, Kansas City, Missouri, November 9, 1881;
New York Herald, *November 23, 1881*

Even in an era that prided itself on the unusual, the miraculous, the spectacular, and the amazing, Paul Boyton—"the Incredible Floating Man"—knew no peer. Regardless of his scores of other exploits, Boyton's 1881 daring voyage from Glendive to St. Louis set a precedent that has never been duplicated. The odds against his successful navigation of that distance, in that kind of weather, were astronomical.

No wonder that the small group of Glendive residents who had gathered beside the Yellowstone River on that crisp, mid-September morning in 1881 thought no one would ever believe them!

SOURCES

A fascinating, but wholly subjective, work is Paul Boyton's autobiography: *The Story of Paul Boyton: Voyages on All the Great Rivers of the World, Paddling Over 25,000 Miles in a Rubber Dress; A Rare Tale of Travel and Adventure* (Milwaukee: Riverside Printing, 1892). Although written in the third person, the prose is vintage Boyton. Chapter 21 of this volume details his float from Glendive to St. Louis.

Contemporary newspaper accounts of "the Incredible Floating Man" are the most factual and vivid. The basic set is the series of installments written by correspondent James Creelman for the *New York Herald*. More than two dozen of these pieces ran in the *Herald* from October 22 to November 21, 1881. Equally useful are the shore-bound newspaper accounts from communities along the Missouri, from Bismarck, Dakota Territory, all the way to St. Louis.

The late Don Miller, professor of English at Montana Tech in Butte, published two short pieces about Boyton: "River Swim Started Here," (Glendive) *Ranger-Review*, May 4, 1986; "The Unsinkable Captain Boyton," *St. Louis* [Chamber of] *Commerce*, May, 1986. The author is especially grateful for the enthusiasm of Don, with whom he began the historical pursuit of "Beaver Boyton" in the early 1980s. See also: Lyman M. Nash, "The Unsinkable Wonder," *Argosy* (December, 1963), 34-36, 114-116.

Finally, the author wishes to thank Ms. Coralee Paull of St. Louis for her Missouri newspaper research concerning Boyton. Without the kind help of such experienced researchers, many historical articles would suffer a paucity of particulars.

CHAPTER THREE

HELENA'S CROSS-DRESSING FOOTPAD, BERTIE MILLER

A man can fall pretty low—but
never so low that there is not a
chance for redemption. But when
a woman begins going down, there
is no stopping the slide, and there
is no way back up.
Bertie Miller,
Helena, 1891

The October 1891 crime wave took Helena completely by surprise—for the community believed itself too sophisticated for such mundane things. A rash of nighttime stick-ups and shootings in the temporary state capital's quiet neighborhoods left the community's almost-14,000 residents shocked, terrified, and vengeful. The streets of Helena no longer seemed safe for honest citizens.

On Tuesday night, October 6, at about midnight, a thief had emerged from the darkness and—brandishing two large revolvers—held up Thomas F. Richardson, a conductor for the Montana Central Railway, at the corner of Ewing Street and Seventh Avenue. The robber escaped with several dollars in silver, some change, and a valuable gold watch. The next morning's *Helena Daily Independent* described the bandit as

a young, thickset man about 5-foot, 7-inches in height, with a small moustache and about a week's growth of beard on his face. He was well-dressed in dark clothes and wore a black slouch hat.

On Wednesday night, on the corner of Shiland and Broadway, the same thief accosted Robert W. Ray, a teamster who lived at 1012 Breckenridge. The footpad (a highwayman or robber who works on foot) demanded that the startled Ray throw up his hands. He then put a nickel-plated pistol to the victim's head and relieved him of several dollars and a silver watch, escaping into the darkness.

On the same night (October 7) police officer John J. Grogan— making his regular east-side foot patrol—encountered a man standing in the darkness near the corner of Ewing and Eighth Avenue. He approached the fellow and asked him his business in the neighborhood. Still silent, the chap pulled a pistol, and the two men grappled for the gun. The suspect then drew a second revolver and shot officer Grogan in the chest. The assailant ran into the darkness—dropping the weapon over which the two had struggled—and escaped.

A bleeding Grogan stumbled to Miss Katherine Carpenter's boarding house at 217 Eighth Avenue and collapsed in the doorway. Soon Miss Carpenter and her tenants were comforting the policeman on a sitting-room couch and had called for both Dr. Edwin S. Kellogg and Catholic priest Lawrence B. Palladino. Dr. Kellogg thought that Grogan would recover from his wound, but advised against moving him from the boarding house.

The Helena city police force and the Lewis and Clark County sheriff's men responded quickly. Early Thursday morning they began checking any suspicious person trying to leave town. And almost immediately they got lucky.

To John Gibson and John A. Back (the two Helena policemen who detained the slight young man near the Northern Pacific Railroad yards) it initially seemed a routine encounter. The fellow—sporting short hair, a smooth face, and baggy clothes—had been picking his way along the tracks toward East Helena. However, he became unusually, visibly nervous upon seeing the officers approach.

When questioned by the policemen, the lad replied in a falsetto voice that his name was "Charlie Miller" and that he was looking for work at the new East Helena smelter. A search of his pockets produced an expensive gold watch. The timepiece fit the description of the watch stolen from conductor Richardson on Tuesday night. On this evidence, the officers arrested Charlie and escorted him to the Helena City Jail, adjacent to City Hall.

A further search of the suspect's clothing at the jail revealed an even more remarkable fact: "Charlie Miller" was really a full-grown woman!

A detective exclaimed (*Helena Weekly Journal,* October 15, 1891), "Why you are a woman!"

And Charlie replied, "Well, it took you a good while to find that out!"

Thus began the unraveling of one of the strangest stories in the annals of Helena crime—the tale of Bertie Miller, the cross-dressing footpad. The terror that had gripped Helena for three long days and two dark nights quickly became a community-wide preoccupation with this strange, titillating character. And the tale rapidly spread to newspapers across the whole country.

The suspect—by this time calling herself "Bertie Miller," although still dressed in men's clothes—unsuspectingly contributed to the authorities' next break. Just after noon on Thursday, she penned a note and asked the officers to deliver it to her companion in their rented room in a small, white, frame house at 104 Ewing. The note, written in Norwegian, read:

> Henry Clark—
> I am in jail.
> Come to me immediately.
> (signed) Charlie Miller.

City detective Nils P. Walters carried the note to Clark's room, while a dozen lawmen surrounded the dwelling. The sleeping Clark offered no resistance—even when Walters' search of his room

Bertie Miller—alias Charlie Miller, Helen Forslund
Photo courtesy of Montana Historical Society, Helena

revealed a .38-caliber Frontier Bulldog revolver, nickel-plated and fully charged, several cases of .38 and .44-caliber shells, and a black mask with eye holes cut in it.

Bertie Miller
*Photo courtesy of
Montana Historical Society, Helena*

Within the hour, the detective escorted Clark from the City Jail to Mrs. Carpenter's boardinghouse. Here a weak Officer Grogan definitely identified the 24-year-old Clark as his assailant on the preceding night. In several days, Dr. Treacy reported that Grogan had improved considerably and was resting easily. At that point, no attempt yet had been made to extract the bullet lodged underneath the officer's shoulder blade. The physician said (*Helena Daily Herald*, October 13, 1891):

> We will remove the slug in a day or two. In the meantime, Officer Grogan will do considerably better if people will not tramp in at all hours of the day and night to disturb his rest!

Unlike Bertie—who was talking to just about anyone who would listen—Henry Clark remained silent in his cell. The *Daily Herald* (October 9) described him as

> a man of medium height and a weight of about 150 pounds. He has a

freckled face and a dark, reddish mustache, is well-built and muscular. But he is very much scared, and he appeared glad to get into one of the cells.

Though Clark does not have the appearance of intelligence that is credited to his female companion, yet he possesses one faculty that Bertie Miller does not—he can keep his mouth shut except when he eats his three meals a day. Except what he has said to his lawyer, which comes under the head of confidence between counsel and client, Clark has not said a word since his arrest that would in the least aid the authorities in obtaining evidence.

Henry Clark
Photo courtesy of
Montana Historical Society, Helena

Clark smoked his pipe almost continuously and kept his own counsel. During the afternoon, a crowd of more than 150 men and boys gathered in front of the City Jail. They milled about and talked loudly of Montana vigilantes, of Helena's former Hanging Tree, of "real justice," and of "Helena tradition."

City police responded to this threat. Under heavy guard, they slipped Clark out the jail's back door, on Clore Street, and whisked him to the more substantial county jail in the old Presbyterian Church, near the new Lewis and Clark County Courthouse.

Meanwhile, Mayor Theodore H. Kleinschmidt—in true "Old West" fashion—faced the mob from the top step of the City Hall staircase and threatened (*Independent,* October 10):

> We propose to hold this prisoner just as long as we have a man left. The first person who makes a step to break into this jail will get the worst of it!

The mayor's diversionary tactic proved effective, and a potential lynch mob became a crowd of curiosity-seekers.

Over the next several days, Bertie Miller worked to resolve her gender. The *Independent* reported (October 10):

> "Charlie," or "Bertie," while in her cell at the City Jail alternatively cried like a woman and blustered around like a reckless tough, boasting of her deeds.

When asked if she would like women's clothing to wear, she responded:

> No. It has been a year since I began dressing as a boy, and I have no woman's clothes now. Besides, if I put on women's clothing, I will break down and make a fool of myself. I want to go into court with these men's clothes on, and then I can face them all. But if I get out of this scrape, I'll put on women's clothing again and keep wearing it.

At an arraignment hearing for Bertie Miller and Henry Clark on October 10, Judge Junius G. Sanders appointed Joseph W. Kinsley as Bertie's attorney. The bright young lawyer immediately engaged in lengthy consultation with Bertie in her cell.

Kinsley emerged with the announcement that Bertie, thereafter, would don only women's clothing. He also asked a number of "the charitable ladies of Helena" to call on Bertie in her cell "to divert her mind from the situation." The cross-dressing footpad immediately became a cause celebre for the do-good leaders of women's clubs and church auxiliaries in the city.

By Sunday morning, Bertie was attired in conventional female garments (*Independent,* October 11):

The dress was a gray cashmere with black velvet collar and cuffs, and the usual high shoulders and puffed sleeves. A white handkerchief was fastened over the little window of the cell while the transformation was going on. When the change was made, the door opened. The boy had disappeared and instead there was a woman—and a rather pretty one, too, but for the short hair. The prisoner loomed up rather large in her new raiment and acted somewhat awkwardly.

Attorney Kinsley confided in an *Independent* reporter (October 11):

My client must have a hat, and a becoming one at that. When she goes into the courtroom, spectators will behold a stunning-looking female who will change some preconceived ideas as to the appearance of a female bandit.

The hat will partly conceal the blond hair, cut pompadour. And the bright colors of the bonnet, and the dress, and the other fetching touches—put on by skilled female hands—will transform this tanned boyish-looking "hands up" individual into a comely young woman.

She will be attractive enough to melt the heart of any stout-hearted juror. In such an array, it would be hard to convince anyone that the woman ever played the part of the brigand.

At the preliminary hearing on October 13, Helena women packed the courtroom and the halls outside. County Attorney Cornelius B. Nolan charged Bertie with complicity in the robbery of conductor Richardson and bound her over for trial. The *Herald* reported (October 14):

Bertie Miller then was ushered in. She was becomingly attired in a light gray dress with a collar and cuffs of black velvet. At her throat was a plain scarf pin, while her feet were clad in a new pair of button shoes. She wore a soft felt hat of narrow rim, the same as are frequently seen worn by women promenading the street.

Bertie appeared perfectly cool and collected, and she exhibited no nervousness whatever. She is taller and apparently heavier than her chum Clark, who sat crouched in his seat opposite. They paid little attention to each other.

The prosecutor charged Henry Clark with highway robbery against Robert W. Ray. The state selected this offense because it carried a possible life sentence—a more severe penalty than the sentence for shooting Officer Grogan. The judge set bail for each of the suspects at $5,000.

While awaiting trial, Bertie Miller told reporters bits and pieces of the fascinating story of her fall into crime. She revealed that her real name was Bertha Helen Forslund and that she had been born in Norway in 1871. She had immigrated with her parents to Minnesota as a child and then moved with them to a ranch near Lockwood, Washington—about 22 miles from Spokane—in 1888.

Bertie said that she had met Clark when he worked at an adjacent ranch about three years ago. He courted her and proposed to her, but she refused to marry him, saying that she was too young and that her father needed her on the ranch. Finally, in the summer of 1890, she took a job at the Eagle Hotel in Spokane, and Clark followed her there.

In December, 1890, Clark convinced her that they should try Montana, "where wages were higher and good jobs more plentiful." At this point Clark persuaded her that they could travel and live together in greater safety as two workingmen. He provided her with male clothing and helped her to cut her hair short. He also christened her "Charlie Miller" when she put on pants. Bertie had not resorted to women's clothing from the time she arrived in Montana until she was jailed.

Bertie first worked as a clerk in the Grand Hotel in Missoula— for $45 per month—and then in the All Nations Saloon there as a bartender. Clark found employment in Missoula as a steam fitter and, in the spring, he took a smelter job in Anaconda. Bertie soon joined him in Butte. At this point Clark accelerated his hold-up activity. And the easy money and the danger drew Bertie into the business.

Prior to reaching Helena on October 1, the couple had held up both men and women in several western Montana communities. Authorities found a partial accounting among Bertie's effects in their rented room (*Independent*, October 10):

Philipsburg	$85.00
Missoula	$27.00
Butte	$200.00
Anaconda	$58.65 and a gold watch

In Helena, Bertie was roaming the newer upper-west-side neighborhood, while Henry Clark worked the east side. Although she had robbed no one in the Capital City, she did accompany Clark when he held up conductor Richardson, as well as when he shot Officer Grogan. Clark had given her Richardson's watch on Wednesday, which policemen Gibson and Back had confiscated on Thursday.

On October 29, District Court Judge William H. Hunt tried Henry Clark on the charge of highway robbery. The suspect:

> was cleanly shaved, and his hair was carefully brushed. He wore the same dark stripped [sic] suit in which he was dressed at his preliminary examination and at the time of his arrest. He kept his left hand up to his face, and he watched the proceedings, glancing furtively about. He looked exceedingly small and not at all formidable (*Herald*, October 29, 1891).

Both conductor Richardson and Officer Grogan adamantly identified Clark as their assailant. When the accused did not testify in his own behalf, the jury quickly found him "guilty as charged of highway robbery." Judge Hunt then sentenced Clark to forty years of hard labor in the Deer Lodge state prison.

> In the afternoon there was a greater crowd than ever to witness the trial of
> Bertie Miller, alias Helen Forslund, alias Charlie Miller. The ladies were out in
> force and occupied most of the available space within the courtroom railing.
>
> Confinement in the small cell at the City Hall has removed the tan from
> her face and hands, and she looks more like a woman than she did when
> first arrested (*Herald*, October 29).

Evidence presented at the trial cleared Bertie of any complicity in
the hold-up of conductor Richardson. Clark returned to court to
testify for the defense. He asserted that his traveling companion had
played no role in the crimes he had committed.

After short deliberation, the jury found Bertie "not guilty." The
sympathetic *Independent* observed (November 3):

> When the jury brought in the verdict, the defendant looked as if a ton
> had been lifted off her shoulders. She stood up, bowed to the jury and said,
> "Gentlemen, I thank you for your verdict."

The *Herald* countered (November 3):

> The so-called highway lady, who has given Helena so much notoriety
> during the past month through the Eastern press, will go free.
>
> It is worthy of remark in this connection that the trial excited more inter-
> est than has ever been manifested in this city in a judicial proceeding. The
> courtroom was constantly crowded to the limit of its capacity, and a con-
> siderable portion of the spectators were ladies.
>
> How far they may have influenced the jury is a matter of conjecture only.

Bertie left the courtroom in the company of Mrs. Robert N.
Adams, representing the local chapter of the Women's Christian
Temperance Union. Mrs. Adams had befriended the young footpad
throughout her ordeal and would care for her until Bertie's sister,
Mrs. Ellen Culdeen, could arrive from Minneapolis.

> *Editorial Comment,* Helena Daily Herald,
> *October 14, 1891:*
> Now that Miss Helen Forslund, alias Bertie Miller, is safely incarcerat-
> ed for a considerable period, and is neither enjoying the possession of a
> revolver nor wandering about the streets o' nights, we are emboldened to
> make a remark that we have hitherto omitted.
>
> The multiplication of female employments is an encouraging sign of
> the times. It is gratifying to observe that women are no longer restricted
> to sewing, teaching, and domestic work when they are obliged to depend
> on their own exertions for a livelihood.
>
> But reforms are apt to go to extremes. As it is necessary to draw the line
> somewhere, we meekly suggest that the gentle sex had better not encroach
> upon the profession of the highwayman.

Bertie's future consumed the attention of many Helena residents.
The *Daily Herald* summarized (November 5):

> It is said that she is anxious to return to her home in Washington. A sum
> sufficient to defray her expenses there will probably be raised among
> Helenans without difficulty. However, she has been offered a position as a
> clerk in a cigar store in this city.
>
> Bertie's career has been a strange and peculiar one. Many believe that she
> will reform and become a better woman, while there are equally as many
> others who expect that she will continue to pursue a downward career.

Bertie Miller visited Henry Clark for 15 minutes in the County
Jail the next morning. She then boarded a Northern Pacific express
to return with her sister to her parents' ranch near Spokane. An
Independent newsman accompanied her to the railroad depot—
where a crowd of about one hundred curiosity-seekers had assembled to witness Bertie's departure—and reported (November 8):

> She wishes to pass the remainder of her days as a woman. She thinks that

her experience in Montana is enough for one lifetime. As a boy, Bertie Miller had opportunities that, as a woman, she could never have possessed: judging life among the vicious classes of society.

Bertie says, "A man can fall pretty low—but never so low that there is not a chance for redemption. But when a woman begins going down, there is no stopping the slide, and there is no way back up."

At any rate, the curtain has been rung down upon this most sensational and somewhat romantic episode.

At the train station, Bertie also told a *Helena Daily Journal* stringer that she harbored mixed feelings about the five weeks she had spent in Helena (*Weekly Journal,* November 12, 1891):

> I feel good, and I feel bad. I feel good, of course, because of being given my liberty. And I feel good because of my acquittal from a criminal offense. And finally I feel good because of the prospects of a happy return home—even with such a stain on my character.
>
> And I feel bad because Henry Clark received such a severe sentence. He did the square thing by me with his evidence. He tried to make the best case he could for me. I shall not forget him.
>
> If only Clark had let me keep on my woman's dress in my travels about with him and not made me put on that boy's dress, then I would not have fallen to these depths. Oh, what I have seen in those clothes.

Ultimately, Bertie Miller—that is, Helen Forslund—apparently kept her word and her resolve. After spending a short period with parents on their Washington ranch, she removed to Portland, Oregon. Here she became a mainstay of the local Salvation Army contingent, under the name of "Sister Bertie." A reporter with Montana experience spotted her on a Portland street corner in 1896, but she refused an interview with him.

And perhaps Bertie's story has a happy ending. For Montana Governor Joseph K. Toole pardoned Henry Clark on Christmas

THE STORY OF THE
BERTIE MILLER/HENRY CLARK PHOTOGRAPHS

On October 8, 1891, authorities captured Bertie Miller and Henry Clark and imprisoned them in Helena's city jail and county lock-up, respectively. The *Helena Daily Journal* immediately sent a sketch artist to the jail cells to capture the images of these notorious brigands. Two rather primitive line drawings of the suspects ran in the *Journal's* October 9 edition. (The *Helena Daily Independent* ran its own primitive line-drawing depictions of the principals on October 18.)

The *Helena Daily Herald* noted (October 10, 1891):

> Clark was heartily disgusted on viewing a reputed portrait of himself printed in a morning paper. He said that he would willingly sit for a photograph by a reputed artist. The woman, Bertie Miller, also stated that she had no objection to having her picture taken.

Russell H. Beckwith, an enterprising young Helena photographer, arranged with authorities to take the pictures on October 15. Because the police would not release Clark, Beckwith arrived at the county jail and photographed the prisoner standing in his cell.

Bertie Miller, however, was permitted to walk over to Beckwith's gallery on Main Street, under police guard. Against the studio background, Beckwith took several shots of her in the men's clothing that she had worn at the time of her arrest. After changing into the gray cashmere dress that she would wear to court, Bertie reappeared for a final studio photograph. These are the extant images of Clark and Bertie that appear in this chapter.

The *Helena Daily Independent* discussed the peculiar situation (October 20, 1891):

> Bertie Miller thinks that she has good grounds for a kick. And almost

everybody that knows what it is about thinks that she is pretty nearly right. The enterprising photographer [Beckwith] who secured pictures of her and Clark is reaping a rich harvest from the sale of the same. Just where the girl profits from this scheme nobody has been able to discover. She has received only one copy of each picture.

It is, of course, customary for officers of the law to have prisoners' pictures taken—to aid in subsequent identifications. However, Helena is the first case on record where a prisoner has been allowed to sit for photographs for the purpose of private speculation.

On the other hand, without Russell Beckwith's enterprising spirit and Bertie Miller and Henry Clark's willingness, we would not today have any timely photographs of these two remarkable footpads.

Day, 1902—after the highwayman had served more than 10 years of his 40-year term. Toole explained that the original sentence was excessive and that Clark had proven a model prisoner at Deer Lodge. The *Anaconda Standard* observed (December 21, 1902):

Helen Forslund never ceased to work for Clark's release. And there is an idea here that it is largely due to her efforts that Clark is to receive what—to a man in his position—is the best Christmas gift that he could ever get.

One would like to think that this remarkable story of Helena's cross-dressing footpad and her stoic accomplice did, indeed, end romantically:

As the Northern Pacific mainliner ground to a stop at the Portland station, a short, tired man in his mid-thirties stepped down onto the platform. Into his arms rushed a slim woman, dressed in Salvation Army gray, with slightly mannish features and tears in her eyes. The two embraced silently as other passengers moved around them. The years of long, painful separation finally were over for the lovers.

SOURCES

Not surprisingly, in the absence of extant court records, newspapers provide the most complete accounts of the Clark-Miller crime spree and trials. A few Montana papers also ran some titillating feature stories in retrospect: *Anaconda Standard,* December 21, 1902; Montana Newspaper Association Inserts, April 30, 1942.

However, the richest information can be gleaned from Helena's three newspapers operating during the relevant time period of October 1–November 15, 1891: the *Helena Daily Independent;* the *Helena Daily Herald;* the *Helena Weekly Journal.*

In an era of avid newspaper journalism, reporters and editors from these three papers dug tirelessly for basic information and followed all possible leads into background information.

This excellent body of first-hand material is available in the microfilm newspaper collection of the Montana Historical Society in Helena. Likewise, the Society's Photo Archives has preserved the controversial photos of Henry Clark and Bertie Miller/Helen Forslund—and made them available for this publication.

CHAPTER FOUR

CHIEF CHARLO AND THE SALISH "TRAIL OF TEARS"

> [The white man's] laws never gave
> us a blade, nor a tree, nor a duck,
> nor a grouse, nor a trout. No. Like
> the wolverine that steals your
> cache, how often does he come?
> You know he comes as long as he
> lives. He takes more and more,
> and he dirties what he leaves.
> *Chief Charlo, 1909*

The most severe ethical burden that the white Montanan currently shoulders is the federal government's historical treatment of the American Indian during the last two hundred years. Acting on behalf of individuals and groups, that government—consciously or unconsciously—consistently treated natives in a despicable fashion. The thread of conflict between Indians and whites winds through American history and continues to inform relations between the two cultures.

Particularly the federal policy of "relocating" native tribes from their traditional lands to new reservations—often far removed—precipitated some truly regrettable, murderous migrations. In 1838-1839, United States soldiers produced the original "Trail of Tears," stretching 1,200 miles from Georgia to Arkansas and Indian Territory (Oklahoma). These troops force-marched 15,000 Cherokee natives west in winter conditions, with the ultimate loss of 4,000 Indian lives to malnutrition, exposure, and disease.

In 1878—in a similarly ill-fated trek known as "the Long

March"—about 300 Northern Cheyennes under Dull Knife and Little Wolf pushed north from Indian Territory in a desperate attempt to cover over 1,500 miles to reach their homeland in southeastern Montana. Pursued by 10,000 soldiers and an additional 3,000 civilians, about 140 of the survivors finally surrendered to troops who escorted them to Fort Robinson in Nebraska. Soldiers then killed more than 50 Cheyenne prisoners when they tried to escape from the compound in January, 1879.

Less well-known, but equally heroic, is the story of Salish Chief Charlo and his followers in western Montana. Long the nonviolent friends of whites, the Salish suffered government duplicity, unfulfilled official promises, and top-level treaty fraud. In the end completely devastated, Charlo's people abandoned their Bitterroot Valley homeland for the current reservation in the lower Flathead Valley. Charlo led the band on Montana's own "Trail of Tears" in October, 1891—comprising one of the darkest episodes in this state's history.

The Salish-speaking "Flatheads"—a name mistakenly applied by early French voyagers and perpetuated by Meriwether Lewis and William Clark—consistently had befriended whites who penetrated their territory. Those lands stretched from British Columbia to the Yellowstone Valley at various times, but centered on western Montana's Rocky Mountain Trench: that long, narrow, valley trough that parallels the Continental Divide to the west and runs from north-west of present-day Whitefish to Sula, at the head of the Bitterroot Valley.

In 1805, for example, the Salish "recvd us friendly," wrote William Clark after the Lewis and Clark Expedition met them at Ross's Hole, in the Bitterroot Valley. Similarly the Salish welcomed British and American fur traders to western Montana.

In 1831 the tribe launched the first of its four expeditions to St. Louis, in search of Christianity. These attempts culminated, in 1841, with Father Pierre-Jean DeSmet's establishment of St. Mary's Mission at Stevensville, in the midst of the Salish led by Chief

Chief Charlo, center, sits in front of Peter Ronan. On left, front to back: Abel, Antoine Moeise, John Hill. Right, front to back: Louis, Michael Rivais.
Photo courtesy of Montana Historical Society, Helena

Victor. Subsequently the Jesuits relocated (1854) St. Ignatius Mission in the lower Flathead (Mission) Valley.

When Isaac I. Stevens—the governor and superintendent of Indian affairs for Washington Territory—convened an assembly of western Montana natives in July 1855, that same Victor represented the Salish population of about 450. The meeting at Council Grove (west of Missoula, near the Clark's Fork River) produced the important Hell Gate Treaty. At this event, Chief Alexander represented the 600 Upper Pend d'Oreilles (Kalispels), and Chief Michael led the 350 Kutenais. Victor (*Alimaken*), the head chief of the lower Kutenais, refused to attend the gathering.

Stevens, on behalf of the United States government, intended to establish a single reservation in the lower Flathead Valley. Called "the Jocko Reserve," it would contain all four groups. By this treaty, the members of this loosely-knit confederacy also would cede their claims to the vast amounts of their tribal lands in western Montana. Alexander and Michael agreed to locate on the Jocko Reserve, but Victor refused. He asserted that the Salish recognized both the lower Flathead Valley and the Bitterroot Valley as their ancestral lands. And he declared that his people preferred to remain in the Bitterroot.

Victor's inherent faith in the wisdom of white leaders, however, suggested a compromise. He proposed that his people would remain in the Bitterroot—above (south of) Lolo Creek—until the federal government could survey the valley. Once examined, the President could decide if that Bitterroot land was better suited to the Salish than was the Jocko Reserve. A frustrated Stevens agreed to this request, which became Article 11 in the Hell Gate Treaty (see Robert Bigart and Clarence Woodcock, eds., *In the Name of the Salish and Kootenai Nation*, 1996):

> ARTICLE 11. It is, moreover, provided that the Bitter Root Valley, above the Loo-lo Fork, shall be carefully surveyed and examined, and if it shall prove, in the judgment of the President, to be better adapted to the wants

of the Flathead tribe than the general reservation provided for in this treaty, then such portions of it as may be necessary shall be set apart as a separate reservation for the said tribe. No portion of the Bitter Root Valley, above the Loo-lo Fork, shall be opened to settlement until such examination is had and the decision of the President is made.

With this provision inserted, Victor signed the Hell Gate Treaty (not ratified by the U.S. Senate until 1859), and his followers remained in the Bitterroot, most of them near St. Mary's Mission. Here many began farming and stock-raising, to supplement their annual bison-hunting expeditions to the plains east of the Continental Divide. Alexander and his Upper Pend d'Oreilles, as well as Michael and his Kutenais, settled on the Jocko Reserve—some near the Jocko Agency (outside present-day Arlee), others close to St. Ignatius Mission, and still others beside Flathead Lake. All awaited the federal survey of the upper Bitterroot Valley.

The government, however, initiated no such examination. The 1860s brought swarms of white placer-gold prospectors to the country and, in 1864, Congress created Montana Territory. Discouraged miners and overland immigrants gradually "discovered" the Bitterroot Valley and settled into its lush, fertile, game-rich environment. Although this settlement directly violated the Hell Gate Treaty, neither the federal government nor the territorial government moved to enforce its provisions.

W. J. McCormick, a special Indian Agent, in 1868 recognized this impending clash of cultures in the Bitterroot. He chastised the federal government for its failure to survey the upper Bitterroot and warned (*Report of the Commissioner of Indian Affairs, 1868, House Executive Document #49*, Serial Set 1366):

> The conflicting interests of the opposite races are becoming every day more and more apparent….Already a feeling of insecurity prevails to some extent among the whites of the Bitter Root Valley. Meanwhile the Flathead

Indians watch with sullen interest the progress and encroachments of the whites upon their ancient domain, restricting and circumscribing the range of their cattle and horses.

That the two races should live together in amity and good accord is not to be expected, as history fully shows that, in all conflicts of races, the weaker must sooner or later yield to, or be destroyed by, the more powerful.

With the valley filling with white settlers, Agent McCormick recommended that the government compensate Victor and his people for their land and improvements—and then remove them to the Jocko Reserve. The federal government failed to act on this advice.

As the years slipped by and the silence from Washington, D.C., deepened, Victor's Salish became increasingly convinced that white authorities had decided to grant them the upper Bitterroot as their own reservation. When Victor died in 1870, his son Charlo (*Slem-hak-kah*, "Little Claw of the Grizzly Bear") assumed leadership of the Salish. From the beginning, he proved as determined as his father to remain in the Bitterroot until the federal government honored its commitment made in Article 11 of the Hell Gate Treaty.

Finally, on November 14, 1871, President Ulysses S. Grant issued an Executive Order directing the removal of the Salish to the Jocko Reserve. Congress followed on June 5, 1872, with an appropriation of $50,000 to compensate the Salish for their Bitterroot holdings and to cover the expenses of removal. In effect, President Grant pretended that the conditions of Article 11 had been met. That is, he acted as if government officials actually had surveyed and examined the upper Bitterroot and as if he then had determined that the Jocko Reserve offered the better choice for the Salish.

When Charlo refused this order—arguing that the government never had assessed the upper Bitterroot as promised—the Secretary of the Interior appointed a special commissioner to negotiate the removal with Charlo. James A. Garfield of Ohio had reached the rank of major general during the Civil War, and he was well into

SPEECH OF SALISH CHIEF CHARLO TO U.S. SENATOR GEORGE G. VEST (MISSOURI), SEPTEMBER 10, 1883, AT STEVENSVILLE, MONTANA TERRITORY

Vest: "...I informed him further that the government did not want to use force, but that I had an order in my pocket to have soldiers brought from Fort Missoula and that he and his 50 or 60 warriors could be tied and carried over to the fort like so many bags of grain."

Charlo: "You may carry me to Fort Missoula dead, but you will never carry me there alive. I heard before that your great father had printed a book showing my name to the treaty, but I never signed nor told anybody else to sign it for me.

"As to carrying me to the fort like a bag of grain, you did not talk that way when your people were going to California and came through my country sick and hungry. I had many warriors then and could have killed them all, but we nursed and fed them and did all we could to make them happy.

"Nearly all my warriors are dead now, and I have only women and children. You have your foot on my head now (Charlo threw on the floor a fragment of an old woolen hat and put his foot upon it), but then I had my foot on your head.

"There is not a drop of white blood on the hands of my people. When Joseph, the Nez Perce, my kinsman, marched through my country on his way to Canada, I refused to take his hand because it had white blood on it. I told him that, if he hurt a single one of the whites in the Bitter Root Valley, I would attack him with my warriors at once. There (Charlo pointed to an old, blind Indian in the room) is a man who drew his revolver and defended the wife of the blacksmith at Stevensville from the Nez Perces at the risk of his life.

"He (Charlo then pointed to the cell of Father Anthony Ravalli, which joined the meeting room) was there, and he knows that I refused to sign the Garfield treaty. I have no faith in what you say now, for the government has broken all the promises made by your great father in 1855."

—Anaconda Standard, *December 20, 1903*

serving his eight consecutive terms in the U.S. House (1863-1879). A dynamic debater, by 1872 he had become one of the most influential members of Congress. Garfield would be elected the twentieth President of the United States in 1880, only to be assassinated less than one year later.

On his 1872 trip to Montana, Special Commissioner Garfield first stopped in Virginia City, the capital of Montana Territory. Between Virginia City and Stevensville, four dignitaries joined his party: Territorial Governor Benjamin F. Potts; Jasper A. Viall, the Indian Superintendent for Montana Territory; Territorial Delegate to Congress William Claggett; and noted Republican attorney Wilbur Fisk Sanders. On August 22, the delegation met with the Salish leaders: First Chief Charlo, Second Chief Arlee, and Third Chief Adolf.

In two days of negotiating, cajoling, and threatening, Garfield failed to persuade the natives to budge from their Bitterroot lands. He broke the deadlock by requesting that the three chiefs meet him at the Jocko Agency, where they could judge reservation conditions for themselves. Once in the Mission Valley, the Congressman succeeded in splitting the Salish leadership by promising new houses, seed grain, and cultivated fields to Arlee and Adolf.

Garfield prepared an agreement dated August 27, 1872. His report of the negotiations states (Report of the Commissioner of Indian Affairs, 1872, *House Executive Document #1*, Serial Set 1560):

> It became evident in the course of this interview that the chiefs had at last become divided in opinion among themselves on the matter of the removal....The provisions of the contract were determined after full consultation with the superintendent [Viall] and the territorial delegate [Claggett]. And finally the chiefs were requested to answer by signing or refusing to sign it [the contract].
>
> Arlee and Adolf, the second and third chiefs, signed the contract, and said they would do all that they could to enforce it. But Charlo refused to

sign. He said that, if the President commanded it, he would leave the Bitter Root Valley, but at present he would not promise to go to the reservation.

Garfield's secretary produced three copies of this agreement. The Special Commissioner delivered one copy to the Salish, a duplicate to J. A. Viall, the Indian Superintendent for Montana Territory, and he carried a third copy back to Washington, D.C., for the Secretary of the Interior. Garfield ordered the immediate construction of twenty houses for the followers of Arlee and Adolf. However, workmen did not complete those structures until 1874. Only then did Arlee and a dozen Salish families relocate on the Jocko Reserve.

During 1873 Charlo's enduring faith in the wisdom of the United States government finally disintegrated. He became disillusioned, angered, and embittered—for good reason. First, Daniel Shanahan, the Indian Agent on the Jocko Reserve, engineered the official replacement of Charlo, as head chief of the Salish, with Arlee. He reasoned (Report of the Commissioner of Indian Affairs, 1873) that Charlo had "forfeited his right by refusing to remove...." Thus Arlee and his people benefitted most from the $50,000 removal appropriation. As a result of Shanahan's administrative maneuver, Charlo and Arlee remained bitter enemies for the rest of their lives.

Second, in 1873, when the Commissioner of Indian Affairs published his annual report for 1872, he included a copy of the agreement negotiated by Special Commissioner Garfield. Lo and behold, the contract contained the mark of Charlo—as if he had signed the agreement!

Quite obviously, Special Commissioner James A. Garfield—soon to be President James A. Garfield—had affixed Charlo's mark to the published document. Critics might have considered Garfield's mission to Montana a failure without Charlo's approval, so the Congressman simply provided that approval himself.

Charlo was outraged. He dug his heels even further into the Bitterroot grasslands and refused to abandon his ancestral lands. As more and more whites settled the area, he remained furious and obdurate. In 1876, when the federal government issued land patents to 51 Salish for the Bitterroot property on which they were living, Charlo refused to honor the documents. The land agent deposited them with Father Anthony Ravalli at St. Mary's Mission. The chief reasoned that his people should pay no taxes on land that they already owned by treaty.

Through the 1870s, Charlo's families barely survived by farming in the Bitterroot, while hundreds of additional whites took up land around them. Yet, in 1877, when the Nez Perces under Joseph and Looking Glass dashed through the valley, Charlo refused to aid them and protected his white neighbors.

Finally, in 1883, the U.S. Senate created a select committee to examine conditions among natives in Montana. In September, Senator George Graham Vest of Missouri and Territorial Delegate to Congress Martin Maginnis arrived in Stevensville. They first interviewed Father Ravalli on his deathbed. The Jesuit admitted that he had attended the 1872 Garfield negotiations and that Charlo adamantly had refused to sign the agreement.

Commissioner Vest then met with Charlo and attempted to persuade him to remove to the Jocko Reservation. The chief, however, staunchly refused. He proudly referred to his copy of the 1872 Garfield contract—without his mark—held by Agent Peter Ronan at the Jocko Agency. Before leaving, the Senator invited Charlo and his subchiefs to Washington, D.C., to talk with the President and the Secretary of the Interior.

Once back in the capital himself, Vest retrieved the third copy of the 1872 agreement from the Department of the Interior's files. On it too, Charlo's signature was conspicuously absent. Further, Vest discovered an August 27, 1872, letter written by Special Agent Garfield to Jasper A. Viall, the Superintendent of Indian Affairs for Montana. It provided the "smoking gun" (Commissioner of Indian Affairs, 1872, Serial Set 1560):

> In carrying out the terms of the contract made with the chiefs of the
> Flatheads for removing that tribe to this reservation, I have concluded, after
> full consultation with you, to proceed with the work in the same manner as
> though Charlo, the first chief, had signed the contract. I do this in the belief
> that when he sees the work actually going forward, he will conclude to come
> here with the other chiefs and thus keep the tribe unbroken.

Historians since have discovered another letter, written by
Garfield to his wife on August 23, 1872. It includes lines that
attempt to justify his subsequent actions (Helen Addison Howard,
Northwest Trail Blazers, 1963):

> I feel bound to do all in my power to save these noble Indians from the
> mistake they will make if they refuse [to remove to the Jocko]. Moreover I
> greatly dislike to fail in anything I undertake....

Early in 1884, a nearly blind Charlo, several subchiefs, and an
interpreter accompanied Agent Ronan to Washington, D.C. There
they met with Secretary of the Interior Henry M. Teller and with
President Chester A. Arthur. Between meetings, a top surgeon
removed the cataracts from Charlo's eyes, restoring his sight.
Despite other kindnesses, Charlo refused to abandon his beloved
Bitterroot, and the delegation returned to Montana.

Although vindicated, Charlo and his people faced poverty and
starvation. Between 1884 and 1887, 25 Salish families slipped away
from the Bitterroot and relocated on the Jocko Reserve. Agent Ronan
offered the head of each family 160 acres, a new house, assistance in
fencing and breaking 10 acres of land, two cows, a wagon, a plow,
and seed for the first year. In 1885 Ronan also supplied Charlo's
Bitterroot Salish with food, wagons, plows, and harness (see Peter
Ronan, *Historical Sketch of the Flathead Indian Nation*, 1890).

Congress could conceive no solution to the plight of Charlo's
Salish except removal. In 1889 that body passed legislation to buy

out all Salish lands in the Bitterroot Valley. The Department of the Interior detailed General Henry B. Carrington of Massachusetts as special commissioner to settle title to the Salish properties. Finally Charlo would deal with an ethical government representative. Carrington performed his duties with sympathy, fairness, sensitivity, efficiency, and apology. Charlo subsequently conferred on him a Salish name meaning "Big Heart."

The summer of 1889 brought devastating drought to the Bitterroot Valley. In desperation, Charlo capitulated and signed an agreement (November 3) with Special Agent Carrington to remove his 32 remaining families to the Jocko Reserve. Since Arlee had died in August, Charlo could avoid confronting him on the reservation. More important, authorities again would designate Charlo the lead chief of the Salish. The somber Salish leader declared (Arthur L. Stone, *Following Old Trails*, 1913):

> I will go—I and my children. My young men are becoming bad; they have no place to hunt. My women are hungry. For their sake I will go. I do not want the land you promise. I do not believe your promises. All I want is enough ground for my grave. We will go over there.

Anticipating removal, the Salish sowed no crops in 1890—only to have their relocation delayed by bureaucratic red tape. Agent Ronan prevented widespread starvation among the families by distributing foodstuffs and clothing throughout the following winter. In fact, Ronan consistently stretched the rules to treat the Bitterroot Salish with logic and compassion.

Finally in 1891, Special Agent Carrington organized the Salish march from the Bitterroot to the Jocko Reserve. On October 14, at St. Mary's Mission, the Salish engaged in an all-night prayer vigil and feast. The next morning Charlo and his 225 remaining followers assembled their 100 wagons and 400 head of livestock.

After receiving the blessing of the Catholic priest, the natives sang

Dies Irae—"The Day of Wrath," a funeral dirge. Down the main street of Stevensville, the procession trailed slowly out of town. Charlo, mounted on a pony, led the entourage, which included small bands of mounted young men and Special Commissioner Henry Carrington in a spring wagon. As the party descended his beloved Bitterroot Valley, the chief never looked back. Journalist A. L. Stone described the scene (*Following Old Trails*):

> Not in haste, not in disorder, not in an uproar, but slowly, with dignity and in silence they moved out from the mission. Out past [Fort] Owen and across the river and then down the valley, ever amid scenes which had been their daily environment for a lifetime—each step reluctant and each mile a pang.

Charlo's "Trail of Tears" wound 55 miles, through Missoula, up the Coriacan Defile, and onto the Jocko Reserve near Evaro. On October 17, the party reached the Jocko Agency, outside Arlee. Mary Ronan, the wife of Agent Peter Ronan, witnessed the long-awaited arrival (Margaret Ronan, *Frontier Woman*, 1973):

> It was a unique and, to some minds, a pathetic spectacle when Charlo and his band of Indians marched to their future home. Their coming had been heralded, and many of the Reservation Indians had gathered at the Agency to give them welcome. When within a mile of the Agency church, the advancing Indians spread out in a broad column.
>
> The young men kept constantly discharging their firearms. Meanwhile a few of the number, mounted on fleet ponies, arrayed in fantastic Indian paraphernalia, with long blankets partially draping the forms of warriors and steeds, rode back and forth in front of the advancing caravan, shouting and firing their guns until they neared the church, where a large banner of the Sacred Heart of Mary and Jesus was erected on a tall pole....
>
> Chief Charlo's countenance retained its habitual expression of stubborn pride and gloom, as he advanced on foot, shaking hands with all who had come to greet him.

Agent Ronan built a new house for Charlo a few hundred yards north of the Agency square, on Arlee's former claim. The other families ultimately took up sites in the southern portion of the reservation—after 1891 called "the Flathead Indian Reservation." Although Mary Ronan observed that Charlo "bore himself with reserve, dignity, and pride of race…like a king in exile," the aging leader grieved, every day, for his abandoned Bitterroot Valley.

Charlo never reconciled to the removal or to the federal government's treatment of the Salish—from 1855 on. He would discuss no aspect of his Bitterroot life with whites. Yet he might have found some solace in the improved conditions of his followers.

In September 1911, many Salish returned to Stevensville to commemorate the twentieth anniversary of their "Trail of Tears" march. Here they danced, feasted, visited old white friends, worshiped at St. Mary's Church, and performed rituals at the graves of their ancestors. Charlo did not suffer the indignity of this return to his beloved Bitterroot Valley. After spending his last years in blindness, he had died on January 10, 1910, at Jocko.

Of Charlo's lifelong battle to retain his ancestral homeland, Arthur Stone wrote (*Following Old Trails*):

> Deceived by the agents of the government, betrayed by the special representative of the President, conspired against by some of his own people, trusting only the few whites who were his close neighbors, Charlo had resisted steadfastly.…If the whites had been as honest with him as he was with them, his last days would have been happier.

A regrettable epitaph for a gallant leader and his proud people.

SOURCES

All of the general works on the Salish address the issue of the removal of Charlo's people from the Bitterroot. See: L. B. Palladino, S. J., *Indian and White in the North West: A History of Catholicity in Montana, 1831-1891* (Lancaster, Penn.: Wickersham, 1922), 77-90; John Fahey, *The Flathead Indians* (Norman: University of Oklahoma, 1974), 149-166, 227-250; Olga Weydemeyer Johnson, *Flathead and Kootenay: The Rivers, the Tribes, and the Region's Traders* (Glendale, Calif.: Arthur H. Clark, 1969), 337-359; Arthur L. Stone, *Following Old Trails* (Missoula: Elrod, 1913), 76-96.

See also: Helen Addison Howard, *North West Trail Blazers* (Caldwell: Caxton, 1963), 175-202; Peter Ronan, *Historical Sketch of the Flathead Indian Nation, 1813-1890* (Helena: Journal, 1890), 54-72; Margaret Ronan, *Frontier Woman, the Story of Mary Ronan*, H. G. Merriam, ed. (Missoula: University of Montana, 1974); James P. Nugent and Margery H. Brown, *The Confederated Salish and Kootenai Tribes of the Flathead Reservation in Montana: An Analysis of Tribal Government in Relation to Pre-Reservation and Reservation Life of the Principal Tribes of Western Montana* (Missoula: UM Law School, Indian Law Seminar, 1975).

Several periodical pieces supply supplementary information: Oliver W. Holmes, ed., "Peregrinations of a Politician [Garfield's trip]," *Montana: The Magazine of Western History,* 6, #4 (October, 1956), 34-45; Michael Harrison, "Chief Charlot's [sic] Battle with Bureaucracy," *Montana: The Magazine of Western History,* 10, #4 (October, 1960), 27-33; Albert J. Partoll, "The Flathead Indian Treaty Council of 1855," *Pacific Northwest Quarterly,* Vol. 29 (1938), 283-314; Mark Boesch, "The Forged Signature of Chief Charlot" [sic], *Empire Magazine, Denver Post,* November 3, 1974, 28-31; "Sullen Old Chief Charlot [sic] Nurses Many Wrongs," *Anaconda Standard,* December 20, 1903.

Government documents necessarily provide some of the pivotal sources for this study. The story of Charlo's Salish appears within the run of annual reports from the Flathead Agency, beginning in 1868. See particularly: U.S. Office of Indian Affairs, *Annual Reports of the Commissioner of Indian Affairs to the Secretary of the Interior* (Washington, D.C.: General Printing Office)—for 1868 (Serial Set #1366), for 1872 (Serial Set #1560), for 1873 (Serial Set #1601), for 1874 (Serial Set #1639), for 1877 (Serial Set #1800), for 1889 (Serial Set #2841), for 1890 (Serial Set #2934), for 1891 (Serial Set #3088).

The 1855 Flathead Treaty can be found in: Charles J. Kappler, ed., *Indian*

Affairs, Laws and Treaties (Washington, D.C.: General Printing Office, 1904), II, 722-725. The Kappler series appears as Senate Document #319, 58th Congress, 2nd Session, Serial Set #4624. President Grant's November 14, 1871, Executive Order to remove the Salish appears in: *Executive Orders Relating to Indian Reservations, 1855-1912* (Washington, D.C.: General Printing Office, 1922), 89.

Senator Vest's report is included in: U.S. Senate Committee Reports, 1883-1884, 48th Congress, 1st Session, *Report of the Subcommittee of the Special Committee of the U.S. Senate, Appointed to Visit the Indian Tribes of Montana, #283* (Washington, D.C.: General Printing Office, 1884), Serial Set #2170 and #2171. General Carrington's report of his 1889 negotiations appears in: U.S. Senate, *Executive Document #70, 51st Congress, 1st Session* (Washington, D.C.: General Printing Office, 1890), Serial Set #2686.

Finally, contemporary accounts of the various episodes in this saga can be tracked in Montana's daily and weekly newspapers. Garfield's 1872 trip is covered in the *Helena Daily Herald*, the *Missoula Pioneer*, and the (Deer Lodge) *New North West*. See the (Missoula) *Weekly Missoulian* regarding Senator Vest's 1883 negotiations.

For the 1891 removal, see especially the (Deer Lodge) *New North West*, the (Missoula) *Missoulian*, and the Missoula *Weekly Gazette*. Regarding the 1911 return of the Salish to Stevensville, see: (Missoula) *Missoulian*; (Stevensville) *North West Tribune*.

CHAPTER FIVE

THE GREAT GREY CLIFF TRAIN ROBBERY

As Montanans well know, the "Wild West" lives strong and long here, right into the twenty-first century. That is because just enough truth existed in the real nineteenth-century American West to fuel today's myths of the "Wild West."

Town marshals did shoot it out with gunfighters on dusty streets; cattlemen did battle sheepmen for prime rangeland; some saloon-owning madames did have "hearts of gold"! And, epic train rob-beries and manhunts—reminiscent of the 1969 film classic "Butch Cassidy and the Sundance Kid"—did occur, right here in Montana.

This confusion of art and reality produced an early-1890s Montana in which each realm imitated the other. Truly, the brand-new state of Montana found itself caught in a cultural warp. The federal Superintendent of the Census had declared an end to the frontier in 1890. Yet Montanans had just begun to ride the euphoric tide of new railroad links to the Midwest and both coasts. And, simultaneously, the Montana economy took tough hits from the national Panic of 1893.

The halcyon days of Montana's open-range cattle industry had faded with the Hard Winter of 1886-1887, but a struggling "cowboy culture" still blanketed much of the state in the early 1890s. Meanwhile an Eastern trend in popular literature and culture exploited the cowboy's lifestyle. Primarily through shoot-em-up "dime novels" and itinerant "Wild West shows," a romantic image of the cowboy emerged that featured open gunfights, cattle stampedes, bandit women, bank holdups, bounty hunters, range wars, daring outlaws, and train robberies.

Gradually, almost unconsciously, Westerners began to accept the "Wild West" image as their own—and to live it. That element of "living the myth" is clearly at work in the little-known 1893 Montana train robbery and manhunt: the Grey Cliff affair.

In this episode, the Northern Pacific Railroad's passenger-express #4 left Helena, heading east, on the hot afternoon of August 26, 1893. By evening it had run through the division point at Livingston and was pushing toward Billings. At Big Timber, in the dark, a clutch of passengers that included two cowboys boarded the express. Calmly, unnoticed, the two men walked forward through the cars, climbed over the coal tender, masked their faces with handkerchiefs, and seized control of the locomotive at gunpoint.

The hold-up men ordered engineer John Brown and fireman Alex Wilson to keep the train moving until they spotted a signal lamp beside the tracks. Just east of Grey Cliff—a small community on the Yellowstone River, eight miles east of Big Timber and fourteen miles west of Reed Point—the lantern appeared out of the darkness. Express #4 screeched to a stop in front of two more masked cowboys, each armed with two revolvers and a Winchester rifle. Then the four holdup men, with the engineer and the fireman, marched directly to the baggage car.

After a short delay, the expressman opened the sliding door to the car, and the thieves rifled its contents. They could not bust into the through-safe, but produced some dynamite to blow it open. The leader, however, abandoned that plan because it would take too long. (Northern Pacific officials later revealed that the safe

A Northern Pacific locomotive in service in 1893.
Photo courtesy of Montana Historical Society, Helena

contained more than $60,000.) He opted instead for a sweep through the passenger cars in search of personal belongings.

So the cluster of outlaws and trainmen walked back down the track toward the last sleeper car. Whenever a curious passenger stuck his head out a window, a bandit shot into the air over the train, and the fellow scuttled back into his seat. The four outlaws then worked through the cars, collecting men's gold watches, cash, and women's jewelry. When reluctant passengers hesitated, a few shots fired through the ceiling of the car persuaded them to donate to the burlap sack bulging with booty.

The *Livingston Post* recounted (August 31, 1893):

> Not a passenger escaped the stern command to "shell out." There was no deviation on account of age, sex, or color. Those who had not taken warning, and secreted their money and valuables, were soon relieved of those things. Numerous gold watches and diamond pins were secured, and in several instances, rings were snatched from the fingers of half-dressed, deathly pale, and thoroughly frightened lady passengers.

The thieves joked with the passengers and occasionally apologized for confiscating a particularly hefty wallet or an especially attractive pocket watch, chain, and fob. While passing through the dining car, the leader ordered four sack lunches "to go." None of the trainmen was robbed, except for conductor John M. Rapelje, who throughout had acted extremely resentful and combative.

At one point during the holdup, the unwritten "code of the West" surfaced. When one of the bandits swore at a recalcitrant passenger, the leader admonished him, "There are ladies present. Remember that you are a gentleman." In the same "Wild West" vein, the *Helena Daily Herald* editorialized (August 28, 1893):

> There is certainly some style about Montana highwaymen. After going

through a train near Grey Cliff on Saturday night, and being in need of
refreshments, they held the engineer until they could order and carry away
a good square meal from the dining car—which they ordered as if they were
accustomed to dining cars all their lives.

During the fifty-minute holdup, the gang sacked up a bit more
than $1,000 in money and goods—as well as their traveling lunches.
They thanked the trainmen for their cooperation and rode off north,
toward the Yellowstone River, into the darkness. Engineer Brown ran
#4 at top speed into Reed Point, where he telegraphed news of the
daring train robbery to authorities up and down the line.

In the darkness, the four outlaws swam their horses across the
Yellowstone, bypassed Melville, looped west of the Cayuse Hills,
and pushed toward the upper Musselshell Valley. About forty miles
from the Yellowstone, just south of Merino (present-day
Harlowton), they had stashed four fresh horses, and by dawn they
reached this relay camp.

Around the campfire that morning sat an unlikely assemblage of
men. The acknowledged leader was Charley Jones (alias Charles
Kinkaid; alias John Charles), a short burly cowhand in his mid-thirties, with a full head of red hair. A Texan, Charley had wintered in
Helena in 1891 and had worked for the "79" outfit in Custer County
for several seasons. Next to Jones sat an exhausted Jack White (alias
Bob Taylor; alias Ben Hall). White had ridden for several ranches
along the Yellowstone and knew Jones from the "79" outfit.

Across the fire sprawled the tallest of the fugitives, Jack Chipman.
An Englishman by birth, Chipman was in his mid-twenties, slim,
and over six feet tall. He wore eyeglasses and was rather dressy—in
fact, he was known in Red Lodge as "the dude cowboy." Chipman
had arrived in Montana in 1890 and had worked for cattlemen in
the upper Shields Valley. Local lawmen thought that Chipman was
the sneak thief who had been robbing sheep camps in the area.

The last of the outlaws was the quiet Sam Shermer (alias Ben

Mattock; alias Joe Mattocks; alias Sam Holliday). He had worked as a sheepherder in Fergus County for several years. In 1891 he had been arrested in Big Timber on a warrant for an Ohio post-office robbery, but the Ohio jury found him not guilty, and he had returned to Montana.

Jones, White, and Chipman had asked Shermer to join the gang after their original accomplice—the one-armed Jack Flynn, a foreman for the "79"—had drowned in June while swimming some strays across the Yellowstone River near Laurel. The four men had planned to rob a Big Timber bank, but Flynn had been their "inside man." Without him, they had approached Shermer and substituted the Northern Pacific express as their target.

Riding four fresh horses and leading their spent mounts, the gang abandoned their relay camp, crossed the Musselshell River below Two Dot, and pushed northwest. Once in the Little Belt Mountains, the men separated. They agreed to reunite at Blackfoot, a small town on the Blackfeet Indian Reservation, in about three weeks.

Meanwhile "the good guys" assembled. By coincidence Yellowstone County sheriff John M. Ramsey was visiting in the town of Stillwater (just east of Reed Point) on August 26. Upon hearing of the train robbery, he gathered a posse of 13 men, loaded their horses in a local-freight boxcar, and steamed up the line to Grey Cliff. He was joined there early on August 27 by Park County sheriff John M. Conrow and his posse of 15 men from Livingston.

Northern Pacific division superintendent J. D. Finn, located in Livingston, arranged for a special train to shuttle lawmen along the mainline. He ordered that the "special" had "highball rights": that is, preference over all N.P. traffic, including express passenger trains. Further, he put a reward of $500 on the head of each robber and pledged $100 per day in expense money to underwrite the posse.

The posse included deputy sheriff Sam Jackson from Livingston, who had some experience in bounty hunting. Jackson—"heavy-set, jovial, and sporting a full beard"—had been deputized in Park,

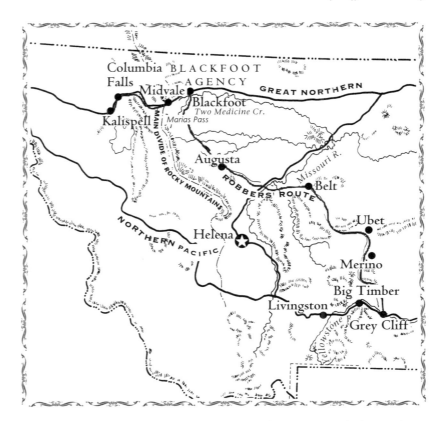

Yellowstone, and Meagher counties. In the morning light, Jackson recognized that one of the fugitives was riding a horse with "plated or running shoes." These lighter, narrower shoes were usually used for horse racing and left distinctive tracks, without heel-caulk marks.

As the composite posse pushed north, toward the Musselshell, rumors circulated that they might be pursuing notorious criminals. Local newspapers speculated that the train robbery had been committed by members of the Dalton Brothers' gang, from Kansas and Oklahoma. Or, at least, it was the work of Harry Gross and Bill Gay, two desperadoes from the mining camp of Castle, whom Meagher County authorities then were hunting.

At an overwhelming advantage of 30-to-4, the large posse fearlessly pursued. A jocular, holiday atmosphere pervaded as they trailed north during the day, only to set camp at dark. Shortly after noon on August 28, they found the thieves' relay camp south of Merino. Here Sheriff Ramsey discovered pieces of a torn letter buried near the campfire. When reassembled, they revealed the name of Jack Chipman.

At the gang's next cold campfire, one of Sheriff Conrow's deputies found a Masonic watch fob in the ashes. It fit the description of the fob stolen from conductor Rapelje near Grey Cliff. The evidence was beginning to accumulate. However, because the posse traveled only in daylight, the criminals—who rode day and night—quickly out-distanced them. Gradually the trail became older, colder.

After eight days in pursuit (on September 3), the lawmen reached Ubet (Judith Gap) and abandoned the chase. They concluded that they never would catch the fugitives, whom they believed were heading for Canada. More important, the Northern Pacific refused to subsidize the sizeable posse any longer.

Deputy Sam Jackson immediately returned to Livingston and struck a deal with N.P. Division Superintendent Finn. In return for a daily stipend from the Northern Pacific, Jackson would hunt the train robbers alone. In addition Finn would appoint him a "special agent" for the railroad and arrange for his commission as a Deputy U.S. Marshal. Jackson then took the train to Dodge (a Montana Central Railway station southwest of Great Falls), where he tried to pick up the trail of the fleeing criminals.

Over the next three weeks, Jackson received news of gang members in various locations. One fugitive had purchased supplies in Belt on September 10—and bragged about a train robbery. Jackson then picked up the distinctive "running shoe" tracks where they crossed the Montana Central line, near Cascade. He followed them northwest, into Augusta, where he learned that two men with six horses had spent September 15.

In Augusta, the two strangers bought whiskey, flour, and bacon, had all their horses reshod, and lost $80 in a local poker game. They also asked for local newspapers published at the end of August, so they could read about the train robbery. The men then rode out in the direction of the town of Sun River.

By this time Jackson had collected enough information to know that he was tracking Charley Jones, Jack Chipman, Jack White, and Sam Shermer. The deputy still believed that the gang was trying to escape to Canada, so he leap-frogged north by rail to the Blackfeet Indian Reservation. This area had become a lively place after the Great Northern built its mainline across the reserve in 1890. During the next year, contract crews—using a parallel tote road— had constructed the tracks west, over Marias Pass and down Bear Creek and the Middle Fork of the Flathead River, toward Kalispell.

On the Blackfeet Reservation, on September 29 (more than one month after the holdup), Jackson contacted interim Indian Agent Lorenzo W. Cooke, who was moving the reservation office from Old Agency on Badger Creek to Willow Creek, near Browning. Cooke informed the lawman that, indeed, he had encountered the four cowhands who fit Jackson's description. Just the preceding week, he had ordered them to leave the agency grounds at Browning because they looked like trouble. Cooke said that he did not know where the suspicious fellows had gone.

In truth, Jones and his men had reunited in the town of Blackfoot—eleven miles east of Browning, on the Great Northern Railway mainline—on September 25. After receiving Agent Cooke's warning, they had returned to Blackfoot to frequent the town's three saloons. And that is where Deputy Marshal Jackson ran into them, face-to-face, on September 30!

With composure reminiscent of Clint Eastwood in *Hang 'Em High* (1968) and *High Plains Drifter* (1973), Jackson never tipped his hand. Rather, he sent Blackfoot restaurant owner Henry Schubert to request a contingent of Indian police from Agent Cooke. When the gang rode out of town on October 1—accompanied by an 18-year-old boy named Jimmy Moots—Jackson detailed two Blackfeet, Dick Kipp and George Cook, to follow them. Moots had met Jones and the others in Blackfoot several days earlier. Alternately frightened and thrilled by their "badness," the bedazzled young man eagerly joined the renegade band when invited.

On the afternoon of October 2, Jackson assembled his posse at Blackfoot: restaurateur Schubert; Duck Head and ten members of his police force, including Frank Monroe, John Brown, Running Crane, Wades-in-Water, Irving Little Plume, and Pete Champine. The Great Northern, at the request of Superintendent Finn and the Northern Pacific, had created a three-car "special" and placed it at Jackson's disposal. The "special" carried Jackson, the posse, and all their horses up the line 32 miles to Midvale (present-day East Glacier).

Kipp and Cook had shadowed the gang to Midvale and then to a log cabin where Moots had been staying—two miles east of town, on Two Medicine Creek, within several hundred yards of the Great Northern tracks. On the crisp, clear morning of Tuesday, October 3, the posse surrounded the cabin. Jackson and Duck Head approached the shelter, through the brush, while two possemen ran off the gang's horses. Suddenly Jackson shouted, "Hold up your hands and come out!" Men in the cabin quickly broke chinking from between the logs to create portholes. The shooting began right on the stroke of 10 o'clock.

Almost at once Duck Head took a bullet through his shoulder, and he and the rest of the Indian police retreated out of range. For the next thirty minutes, Jackson and Schubert exchanged fire with the five men in the cabin. Then Schubert shouted and fell, fatally wounded, and Jackson stopped shooting. During the gunfight, Jones and Chipman had dug a hole under the back wall of the cabin. While Jackson hesitated, considering how to aid Schubert, the five outlaws escaped into the trees on foot. They headed for Midvale and then southwest, along the Great Northern right-of-way, toward Marias Pass.

Jones' gang had accepted Jimmy Moots' hospitality at the cabin while they planned a second train robbery—that of a Great Northern express near Midvale. Because Jones had anticipated a mad dash for the Canadian line after that holdup, the men had stashed almost 1,500 rounds of ammunition, a dozen new blankets, their heavy coats, 10 hams, a side of beef, 7 saddles, and 8 horses at the cabin. They abandoned all of these supplies and equipment when they fled west on foot.

Marshal Jackson remained concealed in the brush for hours because he believed the criminals were still in the cabin. Finally, in mid-afternoon, he crawled to Schubert's side, found him barely alive, and loaded him on a horse. Henry Schubert died on the ride to Midvale—where Jackson discovered the Blackfeet police contingent waiting for a doctor to treat Duck Head's wound.

Once Marshal Jackson wired news of the shootout to Livingston, the manhunt commenced in earnest. That evening, Indian Agent Cooke arrived in Midvale with an additional 15 Indian police. From Helena, Lewis and Clark County Sheriff Charles D. Curtis brought a posse of 10 mounted men. Meanwhile Joseph Gangner, sheriff of the new Flathead County, deputized 18 men in Kalispell. He loaded them on another Great Northern "special" and they "highballed" it toward Midvale. That evening, Deputy Jackson told a reporter, "That Charley Jones is a very, very, bad man. He has grey eyes, is quick as a cat, and is the fastest shot I ever saw."

By Wednesday morning, October 4, a determined army of about sixty deputized men left Midvale to scour the rugged country toward Marias Pass. They were aided by recent storms that left several inches of snow at lower elevations, but almost two feet near the summit.

Throughout the day, bands of lawmen spotted the outlaws as they scrambled through the snow, over downed timber, and disappeared in the woods, approaching the pass. Although "the good guys" fired at them repeatedly, the fugitives always slipped into deeper cover. None of the deputies, even in squads, seemed eager to leave the right-of-way and follow the gunmen into the dense, snow-clogged timber.

On a hunch, Sheriff Gangner took a handful of his men, put them on the Great Northern "special," and steamed through Marias Pass to the west-side Java station. As the cold darkness settled on the high country, Gangner and three men began climbing the mainline east of Java, back toward the summit.

In the blackness, they soon encountered several shadows. One of blurred figures shouted, "There are some sons-of-bitches! Kill them!" In the ensuing firefight, Gangner and his men killed Jack Chipman, wounded Sam Shermer seriously in the hip, and shot through the leg of Jimmy Moots, who gratefully surrendered. Only Jack White and Charley Jones slipped away into the falling snow and the darkness.

Montana newspapers fed on the "Wild West" pursuit of the Jones gang and on the gun battles like wolves on a ripe carcass. The *Great Falls Tribune* remarked (October 7, 1893):

> The roundup of the desperadoes was only accomplished after a hard and vigorous chase, lasting about 48 hours, during which considerable shooting was done, and winding up with a hot fight. The endurance of the boys was wonderful. They waded streams, climbed over fallen trees, and went through snow, slush, and mud. Not one of the pursuers was injured yesterday.

After spending a cold, wet night hiding in a pile of railroad ties, a weary Charley Jones walked into the Java section house early the next morning and surrendered to Bill Bracken, the Irish section boss. Bracken fed him breakfast, dried his clothes over the stove, and delivered him to Sheriff Gangner. Jones' opening remark to the sheriff—"Say, Joe, won't you fellows ever stop following a man?"— echoed loudly Butch Cassidy's movie line about his pursuers, "Who *are* those guys?"

Triumphantly Gangner's men rode the "special" into Kalispell that afternoon, with bodies and prisoners under guard. Marshall Jackson accompanied the group and stated (*Helena Daily Independent*, October 6, 1893): "I am elated at our success. This has been one of the hardest and the most exciting times that I have ever had chasing criminals."

Agent Cooke and the Indian-police contingent spent the next three days searching along the Great Northern right-of-way for Jack White, but the fugitive had disappeared. Finally the manhunt ended, and all of the lawmen returned to their respective jurisdictions. Newspapers across the state trumpeted (*Helena Daily Independent*, October 8, 1893):

> The pursuit and capture of these train robbers is the most notable, as well as the most successful, that has ever been recorded in this country. Marshal Jackson is more than modest in regard to the part he took in it. But the fact remains that he started after the robbers the day after the hold-up and never stopped, despite the hardships, until his mission had been successfully fulfilled.

The wounded Sam Shermer delivered a deathbed confession in Kalispell on October 8. He assured authorities that Jimmy Moots had joined the group only a few days earlier, and he fingered Jack Chipman as the killer of Henry Schubert in the Midvale cabin shootout. Authorities buried both Shermer and Chipman in Kalispell. Meanwhile, Sam Jackson escorted the shackled Charley Jones and Jimmy Moots to Helena, by train. At Helena's Montana Central depot, 250 curious townspeople greeted the party—just to catch a glimpse of the desperate gunmen about whom they had read so much.

For almost three weeks, no one heard a whisper about Jack White. During that time he had lived off the land, slowly working his way through the snow and the timber, down the Middle Fork of the Flathead River. Then a truly bizarre sequence occurred. Wholly by coincidence, White stumbled into someone he knew in the woods northeast of Columbia Falls, near Lake Five. In the late 1880s, White and G. P. Gensman had filed on adjacent homesteads in Chouteau County. Although neither had proved up on his claim, they had spent some time as neighbors near Highwood.

Then suddenly these two old acquaintances found themselves face-to-face in the snowy timber on October 20. An elated White believed that he had found a true friend. He explained his plight and begged Gensman for help—in return for the remainder of the train-robbery cash he carried, about $150. Gensman promised to return in three days with clothing, food, and ammunition, and to guide White out of the valley.

On October 23, Gensman did meet White again, just outside of Coram. But he did not bring supplies, and he did not lead an extra horse. Rather he brought a friend, Joe Fitzpatrick, to serve as a witness. Gensman, armed with a Winchester and a pistol, approached White and ordered him to surrender. When White dropped his rifle, Gensman shot him twice, at point-blank range, through the chest. White died instantly. Gensman and Fitzpatrick carried the body to Coram, boarded a passenger train, and rode into Kalispell to collect the $500 reward for White.

Flathead County officials listened to Gensman's story, noted that White's rifle and pistol were empty, charged Gensman with manslaughter, and locked him in a cell. A coroner's jury later exonerated the shooter, and the Northern Pacific ultimately paid him the full $500 reward.

Gensman's greedy actions flew directly in the face of "the code of the West." The Choteau *Montanian* observed (November 3, 1893):

> While the people rejoice over the fact that a desperate character [White] has been run down and given his just desserts, they feel that it is a bad precedent to establish to allow private citizens to shoot down men guilty of crimes. Gensman had ample time to report the whereabouts of White to the proper officers, who could have taken him alive, as White had no cartridges. The slayer's greed to

JUDGE HIRAM KNOWLES' ADVICE TO A
CONVICTED JIMMY MOOTS
JANUARY 12, 1893

"It is usual for a judge, in passing sentence, to deliver something of a lecture to the prisoner with the view to directing him toward a better course of life.

"You claim that you have been a hard-working boy. You were found in the company of men who, according to the testimony presented in court, were of bad character: men who sought to make a living otherwise than by honest labor; men who sought to take property from men who make their living by honest means....You were found with those men and were with them when a fellow being was killed.

"The history of men who commit crime is that, while they may meet with some temporary success, yet in the end their life is a failure in every particular. So they die some kind of a miserable death—either within the walls of a penitentiary or out among their fellow men, deserted and forsaken, none desiring to do for them an act of kindness.

"Now I would say to you—as a matter of policy, if for nothing else— never consort with men hereafter who are criminals.

"The judgment of the court is that you be confined in the penitentiary at Deer Lodge for a term of two years and be fined $100."

—Helena Daily Independent, *January 13, 1893*

secure the $500 reward has lost him much sympathy that he would otherwise have shared. At the very least, the killing was a betrayal of friendship.

The (Kalispell) *Flathead Herald-Journal* (October 27, 1893) agreed:

A train robber or any other species of criminal should be caught and punished. But men should not be too free with their guns, lest some horrible crime be committed in the name of justice....Let this be a warning to Gensman and his ilk: his actions in this terrible affair were not those of a brave man and cannot be commended by law-abiding, law-loving people.

With the deaths of Jack Chipman, Sam Shermer, and Jack White, only Charley Jones remained from the original holdup gang. Jones appeared before United States Court Judge Hiram P. Knowles in Helena in January 1894—as did Jimmy Moots. The federal court held jurisdiction because the two were charged with the shooting of Henry Schubert, which had occurred on federal land, the Blackfeet Indian Reservation.

Prosecuting attorney Elbert D. Weed dramatically asserted (*Helena Daily Herald*, January 9, 1894): "If this evidence against defendant Jones is not strong enough to convict him, then we had better disorganize the courts of justice and let every man carry around a Winchester!"

At the trial, teenager Moots cut a deal with prosecutors and received a light sentence in return for his testimony against Jones. After short deliberation, the jury found Charley Jones guilty of first-degree murder in the death of Henry Schubert.

Deputy Marshal Sam Jackson proved to be the hero of the trial. Exuding an almost–John Wayne aura, he recounted again his tenacious pursuit of the train robbers. One prosecuting attorney declared (*Anaconda Standard*, January 11, 1894): "Marshal Jackson has a reputation for bravery as firmly established as that of [famous Montana lawman] X. Biedler!"

However, Jones' two young attorneys—Edward C. Russell and John R. Barrows—immediately appealed the conviction, on the grounds that Judge Knowles had not properly instructed the jury. The Montana Supreme Court sustained the appeal, and Jones was retried in Helena for the Schubert murder in December 1894. This time Jimmy Moots received a full pardon from President Grover Cleveland prior to testifying against his former compatriot.

Yet attorneys Russell and Barrows proved masterful (*Helena Daily Independent*, December 16, 1894):

> When Jones gave himself up and was brought to Helena [October,

1893], he was ill-clad and unkempt. His bushy red whiskers gave him the appearance of a man of 50 who had been working for some rancher whose provisions of soap had run short.

When he was brought into court for his first trial [January, 1894], he had donned a new suit of clothes and had his whiskers trimmed. It altered his appearance to that of a well-to-do country merchant of about 40 years.

Those who saw him walk into court yesterday saw an entirely different looking man from the one they had seen on either of the two previous occasions. He had removed every vestige of hair from his face and looked like what he really is—a man between 30 and 35 years of age. He took a seat near his counsel and his restless blue eyes took in everything within range in the court room.

In the end, the second jury found Jones guilty of manslaughter, primarily on the basis of Jimmy Moots' testimony. Judge Knowles sentenced him to the maximum ten years in the Deer Lodge prison and fined him $100. Jones observed (*Helena Daily Independent*, December 20, 1894): "It's not as bad this time, but it's still pretty hard. However, I had a fair trial, and that's all a man can ask for."

Train-robber Charley Jones finally was released by authorities on March 15, 1906. His term ran more than two years beyond the ten-year sentence because of "a series of misconduct violations" in prison. At the time of Jones' release, Edwin S. Porter's epic silent film "The Great Train Robbery" had been thrilling audiences for three years.

The 1893 Grey Cliff train robbery and manhunt offer dramatic examples of mixing the myth of the "Wild West" with the Montana reality of the time. Many of the players—on both sides of the law—found themselves acting the roles prescribed by contemporary dime novelists, newspapermen, and "Wild West show" promoters. What an incredible time warp in which to live!

Yet present-day Montanans who believe that the myth of the "Wild West" is dead need only check out the boots, the oversized

CAST OF CHARACTERS

THE "BLACK HATS"
Charley Jones
Jack Chipman
Jack White
Sam Shermer
Jimmy Moots

THE "WHITE HATS"
Sam Jackson, deputy U.S. Marshal
Sheriff John M. Ramsey, Yellowstone County
Sheriff John M. Conrow, Park County
Sheriff Charles D. Curtis, Lewis and Clark County
Sheriff Joseph Gangner, Flathead County
Captain Lorenzo W. Cooke, Agent
Little Dog, Police Captain
Duck Head
Frank Munroe
George Cook
John Brown
Running Crane
Dick Kipp
Wades-in-Water
Little Plume
Pete Champine

INVOLVED CITIZENS
John Brown, Northern Pacific engineer
John M. Rapelje, Northern Pacific conductor
J. D. Finn, Northern Pacific division superintendent
Henry Schubert, Blackfoot restaurant owner
J. P. Gensman, Columbia Falls opportunist

belt buckles, and the cowboy hats worn by state legislators, by computer-company executives, and by school teachers. More than a century later, we have not cleanly severed from Charley Jones, Sam Jackson, and Henry Schubert.

All around us, art is imitating life. Or is that life imitating art? Or are the two just hopelessly entangled in twenty-first-century Montana?

SOURCES

Montana newspapers—both dailies and weeklies—provide a wealth of information on various aspects of the Grey Cliff robbery and the ensuing manhunt. They also are the strongest purveyors of the "Wild West" theme that infuses this episode. The best dailies are the *Helena Daily Independent*, the *Helena Daily Herald*, the *Great Falls Tribune*, the *Butte Daily Miner*, and the *Anaconda Standard*. They felt the need to provide statewide coverage, so (between August 26, 1893, and December 23, 1894) they become essential sources for such a wide-ranging saga.

Weeklies across the state likewise covered the Grey Cliff holdup and pursuit (particularly during the August-December 1893 period). Papers in areas immediately affected by the action proved the most complete—for instance, the *Big Timber Pioneer*, the (Livingston) *Enterprise*, the (Bozeman) *Avant Courier*, the (Lewistown) *Argus*, the (Choteau) *Montanian*, the (Fort Benton) *River Press*, the (Columbia Falls) *Columbian*, the (Kalispell) *Graphic*, and the (Demersville/Kalispell) *Inter Lake*.

Other weeklies that provided graphic coverage of the "Wild West" events include: the (Boulder) *Jefferson County Sentinel*, the (Marysville) *Mountaineer*; the (Missoula) *Missoulian*, the (Miles City) *Stock Growers Journal*, and the (Deer Lodge) *New North West*.

Both Jimmy Moots and Charley Jones can be tracked in the records of the Montana State Prison in Deer Lodge: State Microfilm #36, Reel 2. These records are held by the Montana Historical Society Library in Helena.

It may be so obvious that any direct statement is unnecessary, but: one of the pure joys of historical research is to dig out a story like the Grey Cliff train robbery from diverse Montana newspapers, to rectify the factual discrepancies those sources provide, and to fit all of the pieces together so they make some semblance of sense.

CHAPTER SIX

MONTANA'S VENOMOUS CAPITAL FIGHT

> [Daly] must have spent, in round
> figures, over $2,500,000 in the
> contest. Clark and his friends must
> have spent over $400,000. The
> vote of the state did not exceed
> 53,000 in the capital election. The
> cost of each vote was, therefore,
> approximately $55.
>
> *C. P. Connolly,*
> The Devil Learns To Vote, *1906*

O ver one hundred years ago, the citizens of the fledgling state of Montana engaged in one of the most hotly-contested, flamboyant, corrupt elections in their history. Although "capital elections" were not uncommon in Western states, this contest between Anaconda and Helena for the permanent capital of Montana set the precedent for unscrupulous campaign tactics. Its corruption tainted Montana politics for almost 75 years—until the Anaconda Company pulled out of the political arena in the late 1960s.

Members of the 1889 Constitutional Convention neatly dodged the volatile issue of siting the new capital. They submitted the question (Article X, Chapters 2-3) to an 1892 plebiscite. The 1891 state legislature detailed the mechanics of this election (*1891 Laws*, pp. 291-294), for which seven Montana communities qualified.

Although often overlooked, this 1892 campaign quickly evolved into a head-to-head battle between Anaconda and Helena.

"Copper King" Marcus Daly sought the permanent capital for

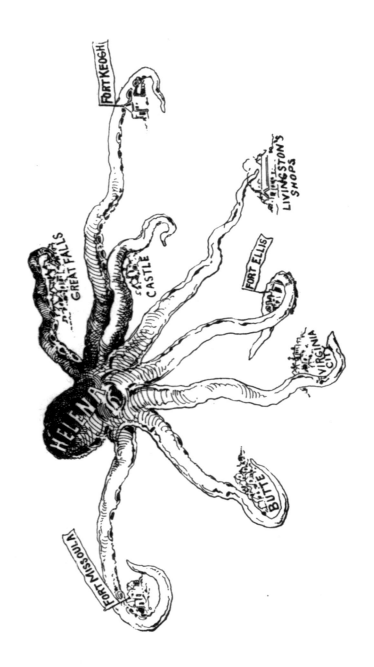

The Helena "octopus" as Anaconda supporters imagined it.
Illustration from pro-Anaconda pamphlet, Helena's Social Supremacy, 1894

his nine-year-old smelter town of Anaconda. Helena businessmen, bankers, and politicians—as well as Butte "Copper King" William Andrews Clark—campaigned to keep the capital where it had resided since 1874, when voters removed it from Virginia City.

In the 1892 capital election, 45,923 votes were cast from a total state registration of 51,500—a remarkable turnout of almost 90 percent! The distribution, however, only compounded the problem:

Anaconda:	10,183 (22.2%)
Boulder:	295 (0.6%)
Bozeman:	7,685 (16.7%)
Butte:	7,752 (16.9%)
Deer Lodge	983 (2.1%)
Great Falls:	5,042 (11.0%)
Helena:	13,983 (30.4%)

Most voters favored the site nearest them. Yet since no town received a majority, Anaconda and Helena squared off again to decide the issue in the 1894 election.

The "capital question" hung ominously over the 1893 legislature as it divided the state-institutions pie: the state university to Missoula; the agricultural college to Bozeman; the normal school to Dillon; the school of mines to Butte; the "deaf and dumb" school to Boulder; prison facilities to Deer Lodge and Billings; the reform school to Miles City.

Great Falls received no slice of the spoils pie because Paris Gibson had argued for a consolidated university (including the state university, the agricultural college, and the school of mines) in Great Falls. He lost, however, to the "segregationists," who wanted to spread the spoils broadly. Neither Helena nor Anaconda received a state institution—as one of them shortly would become the permanent seat of government.

The "capital question" also skulked about the edges of William A.

Clark's attempt to receive the 1893 legislature's appointment to the U.S. Senate (most American voters did not elect senators directly until 1913). Unlike Marcus Daly, Clark held aspirations to high public office. In the 1893 Senatorial contest, Clark came within three votes of a majority. Daly's men, however, blocked a Clark victory.

The legislature adjourned in March 1893, without electing a senator. Clark correctly identified Daly as his nemesis, and he swore revenge. So, from its beginning, the 1894 capital fight promised to pit Clark against Daly, just as much as Helena was pitted against Anaconda.

In preparation for this battle, Daly placed the first Linotypes west of the Mississippi River in the *Anaconda Standard*'s plant. He also hired editor J. H. Durston from the Syracuse (New York) *Post-Standard* and installed crack editorial-writer Charles H. Eggleston as associate editor. The *Standard* fired its first real salvo on July 1, and it did not cease the barrage until mid-November.

William A. Clark's *Butte Miner* similarly marshaled its forces for the campaign during the spring—led by editor John Quinn. The three Helena dailies (the Republican *Helena Herald*, the Democrat *Helena Independent*, and the Populist *Evening Telegram*) forged an uncharacteristic alliance for the duration of the campaign. The *Independent* also created an engraving department to produce the state's first series of home-grown political cartoons.

The campaign battle commenced in earnest after the Fourth of July. Quickly its character turned dirty, then outright vicious. Despite the "Australian [secret] ballot," this election marked the beginning of open political corruption in Montana. The $5 bill became the unofficial election ticket. Supporters of the two locations spent almost $3 million on votes between July 1 and November 6.

The choice for the permanent location of the capital proved a difficult one for most Montanans. Helena represented arrogant money (much of it crippled by the Panic of 1893), old-line political practices, and snooty social airs. Anaconda represented an industrial "company town" created by Marcus Daly and his Anaconda Company conglomerate. Was the voter simply to choose the lesser of two evils?

The battle for the capital occurred on myriad fronts. With the help of Helena organizers, Helena-for-Capital committees sprang up across the state—each responsible for erecting local banners, sponsoring fireworks displays, scheduling torchlight parades, and handing out $5 bills through the late summer. Helena also developed a speakers bureau of noted pioneers and politicians who stumped in every Montana town.

Anaconda-for-Capital committees similarly spread among Montana communities, producing complementary activities. Since the Montana electorate then comprised only legal-age males, Anaconda organizers campaigned regularly in a town's watering holes—a tactic quickly adopted by Helena supporters. Especially in saloons, the $5 bills passed freely.

Helena's spokesmen studiously avoided attacking Marcus Daly directly because of his personal popularity. Rather, they depicted Daly's partner, James Ben Ali Haggin, as the shifty leader of the opposition. And they attacked mercilessly this swarthy president of the Anaconda Company—usually parodying him as a Turkish merchant sporting a fez.

Banners, broadsides, buttons, and ribbons proclaimed a person's preference. Helena advocates used the symbol of the Anaconda snake to great advantage; they crafted thousands of little copper-collar stickpins to represent the corporate ownership of state government. Anaconda-backers countered with an octopus image and resurrected the "Helena Hog" from earlier campaigns—both depicting an insatiable Helena that wished to control the entire state.

Mining magnate/banker Samuel T. Hauser openly subsidized a bureau of noted orators. These spokesmen crisscrossed the state to emphasize Helena's central location, its established railroad access, its economic diversity, and its cultural institutions. Anaconda stumpers, on Daly's payroll, praised their town's strong labor population, its picturesque setting, its youth, and its promise for the future. Ever-present "bag men," armed with $5 bills, accompanied the orators from each camp and "worked the crowd."

On the negative side, Helena speakers derided Anaconda for its pretensions of grandeur, its obvious corporate ownership, and its smoke pollution. Anaconda orators countered that Helena remained a haven for non-union Chinese and Afro-American laborers, a snobbish population of elitists, and a town interested only in self-aggrandizement. After these hyperbolic speeches, the crowd enjoyed drinks on the respective capital committee.

Every innovative ploy tried by one camp brought an immediate, concerted response from the other. When Daly's men distributed special Anaconda-for-Capital cigars at rallies, Helena advocates disclosed that the smokes had been made by non-union "scab" labor. When Helena ministers organized to campaign from the pulpit, Anaconda backers cried "foul" and charged that, for too long, Helenans had believed the Almighty spoke only to them.

Miner Editor John Quinn conceived of the "Women's Helena-for-Capital Committee," and Sam Hauser bankrolled the effort. Through the existing network of women's clubs across the state, Helena women proved most effective in broadcasting the Helena argument. Although women could not vote in Montana until 1914, they certainly could influence their husbands, brothers, and lovers!

In early October, two well-meaning groups from Anaconda and Helena met to develop ways to halt illegal naturalization applications, unlawful voter registrations, and unauthorized voting practices on November 6. By this time, however, neither camp of organizers intended to play by any rules! When money could purchase a vote, it became the most direct means of persuasion. And there was plenty of money available.

Perhaps the hottest forum for capital-fight confrontation

remained the blistering editorial pages of Montana's newspapers. Daly's *Anaconda Standard* served as his flagship—although he also purchased the *Great Falls Tribune* for the duration of the campaign. Clark's *Butte Miner* allied itself with the three Helena dailies to carry Helena's colors. Flaming editorials that appeared first in the "core" publications then were distributed to papers across the state that supported the two respective sides.

J. H. Durston and Charles H. Eggleston of the *Standard* fired salvos at Helena, only to have them returned in kind by the *Miner's* John M. Quinn and the *Independent's* Martin J. Hutchens. When Durston charged that the Northern Pacific Railroad was supporting Helena by giving passes to members of its speakers bureau, Quinn countered that the Great Northern's Jim Hill was pumping money into Anaconda's campaigns in Great Falls and the Flathead Valley.

When the *Herald* and the *Independent* reported that Helena's women's clubs had corresponded with their counterparts across the state, urging them to implore their men to support Helena, the *Standard* ridiculed it as the act of naive, misguided suffragettes. When Quinn charged that Daly had hired scores of "thugs" from the Pinkerton Detective Agency to register voters and guarantee their votes for Anaconda, Durston responded that the Helena agents were rushing the naturalization of hundreds of immigrants and purchasing their votes.

In this no-holds-barred arena, other Montana papers crossed traditional party lines. For example, Helena was supported by such diverse papers as the prohibitionist (Bozeman) *New Issue*, the independent Dupuyer *Acantha*, the Republican *Billings Gazette*, the Democrat (Deer Lodge) *Silver State*, and the agricultural (White Sulphur Springs) *Rocky Mountain Husbandman*.

The capital battle also prompted innovation in Montana newspaper style. The *Independent* pioneered a series of political cartoons. The *Anaconda Standard*, under the direction of is associate editor Charles H. Eggleston, countered with a barrage of epigrams

THE TROUBLE WITH HELENA

In his 1894 satirical booklet Helena's Social Supremacy, *anonymous author Charles H. Eggleston, associate editor of the* Anaconda Standard, *provided some comparisons between the residents of the two communities.*

	HELENA	ANACONDA
Men who wear silk hats	2,625	3
Men who wear cotton night shirts	186	3,016
Men who wear silk night shirts	2,910	4
Men who wear kid gloves	4,552	4
Men who wear overalls	0	3,220
Dinner buckets in daily use	2	4,028
Manhattan cocktails in daily use	17,699	127
Champagne (quarts) in daily use	1,245	2
Beers in daily use	4,088	8,854
Ladies who nurse their babies	124	2,876
Ladies who dance the Minuet	3,773	82
Ladies with poodle dogs	2,285	3
Average number of children per family	.5	3.75
Children with Shetland ponies	590	0
Children who make mud pies	0	2,773
Skeletons in closets	1,343	16
People who eat dinner at 6:00 p.m.	8,658	456
People who eat dinner at 12 noon	370	6,954

shotgunned through its columns. Typical quips highlighted several of the campaign issues:

"The Northern Pacific Railroad Company owns 47,000,000 acres of land, but it doesn't own quite that many people."

"The reason Helena calls this a one-man's-town is because there is only one Chinaman left in Anaconda."

"Tuesday will show that a large majority of the voters of Montana are 'Anaconda thugs'."

"Keep cool, keep sober, keep your shirt on, keep in the middle of the road, and keep working for Anaconda."

At the height of the capital fight, Helena's backers flooded the state with four different pamphlets, each touting the advantages of Helena's history, economy, society, culture, and government. These relatively expensive publications featured maps showing Helena's central location and railroad accessibility, charts demonstrating her financial stability and diversity, and engravings of the town's public buildings, luxurious westside homes, and bustling commercial streets.

To the Helena Capital Committee's pamphlet *An Address to the People of Montana: Reasons Why Helena Should be the Permanent Capital of the State*, Eggleston responded with a satirical publication entitled *Helena's Social Supremacy* (please see sidebar). Playing on Helena's reputation for snobbery, it found a receptive audience across the state.

Montana's 1894 capital fight proved rife with corruption. Not only had the legislature been infected by the bribery of the "Copper Kings," but the state's press also had been tainted. The electorate became the next target. Some independent men formed "capital groups" and sold their votes in a block to the higher bidder. Both Anaconda and Helena money funneled into the saloons. Samuel T. Hauser subsequently remarked,

> It is pretty nice to get the saloons....We simply hand them money to give the boys a drink. If you get the saloons on your side, it is quite an element.

In September and October, hundreds of out-of-state woodsmen appeared in the Anaconda Company's logging camps in western Montana—just in time to register and then to vote for Anaconda on November 6. Great Northern and Northern Pacific railroad men from across the country declared permanent residences in Montana, and voted for Anaconda and Helena, respectively.

During the last weeks of the campaign, the attention of both camps focused on Butte, because its large electorate of miners formed the obvious swing vote. Marcus Daly held an advantage in Butte because his mines employed so many men, but Clark and his allies at the Butte and Boston Company and the Boston and Montana Company could cut into that majority.

At this point in the campaign, Clark committed an additional $50,000 to Helena's coffers; Hauser added another $25,000. In Butte, organizers from both sides gave barrels of whiskey to groups of miners, and agents simply handed out $5 "election tickets" at torchlight parades and rallies. Campaigning in Butte became a 24-hour-a-day proposition during the first week of November.

On election day—November 6—the bitter campaign temporarily quieted, because saloons closed during voting hours. Still, rumors swept through Anaconda of Clark's men voting their hordes in multiple locations. And one Anaconda supporter—a hog salesman who had shouted his preference loudly, repeatedly on Helena's Last Chance Gulch—had to be rescued by the police from an irate Helena crowd. However, the real election focus remained on Butte.

On the night of November 6, hundreds of Helenans filled lower Broadway Avenue. They gathered to watch the election returns appear on a large canvas hanging from the Masonic Hall—projected by stereopticon from the third floor of the *Helena Independent* building across the street. Elsewhere in Helena, special telegraph wires had been run into business offices, into several homes, and into the Auditorium—where various groups had assembled to learn the results. The *Helena Independent* remarked (November 7, 1894):

> All Helena seemed downtown. People ate their dinners at an unusually early hour and hurried to the business portion of the city to get the latest capital returns. The local and state elections were nearly forgotten, for all interest centered in the capital vote. The greatest enthusiasm prevailed. From the Bristol [Hotel, at State and Main] to Sixth Avenue, the street was black with people, and loud shouts for Helena were heard on every hand.

Through the evening, the telegraphed returns from the counties proved the election just too close to call. Helena broke into an early lead, but by 11:00 p.m. that margin had disappeared, as figures arrived from Anaconda strongholds Great Falls, Bozeman, Kalispell, and Sand Coulee—places where the Anaconda Company and the Great Northern Railway were important employers. The crowd finally dispersed about 3:00 in the morning, in a light rain.

But it reassembled by 7:00 a.m., braving the same light rain. Finally, by Thursday afternoon, the outcome became clear: Helena had polled 27,024 votes to 25,118 for Anaconda. By a margin of just 1,906 votes (less than a 2% plurality), Montanans transformed the "temporary capital" into the "permanent capital." Anaconda won relatively small majorities in the key counties of Cascade, Flathead, Missoula, and Silver Bow—but the Clark/Hauser forces secured just enough votes in Great Falls and Butte to offset any landslides, assuring Helena's victory.

A "spontaneous celebration" erupted in Last Chance Gulch

WHY HELENA SHOULD BE THE CAPITAL

One of the several pamphlets produced by the Helena-for-Capital Committee in 1894—entitled Helena as the Capital City—*compares the two candidates:*

- Helena is a city—Anaconda is a village.

- Helena is everybody's town—Anaconda is one man's town.

- In Helena the people rule—in Anaconda a corporation rules.

- Helena wants the capital for the capital—Daly wants the capital to boom his real estate.

- Everybody can run a business to make money in Helena—nobody but a Dalyite can run a business in Anaconda.

- The people are the same in both towns, but Helena has more of them with no strings to their collars.

- Helena is governed by whichever political party the people choose— Anaconda is governed by the same old party and always will be: the Daly party.

- This fight for the capital is not Helena vs. Anaconda—it is the people of Montana vs. Marcus Daly.

involving thousands of revelers. It ran until 4:00 a.m. and featured marching bands that wound through the streets, carousing crowds in white hats, blowing screechy horns, and street-corner orations from members of the "Helena for Capitol" speakers bureaus. The *Helena Daily Herald* noted that this was the first town celebration in which its reporters had seen women marching.

The several "Helena for Capital" committees scheduled a formal celebration for the following Monday night, November 12. The Northern Pacific discounted excursion tickets to Helena supporters

A SONG OF HELENA

In October 1894, the (Kalispell) Flathead Herald-Journal, *which supported Anaconda for the permanent state capital, published the following verse. The editor of the (Choteau)* Montanian—*likewise an Anaconda backer—ran the doggerel on October 26.*

Sing a song of Helena,
        The town that has so much
Refinement, culture, elegance,
        Society and such;

She never opens her classic lips
        Except to educate;
Now isn't that a dainty dish
        To set before the state?

Her business man sits at the "Club"
        Playing "harmless games,"
Or else he spends his time in calling
        Marcus Daly names.

He hasn't anything else to do;
        He wears the best of clothes,
And at the thought of other towns
        Turns up his Grecian nose.

Sing a song of Last Chance,
        The Gulch that wants so much—
Railroad shops, and capitals,
        And focal posts [sic] and—such;

She says that Daly's collar
    Will be on all our throats.
Now isn't that a dainty trap
    She sets to catch our votes?

Our votes you'll find within the mines,
    On railroads or in shops;
Another class who'll vote with us
    Are garnering their crops.

We never thought it was disgrace
    To labor ere we sup,
Till came along that Helena crowd
    With noses all turned up.

Then sing sad songs of Helena,
    She'll need them, O, so much!
Loud cries and lamentations,
    And groans, and howls, and—such;

For when the votes are counted,
    And results are all boiled down,
We'll set a dainty dish of crow
    Before that cultured town.

The Helena "committee"
    Will weep for mis-spent money;
The Anaconda man will smile
    And eat his bread and honey.

John Chinaman will still go on
    A-washing Helena's clothes;
Our turn will come, November 6th,
    To elevate our nose.

from around the state, and the Great Northern/Montana Central was forced to follow suit. Over the weekend, thousands of celebrants poured into the capital.

Residents decorated their houses, and businesses shut their doors. On Monday evening, a torchlight parade of 15,000 persons wound through Helena's streets. They celebrated beneath light from massive fireworks displays and huge bonfires on the slopes of nearby Mount Helena. Speeches, bands, and street dancing filled the night. A carnival atmosphere enveloped the town.

When William A. Clark and *Butte Miner* editor John M. Quinn arrived at the Great Northern depot, they found downtown Helena sporting decorative arches and large, broadside likenesses of Clark under the heading "Our Friend." Enthusiastic celebrants quickly unhitched the horses from the Clark/Quinn carriage; they attached a rope and, by hand, pulled the flower-bedecked coach through Helena's streets, thronged with raucous crowds. The *Helena Independent* reported (November 13, 1894):

> When they turned onto Lawrence [Street] and up Main, the latter street was packed with cheering crowds. The guns boomed, the bands played, and amidst the general uproar could be heard the measured shouts of the white-hatted brigade as it pulled the carriage to the cry of "CLARK—CLARK—W.—A.—CLARK." The crowds parted as the procession moved up Main Street, on its way to the Helena Hotel.

After a series of victory speeches, the merrymakers lined up for free food at the Auditorium's public reception. From there, celebrants adjourned to Helena's saloons, to drink on Clark's open tab. Observers estimated that his liquor bill ran to more than $30,000 for the extravaganza. Some have called this "Montana's drunkest night."

But the cost to Clark, Hauser, the Northern Pacific, and Helena's other supporters proved plainly justifiable. Clark finally had caught the politically gossamer Daly in a public arena and trounced him. On November 7, editor Quinn had trumpeted:

THREE CHEERS! THE PEOPLE ARE SUPREME!
THE CITIZENSHIP OF MONTANA IS VINDICATED!
TYRANNY HAS REACHED ITS WATERLOO!!

Ultimately, however, a more measured analysis of the corrupt, venomous capital fight of 1894 is that of Montana historian K. Ross Toole:

> The victory of political rectitude was more apparent than real....The edge of political integrity was dulled to the precise extent to which the capital fight encouraged popular acceptance of the alliance between the dollar and the vote. For the next 75 years, the people of Montana would suffer the corrupt politics popularized by the capital fight of 1894. What historians have called "the greatest election in the history of Montana" set a shameful precedent for the fledgling state.

SOURCES

The "capital fight of 1894" is addressed in all of the standard Montana histories, as well as in the several twentieth-century "subscription history" narratives. It receives particular attention in: Christopher P. Connolly, *The Devil Learns To Vote* (New York: Covici Friede, 1906/1938). Pertinent periodical pieces include: William L. Lang, "Spoils of Statehood: Montana Communities in Conflict, 1888-1894," *Montana: The Magazine of Western History*, 37, #4 (Autumn, 1987), 34-45; Rick Newby, "Helena's Social Supremacy," *Montana: The Magazine of Western History*, 37, #4 (Autumn, 1987), 68-72.

Another rich source is the barrage of publications produced by the two respective camps during the campaign. For instance, see: Helena Capital Committee, *An Address to the People of Montana: Reasons Why Helena Should be the Permanent Capital of the State* (Helena: Thurber Printers, 1894). The best Anaconda example remains the satirical work: [Charles H. Eggleston], *Helena's Social Supremacy* (Anaconda: Standard Printers, 1894).

Statewide newspapers, however, provide the most fruitful sources. The "core" papers for the Helena cause include Clark's *Butte Miner* and the three Helena dailies—the (Democrat) *Helena Independent,* the (Republican) *Helena Herald,* and the (Populist) *Helena Evening Telegram.* "Helena for Capital" papers across the state were: the *Big Timber Pioneer,* the *Havre Herald,* the *Billings Gazette,* the (White Sulphur Springs) *Rocky Mountain Husbandman;* the *Chinook Opinion,* the (Virginia City) *Madisonian,* the (Deer Lodge) *Silver State;* the (Missoula) *Missoulian;* the (Great Falls) *Leader;* the (Miles City) *Yellowstone Journal;* the (Kalispell) *Inter Lake;* the (Lewistown) *Fergus County Argus.*

The "core" newspapers for the Anaconda effort were Daly's *Anaconda Standard* and the (Butte) *Inter Mountain.* Supporting papers around Montana include: the (Kalispell) *Flathead Herald-Journal;* the (Kalispell) *Graphic;* the *Great Falls Tribune;* the (Bozeman) *Courier;* the (Livingston) *Enterprise;* the (Livingston) *Post;* the *Philipsburg Mail;* the (Deer Lodge) *New North West;* the *Dillon Examiner;* the *Billings Times;* the (Hamilton) *Western News;* the (Lewistown) *Democrat;* the (Choteau) *Montanian;* and the *Boulder Age.*

CHAPTER SEVEN

THE CEDED STRIP
BLACKFEET INDIANS,
GLACIER NATIONAL PARK, AND
THE BADGER-TWO MEDICINE

Those mountains will never disappear.
We will see them as long as we live.
Our children will see them all their lives.
And when we are all dead, they will still be there.
Little Dog, Blackfeet spokesman,
to federal commissioners at the
Willow Creek negotiations,
September 23, 1895

The typical visitor to Glacier National Park—and there are more than one million of them each year—spends less than two days there. Drawn by the spectacular alpine scenery, he breaches the Continental Divide via the breath-taking Going-to-the-Sun Road, descends to the opposite valley, and then sets his sights on the next scheduled destination.

Whether our harried traveler crosses from West Glacier to St. Mary or from east to west, some of the most spectacular vistas he photographs fall within the "Ceded Strip." Relinquished by the Blackfeet Indian Tribe to the federal government in 1896, this 550,000-acre tract is one of the most dramatic sections of Montana's Rocky Mountain Front. The Blackfeet refer to these mountains as *Mistakists*—"the Backbone"—home of a long-standing sacred presence.

The "Strip" comprises a parcel from five to twenty miles wide that nestles along the east side of the Continental Divide and stretches more than 65 miles from the Canadian boundary south to Birch Creek. It now includes both the entire "east side" of Glacier National Park (about 425,000 acres) and the controversial Badger–Two Medicine area (about 130,000 acres).

The "Strip" contains aspen-covered foothills, heavily timbered ridges, well known Glacier Park lakes (Waterton, Swiftcurrent, Sherburne, Upper St. Mary, and Two Medicine), abundant wildlife, and a vertical disparity of more than five thousand feet. Although past exploration in the "Strip" has proven unprofitable, several oil and gas companies continue to harbor the hope of drilling opportunities there.

To the fleeting tourist, the "Ceded Strip" matters little. Yet the people living in the area daily contend with the "Strip" and its emotionally-charged story. For the 1895 negotiations that created this phenomenon remain a controversial chapter in the histories of both Glacier Park and the Blackfeet Tribe.

When federal officials severed the "Ceded Strip," it represented just the last in a series of delineations of Blackfeet lands that had begun decades earlier. By the Fort Laramie Treaty (1851), Blackfeet lands received definite boundaries, stretching from the Continental Divide east to beyond the North Dakota line and extending from the Canadian border south into Wyoming—encompassing much of central Montana.

The Blackfeet lost the southern component of this block four years later in the 1855 Lame Bull's Treaty, while establishing a precedent of annuity payments to the tribe. In 1871 a Congressional act removed Indian tribes from the status of foreign powers and designated them domestic wards of the federal government. Thereafter formal U.S.-Indian relations relied on executive orders and negotiated agreements, rather than treaties. Immediately President Ulysses S. Grant used two executive orders (1873/1874) to relocate the southern boundary of the Blackfeet reserve farther north.

Then, in 1887, government officials negotiated an agreement

Blackfeet tipis in the
Two Medicine area of Glacier National Park, early 1900s.
Photo courtesy of Montana Historical Society, Helena

with the Blackfeet that established the reservation's eastern boundary at its current location. In return for this massive cession of land (known among the Blackfeet as "the time we surrendered the Sweet Grass Hills"), the government promised $1,500,000 in ten annual expenditures.

This 1851-1887 series of federal land reductions accurately parallels the disintegration of the tribe's hegemony in the region. A succession of cultural disasters simultaneously devastated the Blackfeet: the Smallpox Epidemic of 1869, the 1870 Baker Massacre on the Marias, the systematic eradication of the northern Great Plains bison (1880-1883); the "Starvation Winter of 1883-1884."

In this specific context, the tribe had negotiated the Agreement of 1888. And with this agreement the dependence of the Blackfeet on the federal government became complete. Then, in 1895, the Commissioner of Indian Affairs detailed federal commissioners once again to visit the Blackfeet. This time they would discuss the cession of the western portion of the reservation. Government negotiators hardly could have selected a more desperate people.

The social and cultural flux that the Blackfeet encountered—as they reluctantly shifted from a nomadic, bison-hunting lifestyle to one based on agriculture, irrigation, and livestock-raising—resulted in their very real dependence on the local Indian agent's leadership and advice. Yet, this was a time when reservation positions were ripe political plums, and the Blackfeet endured a rapid turnover of agents. Some of these administrators stayed less than a year!

One agent who stayed longer was "Major" George Steell. A Fort Benton trader who had married an Indian woman, he served as the Blackfeet agent from 1890 to 1893 and again from 1895 to 1897. In fact, it was Steell who initially had alerted federal authorities to a serious threat to the Blackfeet Reservation.

Since the 1880s, miners seeking gold, silver, and copper had prospected on the west side of the Continental Divide, just beyond the reservation line. Soon small parties were slipping east onto the

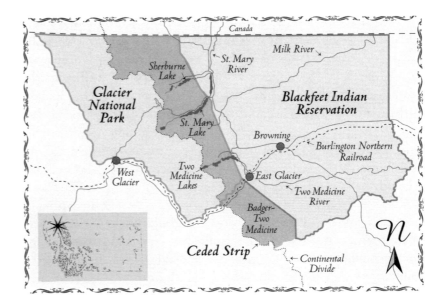

reservation to follow mineral leads that reappeared on the east side. Steell complained, in his 1893 annual report, that his Indian police, Army troops from Fort Assinniboine (located near Havre), and the North West Mounted Police were spending an inordinate amount of time trying to prevent these trespassers from prospecting the mountains of the Blackfeet.

Steell then proposed the sale of these western mountains to the government, to avoid potential Indian-white conflicts. As a result, the Commissioner of Indian Affairs directed Agent Steell to convene a meeting with Blackfeet leaders to gauge their sentiments about such a sale. In a January 25, 1894, gathering, Blackfeet full-blood leaders voted 18 to 3, and mixed-blood headmen voted 8 to 2, to pursue such negotiations. Obviously, with the imminent end of the precious annuity payments from the Agreement of 1888, the temptation to profit from the coveted western portion of their reservation increased among the Blackfeet.

As white pressure increased through 1894 to open these mineral fields to development, it was Montana politicians who led the charge for federal acquisition. Finally, in its Indian Appropriations Act of March 2, 1895, Congress designated $3,500 to finance the discussions. It also appointed a federal negotiating commission composed of William C. Pollock, George Bird Grinnell, and Walter M. Clements. Pollock was a career Bureau of Indian Affairs official from Washington, D.C.; he had negotiated similar agreements with other Indian tribes. Clements came from Georgia and was an attorney with limited arbitration experience.

The appointment of George Bird Grinnell reflected the wishes of at least the older, full-blood faction of the Blackfeet. Grinnell—an Eastern writer, sportsman, and conservationist—and some of the Blackfeet enjoyed mutual respect. He had aided the tribe during the "Starvation Winter of 1883-1884," and, in 1889, he had filed charges against a particularly corrupt reservation agent, Mark W. Baldwin. Those actions ultimately resulted in Baldwin's dismissal. The Blackfeet had conferred on Grinnell the honorary name *Pinotuyi Iszumokan* ("Fisher Cap").

Grinnell had been traveling out to Montana's Rockies and tramping around the "Ceded Strip" since 1885. He was constantly impressed by this spectacular mountain wilderness and, on September 17, 1891, had written in his diary (Gerald A. Diettert, *Grinnell's Glacier*, 57; emphasis mine):

> How would it do to start a movement to buy the St. Mary's Country, say 30 by 30 miles, from the Piegan Indians at a fair valuation and turn it into a National reservation or park?...*certainly all the Indians would like it.* This is worth thinking of and writing about.

On August 30, 1895, the three negotiators hired by the Department of the Interior arrived at the new agency on Willow Creek (Browning). At a meeting called by Agent Steell on

"BLACKFOOT"/"BLACKFEET"

In answer to the question "Who are the Blackfeet?", perhaps the clearest reply comes from Mr. Darrell Robes Kipp, the director of Browning's Piegan Institute, created to preserve the Blackfoot language. In a piece that appeared in the May-June, 1993, issue of *Montana Magazine*, Mr. Kipp wrote:

> The Blackfoot Confederacy consists of five tribes: the North Blackfoot, the Bloods, the North and the South Piegans, and the Small Robes. The Small Robes, once 10,000 strong, were exterminated by smallpox and warfare....
>
> Today, the North Blackfoot, the Bloods, and the North Piegan tribes live in Alberta, Canada, on tribal reserves. The South Piegan—now called the Blackfeet—reside on a tribal reservation in Montana, adjacent to Glacier National Park and the Canada-United States border.

Usually the next question asked is: "How should I use the terms 'Blackfoot' and 'Blackfeet'? Again Mr. Kipp's explanation is instructive (letter to the author, February 10, 1993):

> I use this guideline: when referring to the Confederacy (Alberta + Montana), use "Blackfoot," and when referring specifically to the Montana tribe, use "Blackfeet." For example, we call ourselves "Americans," but could also call ourselves "Montanans"—"Americans" being the collective; "Montanans" being the specific. So, just as "Montanans" are also "Americans," "Blackfeet" are also "Blackfoot." "Blackfeet," when used to describe the South Piegan, is an exclusive term. The "Blackfeet Tribe of Montana" is nomenclature with legal grounding— the Blackfeet Tribal Business Council, the official title of government. So, use "Blackfoot" to refer to the general Confederacy, and use "Blackfeet" specifically for the Montana references.

September 2, more than 200 Blackfeet selected a group of four full-bloods and four mixed-bloods to represent them.

These delegates departed immediately with Commissioners Pollock and Grinnell, Agent Steell, post trader Joe Kipp, and Agency Engineer Ross Cartee to inspect some of the country included in the proposed "Strip." Despite cold, windy, rainy weather, the party collected some mineral samples and hunted bear and mountain goat. Before returning to the Agency, they tried to understand where the "Strip's" eastern boundary could be drawn to separate mountainous mineral areas from timber and high-plains grazing lands.

The initial negotiating session convened on Friday, September 20, and the Blackfeet immediately requested a delay to complete the election of their 35-member negotiation team. On Saturday, September 21, the first working session began at 10:00 a.m. in the Agency's hospital building. Blackfeet leader White Calf spoke eloquently about the plight of his people and their obvious disadvantage at the white man's bargaining table. Indian policeman Little Dog set a more direct course, declaring (*Senate Document 118*, 54th Congress, 1st Session, Serial Set #3350, 9): "The Indians did not ask the Government to come here and buy their land...."

In addition to their own spokesmen, the Blackfeet had selected Kalispell banker Charles E. Conrad and Agent Steell as their representatives. Although not always present at the negotiations, several other advisors influenced the various Blackfeet factions: Joe Kipp; local white trader Alfred B. Hamilton; respected mixed-blood Horace Clarke; the Agency butcher, Joe Cook; local Methodist minister Eugene S. Dutcher; Jesuit Fathers Joseph Damiani and Peter Paul Prando from Holy Family Mission on the reservation.

Using a map of the region drawn by Ross Cartee, the commissioners described the suggested limits of the "Strip," beginning with the International Boundary on the north and the Continental Divide on the west. To fashion the eastern limit, the commissioners started at the International Boundary and ran a line south/southeast, using natural landmarks—Chief Mountain; Flat Top Crag (Napi Point); Divide Creek; Divide Peak; Lower Two Medicine Lake.

With these lines described, discussion focused on the southern limit of the purchase. The commissioners proposed a southern boundary along the mainline of the Great Northern Railway, constructed through the reservation in 1891. As an alternative, Pollock suggested a southern boundary that extended to Birch Creek, thus encompassing all of the Blackfeet's potential mineral land and avoiding future conflict between the Indians and the white prospectors. He reasoned (*Senate Document 118*, 9):

> The white men will come after minerals in spite of all that you and the Government can do. I say this that you may understand all that may come.

Blackfeet spokesman Little Bear Chief countered with an offer to release all of the proposed "Strip" north of Cut Bank Creek. Subsequent discussions, on both Saturday and Monday, addressed the complementary issues of the southern boundary and the compensation amount.

While the proposed boundary moved progressively south—from Cut Bank Creek to the railroad mainline to Birch Creek—the Blackfeet asking price grew from $2 million to $3 million. Pollock countered within a range of $1 million to $1.25 million. When pressed to explain their lower bids, the federal negotiators responded (*Senate Document 118*, 13): "It would be useless for us to offer you more, for Congress would not ratify it if we did."

Amid references to the demonstrable benefits gained by the government in the 1887 negotiations, Blackfeet spokesmen cited their need for transitional funds to develop their livestock economy. As Curly Bear said (*Senate Document 118*, 16):

> That is the reason we sell, to provide for our children. You are trying to get this land for a small sum....We will not sell any grazing land, as our cat-

tle feed on it. We will not sell the timber, as we use it.... We have set the price at $3,000,000 and will stick to it.

Neither side would retreat. By the end of discussions on Monday evening, a stalemate had developed that no suggested compromise could resolve. Both sides left the meeting hall convinced that the talks had concluded in failure.

Another official negotiating session convened on Wednesday morning. In a complete and surprising reversal, White Calf announced that the Blackfeet would relinquish the entire portion of the "Strip" north of Birch Creek for $1.5 million. The forewarned commissioners—eager to conclude a deal—agreed to these terms. White Calf then delivered the pivotal speech of the entire negotiations (*Senate Document 118*, 19):

> Chief Mountain is my head. Now my head is cut off. The mountains have been my last refuge. We have been driven here and now we are settled. From Birch Creek to the boundary line is what I now give you. I want the timber because in the future my children will need it. I also want all the grazing land. I would like to have the right to hunt game and fish in the mountains....
>
> We don't want our land allotted....We always lived here; this is our land....We will sell you the mountain lands, for one and a half million. [Applause.] I shake hands with you because we have come to an agreement, but if you come for any more land, we will have to send you away.

Big Brave then concluded (*Senate Document 118*, 19):

> What these two old men have said, I repeat. I raise my hand for every man, woman, and child on the reservation. What I say, they say....I hope we will have no more talk with the commissioners for fifty years. [Great applause.]

On Thursday morning, September 26, Commissioner Grinnell read the entire agreement aloud to the assembly. As with the negotiation statements, interpreters Charles Simon, James Perrine, and Richard Sanderville completed the translations.

In return for ceding the western portion of their reservation to the federal government, the Blackfeet would receive $1.5 million in ten annual payments of goods and services, to begin upon the expiration of the 1888 Agreement. In effect, the 1896 Agreement simply would extend the terms of the 1888 Agreement for another decade.

The Blackfeet also reserved (1) the right of access to "Ceded Strip" lands and (2) the right to cut timber in the "Strip" for agency, school, and personal use. The tribe further reserved (3) the rights to hunt and fish on "Strip" lands (subject to the State of Montana's fish-and-game laws)—"so long as [those lands] shall remain public lands of the United States."

Other articles of the Agreement addressed the preferential hiring of Indians, the distribution of cattle to the Blackfeet, the granting of public-utility right-of-ways, the postponement of Dawes Act allotments on the reservation until 1907, and the handling of interest paid on annuity funds.

The three commissioners signed the agreement on September 26. Then, for two days, Blackfeet men stepped up to the negotiation table, spoke their names to James Willard Schultz, the recorder, and signed the agreement. Upon completion, 306 members of the reservation's male population of 381 full-bloods and mixed-bloods had endorsed the transaction. Congress approved the Agreement, as written, on June 10, 1896.

Article Six of the Agreement prevented the federal government from opening the "Ceded Strip" to eager prospectors before it had been surveyed. That work engaged surveyors during the summers of 1896 and 1897. Finally, on April 15, 1898, about five hundred prospectors rushed into the "Strip"—most of them staking out likely properties in the Swiftcurrent Valley. They traveled to file these claims in the Teton County seat of Choteau, 130 miles distant.

The mining boom in the "Ceded Strip" produced high hopes, the usual boomer literature, much speculation, and little substantial profit. Gold prospects along Divide Creek lasted long enough to sprout the village of St. Mary. Copper diggings in the Swiftcurrent Valley—most notably near Bullhead and Cracker lakes—resulted in the boom town of Altyn, located near present-day Many Glacier.

Altyn boasted a population that fluctuated between one thousand hopefuls in 1899 and 250 hangers-on in 1901. It sported a half-dozen dry-goods and equipment stores, a post office, several cafes, a hotel, the weekly *Swift Current Courier*, and twice-a-week stagecoach connections to the Great Northern Railway siding at Blackfoot.

By early 1902, the "Ceded Strip's" hardrock-mining boom legitimately could be classified a bust. However, speculative hopes rekindled in late 1902 when Sam Somes, the proprietor of the Altyn hotel, drilled an oil well in the Swiftcurrent Valley and hit a likely pool. He formed the Montana Swiftcurrent Oil Company and lined up financial investors, particularly after his samples won a special award at the 1903 Montana State Fair in Helena.

Somes' modest success fueled a 1904-1907 oil boom, during which speculators filed petroleum claims that carpeted the Swiftcurrent Valley. Roughnecks drilled more than a dozen oil and natural-gas wells in the area now covered by the Sherburne Lake reservoir. Then this boom, like the earlier gold-silver-copper boom, collapsed. Finally, after almost a decade, quiet descended on the mountains of the Blackfeet.

In the meantime, the federal government had included the "Ceded Strip" in its large Lewis and Clark Forest Reserve. This 1897 designation did not restrict homesteading, hunting, mining, or other utilitarian activities, but it did recognize the special character of the area. Historical evidence indicates that George Bird Grinnell influenced the inclusion of the "Ceded Strip" in this new reserve.

Grinnell then embarked again on his decades-long campaign to gain national-park status for this section of the Northern Rockies. Through his articles in *Forest and Stream* and *Century Magazine*, he

THE MACHINATIONS OF
GEORGE BIRD GRINNELL

It borders on the overtly sacrilegious to question any thought or action of the venerable George Bird Grinnell (1849-1938)—renowned writer, ethnologist, sportsman, conservationist, founder of the Audubon Society, and "the Father of Glacier National Park." Nevertheless, circumstances surrounding his role as one of the three government negotiators in the "Ceded Strip" Agreement of 1896 should cause the critical observer some pause.

Grinnell had earned his stripes as a true friend of the Blackfeet even prior to his first trip to the reservation in 1885. Specifically, he had rallied national support for tribal members suffering the "Starvation Winter of 1883-1884." Further, in 1889, he had challenged the administration of Blackfeet Agent Mark W. Baldwin—considered by many tribesmen to be arbitrary and corrupt—and precipitated his dismissal. To honor their friend, the Blackfeet had given Grinnell the name Pinotuyi Iszumokan ("Fisher Cap").

Clearly the Blackfeet asked that Grinnell serve as a commissioner for the 1895 "Ceded Strip" negotiations because they trusted him and believed that he would be fair in dealings with them. Evidence indicates (Michael F. Foley, Indian Claims Commission *Docket #279-D*, 1974, 181-182) that Grinnell initially refused the appointment because he thought that the sale of the "Ceded Strip" would not benefit the Blackfeet. He subsequently changed his mind—reasoning that the tribe would benefit more by having a sympathetic negotiator on the three-man team.

Simultaneously, however, Grinnell was carrying a deep-seated, potentially conflicting agenda. From his first trip to the St. Mary and Swiftcurrent valleys in 1885, the Eastern conservationist recognized the grandeur of the "Ceded Strip." Whether hunting, or mountain climbing, or exploring glaciers, or visiting with hospitable Blackfeet, Grinnell waxed poetic about the special nature of this mountain country. Finally, on September 17, 1891—four years prior to the "Ceded Strip" negotiations—he wrote in his diary (Gerald A. Diettert, *Grinnell's Glacier*, 57):

> How would it do to start a movement to buy the St. Mary's Country, say 30 by 30 miles, from the Piegan Indians at a fair valuation and turn it into a National reservation or park[?] The Great Northern R.R. would probably back the scheme, and [U.S. Senator from Montana] T. C. Power would do all he could for it in the Senate. Mr. [Secretary of the Interior John W.] Noble might favor it, and certainly all the Indians would like it. This is worth thinking of and writing about.

The discovery of gold, silver, and copper deposits in the "Ceded Strip" in the early 1890s certainly dismayed Grinnell. In a July, 1894, letter to Blackfeet Agent George Steell, Grinnell said (Diettert, *Grinnell's Glacier*, 62):

> I had hoped that it might be practicable to set off the mountain part of the Piegan reservation as a national park, or a forest reserve, but if minerals actually exist there,…there is of course no hope that my plan can be carried out.

Then, on his railroad trip west in the fall of 1894, Grinnell stopped off in St. Paul, Minnesota, to sell his national-park idea to F. J. Whitney of the Great Northern Railway Company. He had written earlier to Whitney (Diettert, *Grinnell's Glacier*, 63):

> [I envision] a public park and pleasure resort, somewhat in the nature of Yellowstone National Park, or the Banff National Park on the Canadian Pacific. I presume you are familiar with the St. Mary's Lakes. I am sure that Mr [James J.] Hill [president of the Great Northern Railway] is, for I remember a year or two ago having quite a long talk with him on this subject. The matter is one of great interest to me and to other men in the east, and it should be of interest to intelligent persons of Montana.
> As a member of the three-man, Department of the Interior negotiating

team in 1895, Grinnell spoke sympathetically and sincerely to the Blackfeet (see *Senate Document 118*, 54th Congress, 1st Session, Serial Set #3350, 8-28). When talks broke down on September 23, 1895, Grinnell's dual position as a government negotiator and a confidant of the Blackfeet allowed him to facilitate the Blackfeet reconsideration. At least some credit for the reversal of the Blackfeet position should fall to "Fisher Cap."

On that occasion, Grinnell wrote in his diary (Diettert, *Grinnell's Glacier*, 70): "In the afternoon [the agreement] was accepted, and tonight everybody is glad. Many Indians made good speeches to me, thanking me."

Grinnell never did believe that a full-blown mining boom would develop in the "Ceded Strip." Nevertheless, in the late fall of 1896—only a year after the Blackfeet negotiations—he vehemently lobbied a longtime U.S. Geological Survey friend, Arnold Hague. He implored Hague to persuade the Forestry Commission to include this "important though not very extensive tract on the eastern flanks of the Rocky Mountains" in the Lewis and Clark Forest Reserve recommendation (Diettert, *Grinnell's Glacier*, 73-75).

Quite likely as a result of Hague's work, the "Strip" was included in the 1897 Reserve. This designation limited neither settlement, nor mining, nor hunting, nor other utilitarian activities, but it did signal the government's recognition that the "Strip" contained special, perhaps preservable, qualities.

Commencing again in March 1900—with the publication of his "Ceded Strip" article, "The Crown of the Continent," in *Century Magazine*— Grinnell campaigned for national-park status among politicians, conservationists, and businessmen. His readily-documented crusade to encourage Congress to create a "Glacier National Park" ran from his 1905 articles in *Forest and Stream* to his direct-lobbying efforts in behalf of the 1907, 1908, and 1909 bills to create the park.

Although modest to a fault upon the creation of Glacier National Park on May 11, 1910, Grinnell's 25-year-long plan finally had proven successful. In a *Forest and Stream* piece published shortly after President William Howard Taft had signed the Park legislation, Grinnell wrote (Diettert, *Grinnell's Glacier*, 95):

To receive credit for good work well done is pleasant, but a

> reward far higher...comes from the consciousness of having
> served the public well....

> More to the point, Montana Congressman Charles Pray and U.S.
> Senator Thomas H. Carter—who had piloted the successful legislation
> through the House and the Senate, respectively—wrote congratulatory
> letters to Grinnell.
>
> Given the circumstances and the sequence of events leading to the cre-
> ation of Glacier National Park in 1910, one must ask if Grinnell—as a
> federal-government member of the 1895 "Ceded Strip" commission—did
> not use his position to expedite the removal of his favored area from the
> Blackfeet Reservation. Particularly his practically-simultaneous effort to
> include the area in the Lewis and Clark Forest Reserve indicates a plan
> quietly to move the parcel from reservation status to public-land status to
> national-park status.
>
> If such is the case, the Blackfeet—who admired Grinnell greatly
> throughout his life—were victimized by "Fisher Cap's" duplicity. Perhaps
> it is worth another look at the real motives of "the Father of Glacier Park."

publicized the remarkable nature of the country. Through his
strong contacts among conservationists, businessmen, and politicians, he lobbied for recognition of the Glacier area. In recognition
of his tireless efforts, and the ultimate success of his campaign,
Grinnell today is known as "the Father of Glacier Park."

Glacier National Park, established on May 11, 1910, incorporat-
ed most of the "Ceded Strip." This inclusion created some special
problems for the Blackfeet Tribe. According to the Agreement of
1896, the Blackfeet reserved the right of access to the "Ceded Strip"
and the rights to hunt, fish, and cut timber there—"so long as
[those lands] shall remain public lands of the United States."

However, at the time of the negotiations, Blackfeet leaders may
not have understood the legal definition of "public lands," as used
in this context (*Black's Law Dictionary*, 1979, 1106):

The general public domain; unappropriated lands; lands belonging to the
United States and which are subject to sale or other disposal under general laws,
and not reserved or held back for any special government or public purpose.

A national park is a "reserve of special purpose," exempt from sale
or other disposal. Were the rights of the Blackfeet, negotiated in
good faith in 1895, then extinguished, by a simple federal change
in land classification from "public land" to "reserved land"? This
question has clouded relations between the Blackfeet Tribe and the
National Park Service for more than eighty years.

With the Great Northern Railway's development of a tourist-
facilities network on Glacier's "east side," railroad president Louis
Hill used his powerful international publicity machine to portray
the Blackfeet as "the Indians of Glacier National Park." In the public eye, the Blackfeet were the natural inhabitants of these spectacular mountains. Some tribal members even found seasonal employment around Hill's hotels.

Although perceived by visitors as the historical residents of the
"Ceded Strip," had the Blackfeet lost any and all claims to this land
within the Park? Not necessarily! Many Blackfeet still consider the
1896 Agreement a lease, which either was abrogated by the 1907
allotment of the Blackfeet Indian Reservation or was terminated
after fifty years.

This issue has spawned court cases, independent federal-solicitor
rulings, and "test case" challenges since 1912. Once Indians gained
access to the U.S. Court of Claims (1924), the Blackfeet filed a
"Ceded Strip" claim, but only for monetary damages due to their
lost rights. The 1935 final ruling in this case denied the Blackfeet
claim and has become the basis of all following adjudication.

These subsequent "test cases" and rulings recognize none of the
Blackfeet's reserved rights in the Glacier Park portion of the "Ceded
Strip." However, since Woodrow Kipp challenged the National
Park Service in a 1973 "test case" regarding Blackfeet access to the

"Ceded Strip," the Glacier Park administration has not collected Park entrance fees from enrolled members of the Blackfeet Tribe.

The controversy surrounding the "Ceded Strip" assumes another dimension when it addresses the rugged, roadless Badger–Two Medicine section of the "Strip." This area is a portion of the Lewis and Clark National Forest, administered by the U.S. Forest Service and the Bureau of Land Management. In this wilderness, and on Glacier's "east side," the Blackfeet enumerate long-standing sacred sites. So, compounding the issue of oil and gas exploration in the Badger–Two Medicine area is the unresolved problem of Blackfeet rights reserved in the 1896 Agreement.

More than a century after the signing, several jurisdictional conflicts, derived from the Agreement of 1896, depend on the reservation of Blackfeet rights:

- the right to hunt, fish, and cut timber on the "east side" of Glacier Park;
- the right of access to the "Ceded Strip" to perform sacred ceremonies and to gather traditional plants and medicines;
- the rights of access to, and preservation of, sacred sites;
- the right to influence petroleum exploration/drilling in the Badger–Two Medicine district.

The importance of the Agreement of 1896, which created the "Ceded Strip," cannot be overemphasized—because those issues remain unresolved to the satisfaction of any of the involved parties.

Perhaps our typical out-of-state visitor to Glacier Park need not be concerned with these issues, as he races on to reach Yellowstone Park before dark. However, Montanans can benefit appreciably by understanding the historical background to the Agreement of 1896 and the 'Ceded Strip."

The problem simply will not vanish. As Little Dog noted on September 23, 1895—the second day of negotiations (*Senate Document 118*, 16):

Those mountains will never disappear. We will see them as long as we live. Our children will see them all their lives. And when we are all dead, they will still be there.

SOURCES

The key source for this study is: U.S. Congress, Senate. Agreement with Indians of the Blackfeet Reservation in Montana, *Senate Document 118,* 54th Congress, 1st Session (1896), Serial Set 3350. Other federal documents that pertain include annual reports from the Blackfeet Reservation agent to the Commissioner of Indian Affairs, 1884-1900, Congressional bills and reports involving the creation of Glacier National Park in 1910, and complementary portions of the *Congressional Record.*

Solid background information on the Blackfeet can be found in: Thomas R. Wessel, "Historical Report on the Blackfeet Reservation in Northern Montana," and Michael F. Foley, "An Historical Analysis of the Administration of the Blackfeet Indian Reservation by the United States, 1855-1950s"—parts of U.S. Indian Claims Commission, *Docket #279-D* (Washington, D.C., 1974/1975).

The "Ceded Strip" issue is addressed in: Christopher S. Ashby, "The Blackfeet Agreement of 1895 and Glacier National Park: A Case Study," M.S. seminar paper, University of Montana, 1985; Mark David Spence, "Crown of the Continent: Backbone of the World," *Environmental History,* 1, #3 (July, 1996); Kenneth P. Pitt, "The Ceded Strip: Blackfeet Treaty Rights in the 1980s," manuscript in the Ruhle Library/Archives, Glacier National Park, West Glacier, Montana.

The story of mining within the "Ceded Strip" can be followed in regional/local newspapers from 1894 through 1903: the (Butte) *Inter Mountain,* the *Anaconda Standard,* the *Helena Daily Herald,* the (Fort Benton) *River Press,* the *Great Falls Tribune,* the (Choteau) *Montanian,* and the (Altyn) *Swift Current Courier.* See also two extensive vertical-file collections: Jack Hayne, compiler, "Ceded Strip Mining Items" and "Swiftcurrent Oil Boom Items," Montana Historical Society Library, Helena.

Regarding the twentieth-century repercussions of the 1896 Agreement, see: Mark David Spence, *Dispossessing the Wilderness: Indian Removal and the Making of the National Parks* (New York: Oxford University Press, 1999), 3-41, 71-100; Gene Albert, "Glacier: Beleaguered Park of 1975," *National Parks and Conservation Magazine,* 49, #111 (November, 1975); and Jack Holterman, "Government

Trampled Blackfeet Rights as It Violated Agreements," (Columbia Falls) *Hungry Horse News,* January 14, 1993. The controversy also can be followed in the (Cut Bank) *Pioneer Press,* the *Great Falls Tribune,* and the (Columbia Falls) *Hungry Horse News.* See also: Daniel H. Israel, Sally N. Willett, and Philip E. Roy, "Petition of the Blackfeet Tribe of Indians to the Secretary of the Interior to Approve a Conservation Agreement Providing for the Regulation of Blackfeet Reserved Rights on the Eastern Portion of Glacier National Park" (Browning, 1975).

The best single repository for information concerning the "Ceded Strip" is the Ruhle Library/Archives in the Headquarters Building of Glacier National Park, in West Glacier, Montana. For example, it contains: a copy of the Ross Cartee "Ceded Strip" map; a December 14, 1895, letter from William C. Pollock to the Commissioner of Indian Affairs regarding the Blackfeet negotiations; and the files of L. O. Vaught concerning the "Ceded Strip." Invaluable assistance was provided for this piece from the collections curator, Ms. Deirdre Shaw, of the National Park Service.

CHAPTER EIGHT

CULTURE UNDER CANVAS
CIRCUIT CHAUTAUQUAS IN MONTANA

No institution under the sun takes
the place of Chautauqua. For fine
fun, for rubbing elbows with one's
neighbors away from business
cares, for the delight of untangling
mental snarls, nothing surpasses
Chautauqua. For listening to great
religious and political and educational prophets, for hearing
unusual music, and for attending
worthwhile drama, Chautauqua
is matched by nothing else
in America.
—*Ellison-White*
Chautauqua brochure, 1928

The anticipation had been building among the residents of
Miles City long before the train arrived. In fact, the "advance man"
for the Chautauqua company had been in town for almost three
weeks, coordinating preparations with the Chamber of Commerce.
Yet, when the well-tanned, college men unloaded the mounds of
brown canvas from the boxcar—while bands of jubilant children
swirled around them—then people in Miles City knew that their
first-ever Chautauqua had become a reality.

They were assured that they would be treated to a full six days
of inspirational and informative lectures, quality musical

presentations, humorous speakers, and an elaborate children's program. The Chautauqua had come to town! It promised to bring real culture to a community thirsting for just this kind of educational interlude. As the "advance man" had guaranteed, Miles City would never be the same after the Chautauquans performed in the massive brown tent in Riverside Park from June 29 to July 4, 1910. Why, the Northern Pacific Railroad even offered a reduced "Chautauqua rate" for families coming from out-of-town.

And the people of the Miles City area were not disappointed. For six consecutive afternoons and evenings—for the season ticket price of $3.00—they enjoyed a wondrous feast of education and entertainment. The *Miles City Independent* commented (July 6, 1910):

> The character of the talent was such as to command the approval of all who heard them. They were above the average seen at Chautauqua usually, so that the Chamber of Commerce committee in making the selections is entitled to much credit. It is claimed by many that the price of tickets should have been $5 instead of $3.

Among the highlights of the six-day festival were two performances by the Chicago Operatic Company, both afternoon and evening inspirational lectures by Dr. Charles Lanahan, a talk by Chicago Judge Frank P. Sadler on "crime and wickedness of the big city," an evening of humor with cartoonist and platform comedian Ross Crane, and stirring Fourth of July concerts by the Chautauqua Ladies' Orchestra. The speech of Missouri's reform Governor and Presidential candidate Joseph W. Folk so impressed the editors of the *Independent* that they printed it in its entirety.

In 1910 the people of Miles City were receiving their first taste of a cultural movement that had been spreading across America for more than three decades. The Chautauqua concept emphasized a high level of morality and self-improvement through education and recreation—for people of all ages, but particularly for working

Polson's welcome in July 1914.
Photo courtesy of Montana Historical Society, Helena

"Chautauqua is the most American thing about America."

—President Theodore Roosevelt,
a frequent Chautauqua platform performer

adults. By combining a variety of public lectures, musical and dramatic performances, and first-rate instruction in health and physical education, Chautauquans believed that they could feed popularized knowledge to an American population still quite isolated by primitive communications and transportation.

Moreover, the Chautauqua movement carried a definite messianic fervor: these were morally upright people making personal sacrifices to bring knowledge and quality entertainment to a needy audience. That mission of morality derived directly from the founding of "Mother Chautauqua."

In 1874 two long-bearded gentlemen, the Reverend John H. Vincent and Lewis Miller, conceived an intense summer course of study for Sunday-school teachers. Vincent, a pioneer in Methodist education, and millionaire industrialist Miller (also a Methodist) nevertheless insisted on an inter-denominational camp. Further, they understood the need to vary the heavy diet of religious studies with current topics, inspirational music, and recreation.

They sited the camp in the trees on the shore of Lake Chautauqua in western New York State. From the Seneca Indian name for the lake came the title for the camp and, ultimately, came the label for the entire movement. For better than half a century, the term "Chautauqua" represented a spirited movement of self-education that touted the purity of rural life, the importance of community, and the need for every American's social involvement.

Between 1874 and the mid-1930s, "Mother Chautauqua" spawned three distinct variations. First, based on the annual summer session beside Lake Chautauqua, Vincent and Miller developed a four-year educational cycle under the Chautauqua Literary and Scientific Circle (CLSC). Called "the first of the nation's correspondence schools," the CLSC encouraged people to study history, science, art, foreign languages, music theory, ancient classics, and literature in their own homes and then to meet in local groups to discuss their studies.

Operating from 1878 until the middle of the new century, the CLSC reading program particularly benefited such "nontraditional students" as house-bound women, businessmen, and professionals. By 1940 the cumulative membership of the CLSC exceeded 750,000! A monthly magazine, *The Chautauquan*, tied the local CLSC cells to each and to "Mother Chautauqua."

Second, as the Chautauqua Literary and Scientific Circle expanded, so did the proliferation of fixed-site summer Chautauqua programs, modeled on the New York original. Sites stretched from the Atlantic Coast, through the Midwest, out onto the Great Plains, across the Rocky Mountains, and on to the West Coast. Called "independent Chautauquas" or "daughter Chautauquas," these enterprises sought and received encouragement, advice, and instructional materials from "Mother Chautauqua." Between 1890 and 1910, some fortunate Montanans attended fixed-site "daughter Chautauquas" in: Big Stone Lake, South Dakota; in Odgen, Utah; on Vashon Island, Washington; and in Gladstone, Oregon.

The fixed-site network of summer sessions offered some of America's most dynamic orators—perennial Presidential candidate William Jennings Bryan; suffragette Susan B. Anthony; Progressive Senator Robert LaFollette; muckraker Lincoln Steffens; temperance campaigner Carry Nation; Socialist Eugene V. Debs. Rousing lectures on the values of hard work, Christian piety, and humanitarian service, and on the evils of liquor maintained "Mother Chautauqua's" traditional high moral tone. Known as "Mother, home, and heaven" speeches, their message invariably proved optimistic and uplifting.

REASONS TO ATTEND CHAUTAUQUA, 1920

Reasons why I am going to take my car and drive over to Chautauqua this summer.

Because:

I am sick of war, strikes, and labor unrest. I want to discuss, to decide how to act....

I want to get out of the rut. As in running my car, so in running my life, I do not want to get stuck on the road because of "low clearance." I want to take in the relaxations that refresh and refine and inspire me to fuller speed ahead.

I want the sociability of it all—old neighbors to chat with—new friends to shake hands with—human things of human interest that happen in humans' lives to talk about.

—*John Edward Tapia, "Circuit Chautauqua Program Brochures:*
A Study in Social and Intellectual History,"
Quarterly Journal of Speech, *67, #2 (1981)*

The educational sessions also offered a diversity of current-interest topics, running from the magic of electricity to the advantages of the "single tax," to the woman-suffrage question, to prison reform, to travelogues on Mexico, England, Panama, and Italy—complete with lantern-slide illustrations. Many of the lecturers encouraged the involvement of their listeners in civic reform, ranging from revamped prisons, to slum clearance, to public-school improvement.

The single most popular lecture delivered at the "daughter Chautauquas" was a moral address by Dr. Russell H. Conwell, entitled "Acres of Diamonds." Conwell delivered the talk—which advocated the accumulation of wealth in one's own town and the spending of that wealth for humanitarian purposes—an astonishing six thousand times over a 35-year period!

The third variation that developed from "Mother Chautauqua"

impacted Montana directly. Beginning in 1905, the "circuit Chautauqua" swept the nation. The four- or six- or seven-day session—run by private contracting companies—combined the excellent educational content of the fixed-site Chautauquas with the flexibility of a lyceum speaking circuit. As a result, between 1910 and 1932, hundreds of small towns in the Midwest, in the West, and in Canada hosted the big brown tents of the traveling Chautauquas. In Montana communities, the excitement of "Chautauqua week" rivaled the circus, or the country fair, or the town rodeo.

Under this system, a Chautauqua bureau—like Redpath-Vawter, out of Chicago, or Ellison-White, headquartered in Portland—booked a town when a local committee guaranteed its price. That guarantee ran from about $750 for a four-day session to over $1,400 for a week-long engagement. The local committee could recoup that money by selling full-session tickets, at about $2.00 for four days, or between $2.50 to $3.50 for a seven-day run.

Because the revenue from on-site, single-performance tickets went directly to the Chautauqua company, the sale of season tickets became crucial to the local committees. On occasion, if season-ticket sales fell short, the Chautauqua bureau required the guarantors to make up the difference by self-assessment.

Chautauqua bureaus scheduled each summer circuit very tightly, picking both the dates for a community and the presenters who would appear. Performers often stayed in a town only a day or two, before moving on to the next site. Absolutely vital to the operation of this tight scheduling was an elaborate railroad system that allowed rapid, predictable movement of "the talent" from one town to the next.

The Chautauqua bureau provided other representatives who stayed longer in the community. The "advance man" arrived twenty days prior to the opening of the session. He blanketed the area with advertising, exhorted local-committee members to sell more season tickets, and contracted for a tent site.

The value of an aggressive, imaginative "advance man" became

THE SEASON TICKET

The Amazed One said,
"With prices soaring to dizzy heights,
A pair of shoes is worth as much
As a bride's trousseau in days gone by,
And a suit at the level of a king's ransom...."

Then you say,
"I can hear the Old Fashioned Girls
    in two concerts,
And Burnell Ford, the inventor and scientist,
The Ward Waters Trio in two programs,
And Richard Posey Campbell and the
    Honorable C. H. Poole.

"Then Norman Allan Imrie,
And the Zedeler Quintet in two big concerts,
And the play 'It Pays To Advertise,'
Two programs by Fillion and Tom Skeyhill,
Then Mellinger on Mexico and the Fisk Singers,
All for $2.75."

"Righto!" I said, "There is still one thing
    within reason
On this old earth: the Season Ticket!"

       —*Ellison-White supplement to the*
       Twin Bridges Independent,
       August 13, 1920

obvious to residents of Polson in 1914. Ellison-White detailed G. E. Curtis to assist the local guarantors, and he came armed with ideas—from parades and group photographs to a 90-mile tour as far south as Dixon to solicit season-ticket sales. The (Polson) *Flathead Courier* boomed (July 23, 1914):

> When G. E. Curtis arrived in Polson on Friday, immediately there was something doing. That Mr. Curtis understands the advertising business is shown by the work accomplished here in such a short time. And then his enthusiasm has been met with the same hearty response by our people as is always exhibited by Polson boosters.
>
> At a meeting called Saturday morning, arrangements were made for an automobile parade that same evening. And at six o'clock 26 automobiles were lined up in a semi-circle in front of the Grandview Hotel. They were decorated with Chautauqua pennants and banners, and each auto carried a letter, thus spelling "P-O-L-S-O-N C-H-A-U-T-A-U-Q-U-A B-O-O-S-T-E-R-S."
>
> The band was there discoursing music, while [Polson photographer Herman] Schnitzmeyer arranged the preliminaries for a picture. The parade covered some of the principal streets and finished by going to the Grandview, where the band gave a selection.

Several days before the Chautauqua session opening, the agency superintendent arrived. Remarkable for the age, the superintendent frequently was a pleasant, efficient woman in her twenties or thirties. Her responsibilities covered all of the session preparations and, once the Chautauqua began, she introduced each act and gave two of the afternoon lectures herself. The superintendent's final, important duty involved booking guarantors for the next year's Chautauqua.

The third bureau agent who spent the entire session in town was the Junior Chautauqua director. Young women often filled this position too. The Junior director became responsible for all of the children's morning games and activities, the drilling of youngsters for a pageant production on the sixth day, and the delivering of afternoon story-telling sessions. Frequently called "the story lady," the Junior director also gave at least one adult lecture during the week.

Chautauquas charged little ($1.00), if anything, for a Junior season ticket. Most bureaus considered the Junior program part of their educational mission—as well as good business. When Chautauqua came to town, each child enjoyed a week of education, entertainment, and a costumed role in a Junior Chautauqua production. No wonder Chautauqua left such powerful imprints on an entire generation of small-town children.

Several Chautauqua companies extended their circuits into Montana prior to World War I. Particularly Redpath-Vawter and Britt Chautauqua ran summer sessions in towns along the Northern Pacific mainline. In 1912, however, the mix changed. After that season, J. Roy Ellison left Redpath-Vawter to establish his own circuit in the Northwest.

Ellison joined longtime lyceum organizer Clarence H. White of Boise, Idaho, to establish the Ellison-White Lyceum and Chautauqua Bureau, headquartered in Portland, Oregon. Ellison had studied carefully the Rocky Mountain market and chose Bozeman as his key contract. In the fall of 1912, he booked Bozeman as the first of forty engagements for the following summer. Thus the West's most successful circuit-Chautauqua company began a Montana run that would last for thirteen years. Ultimately Ellison-White became the largest circuit on the continent and extended Chautauqua to Canada, New Zealand, and Australia.

Typical of Montana towns, Red Lodge held its first Chautauqua in 1915 and enjoyed annual engagements through 1923. The (Red Lodge) *Carbon County Journal* trumpeted (July 21, 1915):

> Red Lodge's first Chautauqua, the finest thing in the entertainment line, will open a week from this evening. It will run for seven days, and each day will bring something new and different, amusing or instructive, including performances by magicians and prestidigitators, mind readers and Swiss

Alpine yodelers, concerts by the famous Ciricillo Italian Band and the Berlin Quintet, lectures by noted men and women, and a complete production of the opera "Il Trovatore" in four acts. There will be something doing under the Chautauqua tent morning, afternoon, and evening. Each morning there will be a children's hour, beginning at 9:00 and a lecture at 10:00. At 2:30 each afternoon there will be a concert, which will be followed by an interesting lecture, and in the evening there will be concerts by noted singers and players.

Lectures will be delivered by: Dr. Newell Dwight Hillis, one of the best-known divines in the United States; Nels Darling, the town builder; Father Patrick J. MacCorry; Colonel George W. Bain of Kentucky. Whether or not the Chautauqua is to become an annual institution in Red Lodge depends largely on the advance sale of tickets. Public-spirited merchants and professional men—without any hope whatsoever of reward outside of the progressiveness of the city—have pledged themselves for a guarantee of hundreds of dollars to permit it to obtain a foothold here. Practically every other progressive city in Montana and other states in the Northwest has been having the Chautauqua for several years or will have it this year.

Any doubts in Red Lodge vanished during "Chautauqua week." By the fourth night, signed pledges assured the return of the Ellison-White troupe for 1916 (*Carbon County Journal,* August 4, 1915):

> Superintendent Earl C. Miller started the ball rolling for next year on Saturday evening by announcing his purpose of distributing pledge cards. While torrents of rain descended on the tent, making a roar like Niagara, the twelve hundred people gathered for the evening program listened to an endorsement of the Chautauqua from Principal C. W. Thompson of the high school and another from Charles H. Draper, editor of the *Journal*—both of whom were called on by the superintendent. When the pledges had been turned in, it was found that 340 season tickets had been ordered for 1916.

Some towns abandoned the circuit Chautauqua in 1917 because

of World War I. However, President Woodrow Wilson proclaimed that "the Chautauquas are almost as integral a part of the national defense as men and munitions," so towns like Red Lodge honored their contract with Ellison-White. The *Carbon County Journal* (August 22, 1917) remarked on the week-long session:

> The prevailing notes in every address might be characterized first of all as patriotic and calculated to arouse the people to a sense of the national danger represented in Prussian aggression...."The Chimes of Normandie," the comic opera presented by the Boston Light Opera Company on Saturday afternoon, won the hearts of probably as many of the audience as did any number on the program. This ambitious undertaking represents a new record in Chautauqua work—the first time a full comic opera has been presented under Chautauqua auspices.

The 1918 Ellison-White presentation in Red Lodge provided even greater flag-waving. As the *Journal* warned (August 7, 1918):

> The federal government has recognized the Chautauqua platform as the means of reaching a great majority of the thinking people of America, and it has commissioned the bureau to present two lectures on national issues.

So, mixed in among Thaviu's Exposition Band, the Old Soldier Fiddlers, and a bird-call imitator, Dr. Lincoln L. Wirt spoke on "Accompanying Our Armies in Europe," and Dr. C. J. Bushnell addressed "The Meaning of the Great War." Even the theatrical offering—the Luzerne Actors' "Plays of Our Allies"—carried a heavy patriotic message.

After the war, most Chautauqua companies began to modify their uplifting, informative lecture fare by presenting more dramatic troupes. For example, in Glasgow on August 9, 1922, the Keighley Broadway Players' sermon-play "Turn to the Right" captivated an audience of more than five hundred persons perched on

SEVENTY ACRES OF CANVAS

When you see the big brown tent at Chautauqua, try to visualize an immense field of almost seventy acres covered with canvas, and you will have some idea of how much equipment is used by the Ellison-White Chautauqua Company on their various summer circuits in the United States, Canada, and in the South Seas.

Tent companies credit Ellison-White with having more canvas than any amusement concern of any kind and more than twice as much as any other Chautauqua bureau. We have a total of fifty-nine tents, and in June and July forty of the big khaki tops are up every day in forty different towns. The side-wall and fence, if connected together on all this equipment, would stretch over seven miles and the main guy ropes a dozen miles.

—Ellison-White supplement to the Twin Bridges Independent,
August 22, 1919

rough-board benches. Similarly, in Froid on August 7, 1923, the Comus Players presented "The Shepherd of the Hills" to a record-breaking crowd. At Lewistown, in 1926, the Robert Hardaway Players first offered "Lightin'" and returned two nights later with "Pollyanna"—both presentations to standing-room-only crowds.

The turn from standard educational fare to pure entertainment marked the slow demise of the circuit-Chautauqua in Montana and the nation. For instance, by 1921, Ellison-White had stripped its dynamic last-night show of any inspirational lecturers and provided a concert by the Royal Hawaiian Quintet, followed by Mildred Leo Clemens' illustrated presentation "Rambling Through Paradise." Miss Clemens' stunning performance relied on the technological wonder of "talking motion pictures" of Hawaii's active volcano, Mount Kilauea.

Ellison-White's revenues dropped dramatically in 1922, and again in 1923, despite serving more than 350 towns in the

Northwest. The bureau began to withdraw from its circuits in 1923. The *Froid Tribune* explained (August 3, 1923):

> Froid will not have Chautauqua next season, owing to the fact that many of the guarantors this year were not anxious to sign up for next season. In addition, the Ellison-White people, according to their superintendent Miss Lorraine Taylor, are eliminating all four-day courses as much as possible. So the matter was not urged on either side. Nevertheless, most everybody here believes in Chautauqua and has enjoyed them greatly every year.

Ellison-White abandoned the Chautauqua business completely in 1935, although the corporation survived as a lecture bureau and as the parent of a music school in Portland. Smaller circuit-Chautauqua companies tried to fill the Ellison-White void in Montana, but with little success.

In 1928 Libby promoted two Chautauqua sessions, one by the Cademan Company and the other by Mutual Chautauqua. Neither proved satisfactory, and the editor of the (Libby) *Western News* remarked (September 16, 1928):

> Comes the showman on the scene. You saw and heard the results of his efforts. The effort to sustain the educational content in the programs is rather feeble. Where are the mothers' classes of old, and the earnestness of purpose?

The citizens of Cut Bank used harsher methods in 1930, when they refused to pay the Chautauqua bureau its guarantee (Cut Bank *Pioneer Press*, August 8, 1930):

> Not at all up to the standard of last year was the program of United Chautauqua, which held forth here from Sunday until Wednesday evening. With one or two exceptions, the bill of fare was distinctly third-rate. One performance in particular was reminiscent of explosive farces that used to be presented in the little red schoolhouse back in the Gay Nineties.

> The Chautauqua was underwritten by local businessmen and ranchers, who were theoretically obliged to meet the contract deficit to the full extent. However, with characteristic Cut Bank gameness,...all declared that they had made a mid-year resolution. What that resolution is may be left to the deft imagination of the reader.

The last brown circuit-Chautauqua tent was struck in 1932, with the onset of the Great Depression. However, the demise of Chautauqua was the result of several other factors: the development of radio; automobiles and improved roads, which permitted rural residents to seek entertainment in larger towns; the popularity of talking motion pictures; the spread of quality theater throughout the nation; the wide-spread acceptance of public dancing; the proliferation of public libraries; and the declining quality of Chautauqua productions.

In Montana, the end of Chautauqua signaled a recognition that the state's communities would never be quite as isolated as they were during the 1906-1918 homestead boom. Just as Chautauqua's belief in personal education and self-improvement appealed to Montana progressives, the end of the annual sessions reflects some deflation in the progressive movement. Finally, the national craze for lighter entertainment that rolled out of the Twenties and crashed into the Thirties sealed the fate of circuit Chautauqua.

At the peak of its national popularity in 1924, an estimated thirty million Americans sat in brown tents in 12,000 towns to enjoy lectures, music, drama, and culture provided by circuit Chautauquas. In many Montana communities, "Chautauqua week" became the main social event of the year. The long-term effects of Chautauqua are just as important and measurable. For hundreds of thousands of children and adults, memorable Chautauqua performances literally changed their lives—led them into music and theater, or prompted them to embrace public service, or introduced them to foreign places and topics that they later

CHAUTAUQUA ASSURED FOR HERE NEXT YEAR

It is seldom that people in the small towns are accorded the privilege of attending entertainment of such high class as that furnished to the people of Twin Bridges and vicinity this year by the Ellison-White Chautauqua just closed. Immense crowds filled the tent at every entertainment, and it would be impossible to state which of the performances were most enjoyed.

That the performances were thoroughly appreciated was attested by the frequent and numerous encores accorded the performers, to which they invariably graciously responded.

Another evidence of complete satisfaction may be drawn from the fact that it required but seven minutes to secure sixty-seven guarantors to sign the contract for the appearance of these sterling attractions next year.

—*(Twin Bridges)* Madison County Monitor, *August 29, 1919*

pursued. An Alberta woman who had attended Chautauqua programs as a child captured the Chautauqua spirit: "It was like a light coming into your life—once each year."

On every level, Chautauqua attained its goal of assisting personal education and self-improvement. Further, Chautauqua effectively spread knowledge and information, in an era that otherwise relied heavily on newspapers and magazines.

Some legacies of the 1874-1932 Chautauqua movement remain. University extension courses, summer sessions, and the vast array of private self-improvement businesses (for example, Weight-Watchers, Gamblers Anonymous, and Jane Fonda exercise videos) all can trace their lineage to "Mother Chautauqua." In addition, book clubs, correspondence courses, and the community programs provided by State Humanities Committees derive from Chautauqua roots. Finally, the Elderhostel movement and world's fairs owe similar debts.

The enthusiastic participation of Montana towns in the circuit-

Chautauqua movement ties the state tightly to this phenomenon. In an age of limited communication, "Chautauqua week" brought information to a hungry, small-town public and introduced them—in the most commendable, progressive tradition—to innovation and reform.

Chautauqua proved a powerful influence on Montana popular culture between 1907 and 1932. Regrettably, it became yet another victim of advancing technology.

SOURCES

A body of literature—beginning in the 1880s and running to the present—describes the overall Chautauqua movement and its specific developments across the continent. See, for instance: Jesse L. Hurlburt, *The Story of Chautauqua* (New York: G. P. Putnam's Sons, 1921); Gay MacLaren, *Morally We Roll Along* (Boston: Little, Brown and Company, 1938); Donald Linton Graham, "Circuit Chautauquas: A Middle West Institution," Ph.D. dissertation, University of Iowa, 1953; Harry P. Harrison and Karl Detzer, *Culture Under Canvas: the Story of Tent Chautauqua* (New York: Hastings House, 1958); Theodore Morrison, *Chautauqua: A Center for Education, Religion, and the Arts in America* (Chicago: University of Chicago Press, 1974); Sheilagh S. Jameson, *Chautauqua in Canada* (Calgary, Alta.: Glenbow Museum, 1987).

To fill in the chronological gaps, see also: Rebecca Richmond, *Chautauqua: An American Place* (New York: Duell, Sloane, and Pearce, 1943); Victoria and Robert O. Case, *We Called It Culture* (New York: Doubleday, 1948); Charles Horner, *Strike the Tents: The Story of Chautauqua* (Philadelphia: Dorrance, 1954); Joseph E. Gould, *The Chautauqua Movement: An Episode in the Continuing American Revolution* (Albany: State University of New York, 1961); Alfreda L. Irwin, *Three Taps of the Gavel* (New York: Chautauqua Institution, 1977).

Specific aspects of the Chautauqua movement also have been addressed in periodical pieces—for example: Eldon E. Snyder, "The Chautauqua Movement in Popular Culture: A Sociological Analysis," *Journal of American Culture*, 8, #3 (1985), 79-90; John Edward Tapia, "Circuit Chautauqua Program Brochures: A Study in Social and Intellectual History," *Quarterly Journal of Speech*, 67, #2

(1981), 167-177; Kristine M. Davis, "The Chautauqua Idea: Building Educational Fellowship through Symbol and Ceremony," *Western Journal of Speech Communication,* 47, #4 (1983), 396-410.

See also: Cathleen Schurr, "Chautauqua: Yesterday and Today," *American History Illustrated,* 27, #3 (1992), 40-44, 70, 73; Thomas J. Schlereth, "Chautauqua: A Middle Landscape of the Middle Class," *Old Northwest: A Journal of Regional Life and Letters,* 12, #3 (Fall, 1986), 265-278.

Other periodical pieces look at Chautauqua in a state or regional context and include personal reminiscences of Chautauqua participants: LeRoy Stahl, "The Final Curtain Call: Chautauqua in Montana," *Montana: The Magazine of Western History,* 26, #3 (July, 1976), 52-61; Donald B. Epstein, "Gladstone [Oregon] Chautauqua: Education and Entertainment, 1893-1928," *Oregon Historical Quarterly,* 80, #4 (Winter, 1979), 391-403; Michael R. Schliessmann, "Culture on the Prairie: the Big Stone Lake Chautauqua," *South Dakota History,* 21, #3 (Fall, 1991), 247-262; Louise Day, "My [Idaho] Chautauqua," *Idaho Yesterdays,* 13, #3 (Fall, 1969), 2-5; Janice P. Dawson, "Chautauqua and the Utah Performing Arts," *Utah Historical Quarterly,* 58, #2 (Spring, 1990), 131-144; James P. Eckman, "Promoting an Ideology of Culture: The Chautauqua Literary and Scientific Circles in Nebraska, 1878-1900," *Nebraska History,* 73, #1 (Spring, 1992), 18-24.

The most fertile sources for information on Chautauqua presentations in specific Montana communities are the respective local newspapers. Search these papers from June through September, 1913 to 1930, to discover a particular town's pattern of Chautauqua.

CHAPTER NINE

THE "OVERLAND WESTERNERS"
EPIC TOURISTS IN A TIME WARP

This will be the most amazing
horseback ride in the history of
America! If we can make this
work, we will cover more than
20,000 miles and visit every state
capital in the Union. And it is our
goal to have some of the horses
make the whole go.
There just has never been
anything like the "Overland
Westerners"—not ever!

George W. Beck,
1912

George Beck cooked up this whole crazy idea in 1911. The 36-year-old horse logger from Bainbridge Island, Washington, was frustrated by only seasonal work on the Olympic Peninsula. Plus, he longed for fame and fortune.

And his scheme would produce both! How could anyone resist "the longest horse ride on record"—especially right at the dawn of "the age of the automobile"? Now, if he could just talk his buddies into coming along...

George started with his younger brother. Charles Beck usually worked for the railroad, but recently he had been laid off. Although hesitant, Charles finally signed on for "the horse ride of the century."

Next George approached his 37-year-old brother-in-law, J. B.

"Jay" Ransom. "Slim"—as he also was known—lived in Shelton and thought that a three-year horseback tour of the United States was just the ticket, since he was barely eking out a living for his young family as a logger.

"Jay" suggested that the brothers also include his neighbor and fellow woodsman Raymond "Fat" Rayne. This wispy 20-year-old was itching for adventure and wanted to try "being a cowboy."

Thus was created the mounted quartet that planned to visit every state capital in America—all 48 of them—on horseback, leading a single pack horse. George skillfully had selected the name "Overland Westerners," by which the men would ride into notoriety. The proposed trail covered 20,352 miles—the equivalent of five trips from coast to coast. Montana would contribute almost 700 miles to this total and would provide lots of excitement for the boys.

George had the whole thing figured out. The horsemen would leave Olympia, Washington, on May 1, 1912, follow a carefully plotted—if zigzag—course through the country (please see the map), and finish in Sacramento, California, in May, 1915. By dipping south during the winter seasons, they could keep their schedule and avoid harsh weather and tough road conditions.

After completing their mission in Sacramento, a short ride would bring the adventurers to the gates of the Panama-Pacific International Exposition in San Francisco on June 1. According to George's scenario, the "Overland Westerners" would be received there with great amazement, fanfare, and acclaim. They would become "the toast of the World's Fair"! The boys then would sell souvenirs of their trip from a stand on the midway and make public appearances before thousands of adoring fair-goers. Fame and fortune, indeed—a veritable pot of gold!

George's scheme required documentation for "the Great State House Ride." Thus, the boys would secure postal cancellations at every sizeable community along their route. They would have their photograph taken with each governor (if available) in front of his

The "Overland Westerners": founder George Beck is at lower left, with Jay Ransom behind him. Nip is in the center, Charles Beck behind him and Raymonc Payne in front.

Photo courtesy of Bainbridge Island Historical Museum

capitol and obtain from that governor a "certificate of call." They also would carry a "letter of introduction" from each governor visited to the next governor on the itinerary. And they would collect newspaper articles from local publications covering their progress along the trail.

In addition to the obvious novelty of George's scheme, their three-year trek would demonstrate the quality of horses bred in the Pacific Northwest. George asserted (promotional poster):

> An object of the enterprise is to bring one or more of the original starting horses through the entire journey within the given time. This will accomplish the greatest traveling feat ever known to the history of horse flesh—in consideration of the changes in climate, feed, and water, the conditions of the barns and roads, and the hardships of a ride of this nature.

George's prime candidate for this achievement was "Pinto"—a six-year-old paint horse of mixed Morgan and Arabian stock. This "Morab" stood 15 hands high, weighed about 900 pounds, and began the trip as the crew's only pack horse. Eventually, however, he became George's personal saddle horse. Miraculously, Pinto would travel the entire 20,352-mile route and live to return to Bainbridge Island.

George Beck also conceived an ingenious way to finance the expedition. The Seattle publisher of a small monthly magazine, *The Westerner*, agreed that the quartet could become the publication's "national solicitors." The horsemen would canvass communities through which they passed to exchange "certificates of subscription" for cash.

A subscription to *The Westerner* cost $1.00 a year. The men would split the cash evenly with the magazine. *The Westerner* also would carry exclusive, inside coverage as "the Long Ride" unfolded.

Beck figured that the entire trip would run about $9,000 in out-of-pocket expenses for the group: food; clothing; feed for the horses; tack; film; printing bills; incidentals. Further to offset these costs, the boys created postcard and poster masters, which they carried with them. When their supply of postcards or wall calendars ran low, they would resupply at a print shop along the route—often in batches of 200 to 500. The single-sheet poster/calendars usually sold for 15¢, and the postcards for 5¢ each.

The calendars showed the four years of the journey (1912 through 1915), portraits of the men, a map of their planned itinerary, and an image of Pinto. The caption under Pinto's picture rhymed:

> 20,000 miles, I am supposed to travel,
> Thru mud, sand, rocks and gravel,
> And if I receive the proper care,
> You will surely see me at the Fair.

George Beck's proposed epic journey was especially curious and remarkable for being made on horseback—at a time when automobiles were just being tested for cross-country travel. During the summer of 1912, the Montana Good Roads Congress convened in Anaconda. It promoted improved gravel roads for auto travel and endorsed the new Park-to-Park Highway, linking Yellowstone and Glacier national parks.

Similarly, J. M. Carpenter and E. E. Biles arrived in Helena on July 16, 1912, after covering 3,500 miles of their auto trip from Buffalo, New York, to Los Angeles—a well-publicized test of national road conditions. And Pathfinder A. L. Westgaard, field representative of the American Automobile Association's "transcontinental pathfinding party," chugged into Montana early in August, attempting to prove the feasibility of long-range auto travel.

George's choice of horses over autos obviously fit his party's finances, but he also was making a subtle statement about the Wild West, the personal relationship between a cowboy and his horse, and the "frontier" appeal of the Pacific Northwest—where man still relied on the traditional horse and the "iron horse" for transport.

So, on May 1, 1912, the "Westerners" had their photo taken with Governor M. E. Hay in Olympia, accepted his "letter of introduction" to the governor or Oregon, and struck out for Salem. Oregon in the spring offered good roads, and here "Nip," a 60-pound Gordon setter–Newfoundland cross joined the party. Nip would remain with the horsemen for the duration—covering many more than 20,000 miles because of his penchant for rabbit- and bird-hunting forays.

On good roads, the boys could average 20 to 25 miles a day. They reached Salem, posed with Governor Oscar West before the state house, and pushed on to Boise—encountering seven-foot snow drifts in the Cascades.

On June 18, 1912, the "Westerners" executed their required photograph with Governor James Hawley before the Boise state capitol. They also received his "letter of introduction" to deliver to Montana's Governor Edwin L. Norris. The next morning they left to wend their way through Idaho and into southwestern Montana.

The "Westerners" climbed over Bannock Pass and entered Montana on July 1. By the Fourth of July they had reached Dillon for the annual festivities. En route George took his usual "special pains" to care for the horses. He stopped the party every few hours to graze the stock, and he grained them whenever he had the money. "Fat" Rayne remarked (*Denver Post*, August 30, 1964):

> That man [George] surely knows and loves horses, and cares for them too. We could be choked with thirst, empty-bellied, ready to pitch on our dumb heads from the saddle with weariness, but the broncs always came first. They were fed, rubbed down and blanketed and, if necessary, put under cover. Only then did we rustle for our own eats and shelter.

At the Dillon race track, George noted (George Beck diary, Bainbridge Island Historical Society Archives, Bainbridge Island, Washington): "The [events] committee made arrangements to let us

FROM THE DAILY JOURNAL OF
GEORGE W. BECK, LEAD
"OVERLAND WESTERNER"

July 21, 1912—Got [up] about 7. Went over to the [10-Mile] creek, near the Central Park and washed our clothes and had a bath and now are [sic] writing in our dairy [sic] while the clothes are drying. After our clothes were dry, we hit for camp and to our surprise we found that Fats' saddle was gone. We looked all over for it, but could not find any trace of same.

We afterwards learned that Mr. Lingshire had lost a horse. While away to a dance on Saturday night, it seems as though someone had made away with a white horse, 6 years old and weighed about 1150 [lbs.] with the "5-B" brand on the left hip, with Apoloosa [sic] spots on her nose. After taking the horse, the thief took Fats' outfit, throwed [sic] it on the horse and rode off and heard no more of him. We all notified the county sheriff, who said he would do what he could.

That night we put our things in a shed and slept in a hay loft and tied the dog by them, determined not to run any more chances.

in, free of charge. They wanted us to ride some buckers and do some trick riding, but of course this rot we refused to do." Nevertheless, the celebrities stayed for a full card of exciting match races.

In the afternoon, the boys attended a band concert and a baseball game between Dillon and the Butte Independents (won by Dillon 6 to 2!). And they followed that up with "a 10-cent show" in the evening. This was a euphemism for a "burlesque" performance—a stage production of various acts, featuring low comedy, musical numbers, dancing, and brief nudity. On their journey, the "Overland Westerners" showed a particular weakness for "10-cent shows."

George had 500 copies of the poster/calendar printed by the *Dillon Tribune* jobbers. These items the boys offered for sale when they canvassed a town, selling subscriptions to *The Westerner*. Individual postcards of Pinto, of the mounted quartet, and of their mapped route also sold well. In a lucrative town, the group could make $10 to $25 in an afternoon of canvassing. They also became adept at trading subscriptions to the magazine for food, lodging, and horse feed.

The travelers reached Butte on July 9, and George added a typical entry to his diary:

> Got to Butte about 2:00 P.M. Found a pasture in the lower end of town—about one mile from town and a good one. Got permission to put our things in an old barn that belongs to the fellow that runs the Butte Floral Company's hot houses. Went up town and got a shave and my boots shined. Jay got his horse shod. He came back to camp and declared that Butte certainly had a lot of rubber-necks [gawkers], something fierce.
>
> Butte is quite a sporting town. Mines on all sides—right in the city and all over the Hill. They say that Butte has got a $1,500,000 payroll each month. Wages [are] $3.50 to $4.00 per day, and it is a wide open burg....Butte is a lively town, but not good for our [canvassing] business.

George Beck retrieved a load of the boys' general delivery mail in Butte and sent off a money order to *The Westerner* office for $17.50 in subscriptions. He also ordered $25 worth of postcards printed at the *Butte Miner* shop. The next afternoon, the boys hopped a streetcar up to Columbia Gardens and spent the evening at the dance pavilion there.

On July 17, the "Westerners" reached the capital city of Helena, via Basin, Boulder, Jefferson City, and Clancy. They secured pasture for their five horses two miles north of town, in the Helena Valley. The four travelers established a camp in the meadow and rode the streetcar back and forth to town at 5¢ a trip.

George arranged to have the validating photograph taken in front of the Montana Capitol by Helena cameraman Samuel J. Culbertson. And, on July 22, Governor Norris joined the wayfarers for the photo.

We found Governor Norris to be a prince, and also his secretary [Will Aiken]. We also got introduced to Edgar S. Paxson, the famous cowboy artist who was doing some work in the new [west] wing of the Capitol building at the time. We also saw one of [Charlie] Russell's famous paintings and went all through the Capitol building, and she certainly is a fine one.

The *Montana Record* gave us a swell write-up and also the *Independent*.

In fact, the *Record* had said (July 18, 1912):

Four young men, tanned and bronzed, rode into Helena this morning. Although they attracted no special attention, they were well worth the notice of anyone who admires pluck and courage....

The men are making the trip on Western cow ponies. They are moving leisurely and are riding the same horses on which they started [not so!]. They have encountered some severe weather along the line, and the trip has been fraught with some extreme hardships. So far they have covered about 1,800 miles.

Then tragedy struck! One day, while the quartet was in town canvassing, a thief stole "Fat's" saddle off the pasture fence. The boys had to borrow one from a livery stable for the photo with the governor. Then they purchased a replacement saddle and bridle from noted Helena saddle-maker Fred J. Nye.

To cover this $54 bill, they left their tent, camera, and rifle as security. As they paid off the debt, Nye would ship their collateral to them down the trail. George Beck insisted on this arrangement because he did not want Montanans to think ill of the "Westerners." He said to the boys: "We are gentlemen tourists on horseback with a self-appointed mission. We are not saddle bums."

Finally, on the afternoon of July 22, the party left Helena for Bozeman. In the vicinity of Winston, the boys sought shelter because of a storm that quickly blew in:

We no more than got our things off the horses than she started coming down. [It] thundered and lightened something fierce. We put our things in an old log house nearby and found shelter for the night, although it was full of rats and bugs.

We tore the paper off the walls to lay on the floor, as they were certainly very dirty....We made a bed the best we could and turned in. "Slim" was awakened several times with rats nibbling at his hair, but any kind of a lay-out on such a night was welcomed.

Trailing through Townsend, Belgrade, Bozeman, and Livingston, the intrepid adventurers reached Big Timber on August 2. Along the route, they met scores of hospitable farmers and ranchers who gave them pasture for their horses, meals with the family, and a place to sleep on the front porch, if no barn or haystack was available. Once in the Sweet Grass County seat, George remarked:

Big Timber is a good little town of about 1,800—a farming community....We met a fellow by the name of Bone, and he certainly treated us swell. Went to "a 10-cent show" with him. Saw Nan Aspinwall [a Kalispell native who had ridden her horse across America in 1910] do some of her stunts; pretty good.

Mosquitoes and horse flies plagued the party as it threaded its way down the Yellowstone Valley, headed for Bismarck. The boys recommended Park City for good beer at the Russell Saloon. In that sleepy town, "Fat" lost his wallet on Main Street and then found it there the next day, untouched. Billings provided two different "10-cent shows," but not much profitable canvassing. At Pompeys Pillar, the party:

...Went down to the [Yellowstone] River and had a good swim and a bath. We washed our blankets and had a general wash-up. Had supper at the hotel. A heavy wind came up, and it thundered and lightened [sic] and threatened to rain, but finally blew over. We turned in under an old cottonwood tree.

The night was very cold and heavy dew fell. We got up about 5:30 and headed for Custer....

The alkali water in Hysham caused the horses some problems, but Forsyth proved a gold mine for the canvassers: more than 85 calendars, several dollars in postcards, and 15 subscriptions to *The Westerner*. Along the way, the boys had learned to trade other subscription certificates for oats, dinners, haircuts, smoked meat, and the services of a blacksmith.

In the Miles City general-delivery mail, George received his camera and rifle from Helena saddle-maker Fred Nye—the debt for "Fat's" saddle finally satisfied. The boys spent almost a week in Miles City, noting that the town was "full of cowpunchers, here for the big horse sale," which started on August 19. In Miles City, George "had my teeth fixed; cost $16.00. Also bought a new pair of boots for $7.00."

Farther down the river, the rovers encountered a situation that could have ended the journey right there.

The roads were pretty muddy on account of the recent rains. About 10:30 we came to what is known as the muddy Powder River. This was the largest ford we have had since we started—about ¼-mile across. Slim took a long pole and tested the river for sink holes, and he got pretty wet. We prepared all the horses for the crossing, tied Pinto's head as high as we could, took off our chaps and spurs, and went at it. I took the point, leading Slim's horse, and got across O.K. Jay was leading Pinto who, on account of the heavy pack slipping, turned over in the middle of the stream. Jay flipped him over right side up and headed him upstream—I don't know how—and snaked him to shallow water. Of course, everything was soaked, but we all got across O.K. and had a good rest while things dried out. After this we hit the road again for Terry.

Terry also proved a favorable town for canvassing, and Glendive was even better. The *Dawson County Review* noted (August 30, 1912):

> The people of Glendive warmly welcomed the quartet known as "the Overland Westerners" last week. They are fully a hundred miles ahead of their schedule and, although the effects of hard riding can be seen on them, they are standing it excellently. They say that, when they strike a good town, they generally rest up there. And that is what they have been doing in Glendive during the past several days.

Once the boys left Glendive, they tracked through Wibaux—with front-page coverage in the *Wibaux Pioneer*—and into North Dakota, on their way to Bismarck. They would later remark that some of their greatest adventures had occurred in Montana and some of the most hospitable people they met along the whole route were Montanans. They had covered almost 700 miles and spent almost the entire months of July and August, 1912, traversing the state and visiting the capital.

The "Overland Westerners" persevered through the upper Midwest in the fall of 1912, and then dipped south to Florida during that winter. Through 1913 they rode north along the Atlantic Coast, reached Augusta, Maine, on October 4, and then dropped south to Charleston, West Virginia, for Christmas.

In 1914 the weary travelers pushed up to Michigan and then south again to pick up Louisiana and Texas, before returning north to Iowa. They spent Christmas 1914 on the road between Denver and Santa Fe.

During 1914, *The Westerner* suffered reorganization, and the new owners withdrew their support for the boys' project. But, by this time, the "Westerners" knew that their calendars and postcards—not the magazine subscriptions—were their meal tickets.

On May 24, 1915, the boys had their photo taken before the capitol in Sacramento, California. It was their forty-eighth and last state-house stop on an incredible journey. Their triumph was complete. They had accomplished their goal, and they had done it precisely on schedule.

The "Westerners" had covered 20,352 miles, in the course of 1,127 travel days; the boys had ridden 17 different horses on the adventure; miraculously Pinto and Nip had endured the entire ordeal; the test had been passed without serious injury either to the stock or to the riders. The "Westerners" stood on the doorstep of fame and fortune.

But, on June 1, 1915, San Francisco and the World's Fair proved a bust. George Beck later was quoted in the *Denver Post* of August 30, 1964:

> The pot of gold we had been pursuing had moved out, way out into the Pacific Ocean by the time we reached San Francisco. Unfortunately, we had made no arrangements for a concession at the Fair, and none was available. Also, the concession business was not drawing and, in my opinion, even the Fair was flopping.

No one at the Panama-Pacific International Exposition cared what the "Overland Westerners" had accomplished. Fair-goers were more interested in exotic South Seas dancers, a $350,000 recreation of the Grand Canyon, the latest in automobile engineering, and a life-sized, working reproduction of the Panama Canal.

The discouraged, depressed trio of Charles, "Jay," and "Fat" sold their horses and their tack, and they hopped a freight train back to Washington and to obscurity. George remained in California for several weeks, trying to interest motion-picture producers and such popular writers as Jack London and Rex Beach in the "Westerners'" story. But he could persuade no one of its remarkable character or value.

Finally George Beck raised enough money for passage on a tramp steamer headed for Seattle. With Pinto and Nip he returned to Bainbridge Island a defeated, disconsolate man. Although George tried repeatedly to write the story of the quartet's epic journey, he never could finish the project. He said, "I wrote it sweet enough, but it came up sour."

That characterization likewise could be applied to George's transcontinental scheme. George Beck died a quiet death on the Island. Nip died soon thereafter. Pinto, however, became a community character, for years fed by residents and loved by children.

And perhaps Pinto is the true hero of the "Overland Westerners" story. Perhaps Pinto best exemplifies the vision and the perseverance of this quartet of dreamers—romantics who became the victims of poor timing, rapidly changing technology, and a quixotic public.

SOURCES

Secondary works that cover the national tour of the "Overland Westerners" include: C. A. "Joe" Osier, "20,000 Miles in the Saddle," *Denver Post, Empire Magazine,* August 23, 1964 (Part 1) and August 30, 1964 (Part 2); Cuchullaine O'Reilly, "Forgotten Heroes," *Western Horseman* (August, 1998), 69-75. See also: (Seattle) *The Westerner* magazine, Volumes 1-22 (1904-April, 1915)—particularly Volumes 11-22 (1911-1915).

The "mother lode" of information, maps, journals, articles, and videos is the Bainbridge Island Historical Museum, Bainbridge Island, Washington. Folks at the museum provided great assistance, advice, and research materials—especially copies of: George Beck, "Daily Journal of the Overland Westerners: June 16-August 31, 1912."

For contemporary Montana reaction to the appearance of the Overland Westerners, see the following newspapers: the *Dillon Tribune,* the *Dillon Examiner,* the Butte *Inter Mountain,* the (Helena) *Montana Daily Record,* the *Helena Daily Independent,* the *Manhattan Record,* the *Billings Gazette,* the (Glendive) *Dawson County Review,* and the *Wibaux Pioneer.* Once again, Montana journalism proves a rich source for the historian.

CHAPTER TEN

PATRIOTS GONE BERSERK
THE MONTANA COUNCIL OF DEFENSE, 1917-1918

Fix it so that no longer may the
enemy spies or the peddlers of
sedition and slander go free in
Montana—to insult the patriotism
and to offend the loyalty of our
citizens at home or to send cheer
to the enemy abroad....
We are today either loyal citizens
of this, our native or adopted land,
or else we are traitors. The neutral
or "half baked" citizen, in time of
war, is an impossible conception.
Governor Samuel V.
Stewart, 1918

During World War I, the Montana Council of Defense wrote
one of the very darkest chapters in Montana history.

Under the mantle of "wartime emergency" and "protecting the
public safety," the Council played fast and loose with the civil liberties of all Montanans. The Council imposed restrictions that
today seem preposterous—clear violations of an American's
Constitutionally-guaranteed rights. And the Council did it all by
trading on the war's rampant emotionalism and by cloaking itself in
"patriotism" and "100% Americanism."

For almost two years, the Montana Council of Defense served as
a parallel state government: one that set its own rules; one that

answered to no higher authority; one that seized and practiced all three functions of government—legislative, judicial, and executive. Further, the Council's "reign of terror" took a serious toll on Montana society for years after the war.

World War I began in Europe in 1914. However, the United States did not enter the conflict until April 6, 1917. During the intervening years, Montanans hotly debated war issues that included:

- Should the U.S. enter this foreign war?
- Should the U.S. bankroll the Allies in the interim?
- Does the Constitution allow the U.S. to send draftees overseas?

On the American home-front, a growing wave of hyper-patriotism evolved into anti-German fanaticism and even "German bashing." And, with the entry of the United States into the war, that fervor swept across Montana—because Montanans jumped into the war effort with both feet.

About 40,000 of the state's young men either enlisted or were drafted into service. With booming grain markets and top prices, Montana farmers borrowed to the hilt to expand their acreage. Statewide Liberty Bond drives and Red Cross subscriptions regularly exceeded their quotas. Butte miners (when not on strike) worked three continuous shifts, seven days a week. All of Montana's newspapers were flooded with war news, both from abroad and from the home-front.

In this context President Woodrow Wilson asked state governors and state legislatures to create "state councils of defense"—somewhat along the lines of the National Council of Defense. He directed the state councils to:

- increase food production;
- recruit men for the armed services;
- raise money for war drives;
- promote public support for the war.

But in Montana the 1917 Legislature recently had adjourned. So Governor Samuel V. Stewart created the Montana Council of

Disguised as Uncle Sam, a farmer sows "cowardice" and "treason," while an incongruous group of rats takes food from the fighting troops.
Illustrations published by the National Committee of Patriotic Societies, courtesy of Dave Walter

Indicative of the war hysteria that gripped Montana during World War I is this excerpt from the newspaper piece "Billy Bunny: A Bedtime Story for the Kiddies," written by David Cory. This piece ran in the (Helena) Montana Record-Herald *on May 31, 1918.*

Billy Bunny: A Bedtime Story for the Kiddies

Billy Bunny stepped into the circle of the firelight and said, "I want to sing a song about the war against Germany."

"Go ahead," said Mr. Grizzly Bear.

And Billy did:

> Across in France, with sword and gun,
> Our boys are going for the Hun.
> And so, "On to Berlin" is their cry,
> "For liberty we're proud to die!"

And then Billy Bunny took a little red, white, and blue flag out of his knapsack and waved it in the air and chanted:

> Hip, hip, hurrah, for every star,
> And every bar of red.
> Johnny get your gun, hustle for the Hun,
> And shoot him 'til he's dead, dead, dead.

Defense by executive proclamation. Thus the Council held no legislated authority; it was really just a "governor's advisory panel."

The state's initial Council of Defense well represented Montana's upper middle class. It contained two bankers, a university president, two mercantile executives, a newspaper editor, and a token woman. Governor Stewart appointed himself the chairman of the Council, and he designated his head of the Department of Agriculture and Publicity—Charles D. Greenfield—the Council's executive secretary.

Since there was neither legislative authorization nor legislative appropriation, none of the Council members was paid. The Governor would cover the Council's expenses out of other state-government funds.

The State Council quickly created supporting councils in every one of Montana's 43 counties. Each county council was comprised of three men appointed by the Governor and the State Council. The county councils held the same powers as did the State Council.

In addition, the county councils could certify subordinate town and district groups—"community councils." These local committees were open to anyone who wished to join—and thus drew the most extreme "patriots." The committees did not, however, hold the powers of their superior councils. It would be these community councils that became the "third-degree committees": the best of the self-styled watchdogs of a community's standards of "Americanism" and the harassers of those neighbors whom they found "un-American." During the early months of the Montana Council of Defense's existence, wartime hysteria raged in the state.

One of the most visible purveyors of anti-German hatred was William A. Campbell—a key member of the State Council and the editor of the *Helena Daily Independent*. Because the Council meetings were closed to the public (by decree of Governor Stewart), Campbell became the conduit for Council of Defense news to reach *all* Montanans. And Campbell bordered on the maniacal in his "pro-Americanism."

Campbell excelled in the dissemination of fear. A sample headline from the Independent—in inch-high, bold capitals—read: "YOUR NEIGHBOR, YOUR MAID, YOUR LAWYER, YOUR WAITER MAY BE A GERMAN SPY!"

On September 8, 1917, Campbell reported that Helena residents had seen an airplane "of curious design hovering over the city under the cover of darkness." A month later, the editor revealed to his readers what he figured was a massive espionage operation: Butte spies were sending precious information to a wireless station hidden in the forests somewhere west of Missoula; from here the information was relayed to Germans in Mexico.

On the next day, the *Independent*—in a boldfaced box on the front page—offered a reward of $100 to anyone who could locate the mysterious airplane, which had flown south and east of Helena, and identify its owner. Campbell's statement concluded with an editorial inquiry (*Independent*, September 9, 1917):

> Are the Germans about to bomb the capital of Montana? Have they spies in the mountain fastnesses, equipped with wireless stations and airplanes? Do our enemies fly around over our high mountains, where formerly only the shadow of the eagle swept?

In the throes of extreme anti-German emotionalism, citizens learned quickly how to use the Council to their personal advantage. One could settle any old grudge simply by reporting his personal enemy to the county council! Then he just sat back and watched his fanatical neighbors go after one of their own!

For example, a teacher in Rexford (Lincoln County) had offended the parents of several of his students. The adults reported him to the Lincoln County Council of Defense. J. M. Kennedy of the county council wrote to State Council Secretary Greenfield about the teacher (Record Series 19: Records of the Montana Council of Defense, Box 2, folder 3, letter of February 4, 1918, Montana Historical Society Archives, Helena):

> He is not a good citizen. He is disloyal to this country. He is a rabid, arrogant rebel. He persistently refuses to do his duty as a citizen. As a teacher of the public school at Rexford, he is a public menace. Always he preaches and teaches dangerous doctrines.

Dragged before the county council in Libby, the teacher would admit only to refusing to aid in a campaign to sell thrift stamps and war stamps in the Rexford school. He maintained that children should not be taught that war was worthy of their financial support.

Within two weeks, minutes of the Libby inquiry were delivered to the State Council in Helena. The instructor's teaching certificate then was revoked by the State Superintendent of Public Instruction, and he was fired by the local school board.

To combat Montana's growing wartime problems (both real and imagined), Governor Stewart finally called a special session of the Montana legislature for February 14, 1918. In a frenzy of fanatical patriotism, legislators passed a statewide gun-registration law and an exceptionally tough espionage law.

They also approved an incredible sedition law, with penalties running to a fine of $20,000 and/or 20 years in jail. Because of its severity, this legislation became the core of the federal sedition law later in the year—another dubious honor for Montana.

Special-session legislators also passed a bill that officially created the Council of Defense and made it a legitimate state agency. The legislation appropriated $25,000 for operating expenses and directed the Council to dispense $500,000 in seed loans to farmers. In light of gaining official sanction, the Council reorganized its membership.

The new (second) Council really had gained incredible power, because its enabling legislation permitted it to do "anything not contradicted by the U.S. Constitution or the Montana Constitution." An extra-legal body that already had operated for ten months thus became a legal entity with vast, frightening authority.

To this end, the legislature granted the State Council the power to create "by-laws" or "orders" to regulate Montana's wartime situation (please see the sidebar). Breaking one of these "orders" drew a fine of $1,000, or one year in jail, or both! Violators of these "laws" were prosecuted by county attorneys and processed through the state courts.

Rapidly the new Council set to work creating "orders": 17 in seven months! Most of these "laws" limited or prohibited an activity or a right that the Council deemed "anti-patriotic" or "detrimental to the war effort." They ran from banning parades, to prohibiting fires, to forbidding use of the German language in Montana schools and churches.

Two of the most important of the "orders" were #7 and #8. By these "laws," the Council gave itself the powers to investigate, to subpoena, and to punish violators. It could hold hearings and compel witnesses to attend. It could fine violators and even imprison them. And it did just that in the cases of suspected German operatives Eberhardt von Waldru and Oscar Rohn. Likewise the Council publicly and repeatedly investigated William Dunne, the editor of the radical *Butte Bulletin.*

Just as frightening, the powers invested in the State Council extended to the county councils. So rabid county-level "patriots" also could drag their neighbors before an intimidating county panel and grill them on any subject they wanted!

The second Montana Council of Defense continued its original tasks of increasing farm production, filling draft quotas, and promoting fund drives. But, more and more, it moved into the realm of "creating and maintaining emotional support for the war effort." That is, it whipped Montanans into a pro-American, anti-German frenzy.

Simultaneously the State Council spread fear through Montana society by wielding its self-appointed investigative and punitive powers. The Council's favorite targets were Socialists (especially members of the radical Industrial Workers of the World and the liberal Nonpartisan League), pacifists, Montana's German-Russian population, Mennonites (who, unfortunately, were both pacifists and German!), and suspected German sympathizers of any ethnic background.

The Council kept secret dossiers on "suspicious citizens." It tried, unsuccessfully, to create a 400-man state police force and to attach it to the Council. Either with the enthusiastic support of Montanans or with their acquiescence (often based in fear), the Council controlled everyday life in Montana. And its victims had no recourse—for the Council answered to no one. Mass hysteria and ethnic intolerance fueled Montana's "hyper-patriotism."

Some of the greatest violations of civil liberties occurred during "investigations" run by the county councils. Executive Secretary Greenfield described such an instance involving men who had "under-subscribed" to a Red Cross fund drive in Broadwater County (*RS 19*, Box 1, folder 3, Charles D. Greenfield to Franklin D. Tanner, Hardin, May 18, 1918, MHSA):

> In two cases, these men were brought before the Broadwater County Council of Defense and, while they first persisted in their original decision [not to contribute], nevertheless public sentiment was so stirred up against them that they finally concluded that it was the best part of wisdom to subscribe to the fund drive.
>
> In one case, a genteel boycott was put on a man, in that he was not spoken to by any of his old friends. When he went into a store, the proprietor refused to allow him to be waited on. It took only about 24 hours of this sort of treatment to bring this gentleman to his senses.

"Bond shirkers" were citizens suspected by the county councils of failing to purchase enough Liberty Bonds or savings bonds. "Bond shirkers" received particularly harsh treatment at the hands of the "super-patriots."

In Stevensville, for example, the Stevensville War Service League brought five residents before the Ravalli Council County of Defense. After the extensive grilling of each—designed more to harass than to reveal—the council determined that they all were "money slackers and, as such, deserving of public censure."

The State Council ordered a copy of the county-council findings printed in every newspaper in Ravalli County, to berate the five men.

LEWISTOWN CITIZENS DISPLAY PATRIOTISM

Lewistown. March 27—The pent-up feeling against pro-Germans here found expression this afternoon when an impromptu crowd called Edward Foster in and told him to kiss the flag and take an oath of allegiance. Foster, a prominent real-estate man and an officer in the Montana Regiment during the Spanish-American War, was arrested later upon a charge of having uttered seditious statements a couple of days ago. He gave a bond of $5,000 required by Justice Fred Skalicky.

The crowd went to the high school, secured all the German text books, carried them to the business center, and burned them amid cheers and the singing of patriotic songs. Following this, ten more suspected pro-Germans were required to kiss the flag and take an oath of allegiance. Tonight there was an immense, but very orderly, parade of citizens, headed by the Elks trumpet corps, extending over several blocks.

Roundup Record, *March 29, 1918*

When the editor of the *Stevensville Tribune* questioned this action, he was called to Helena by the State Council for his own hearing!

"Community councils" also ran rampant. These groups of self-appointed patriots created "standards of Americanism" and used them to monitor local actions. Neighbors suspected of pro-German sympathies frequently were brought to the steps of the county courthouse or the city hall. Here—publicly to demonstrate their patriotism—they were forced to kiss the flag, or to sing all the verses of "God Bless America," or to recite the Pledge of Allegiance ten times. The phrase "public censure" became commonplace in Montana's small-town weekly newspapers during 1918.

Both county and community councils also practiced "the delimiting of civil liberties in the name of patriotism" with visiting speakers from suspect organizations. In Miles City, Nonpartisan League organizer J. A. "Mickey" McGlynn was surrounded by members of the local "Third Degree Committee" as he stepped off the train one afternoon.

The patriots hustled him to the basement of a nearby hotel, where they beat him severely. Committee members then dumped McGlynn on the next express to Billings, with the admonition that "Nonpartisan League talk has no place in Miles City." When State Attorney General Sam C. Ford attempted to bring these thugs to task, he was thwarted by the Custer County Attorney, who refused to pursue the case.

Once the anti-German hysteria took root in Montana, it proved hard to control. In the name of "Americanism," community and county councils pursued any citizens whom they considered non-conformists "to make them part of the community's war effort." In Burton K. Wheeler's autobiography, *Yankee from the West*, the U.S. Senator remarks (pp. 147-148):

> In the fall of 1917, so-called "Liberty Committees" were organized in most of the small towns of the state to deal directly with anyone accused of being pro-German or who refused to buy the number of Liberty Bonds that these committees would assess against an individual as his "quota."
>
> The owner of a Billings meat market, who had torn up his Liberty Loan subscription blank, was forced to kiss the flag.
>
> According to the Anaconda Standard, a so-called "Third Degree Committee" in Billings rounded up "pro-Germans and financial slackers" there in November, 1917. A Billings City Council member also was forced to resign his job and to carry an American flag through the streets [to prove his patriotism].

Some of the most vexing violations of rights guaranteed to Americans by their Constitution resulted from Order #3, forbidding the use of the German language. In fact, even before the enactment of Order #3, anti-German fanatics had run Montana's last German-language newspaper, the (Helena) *Montana Staats-Zeitung*, out of business. The weekly folded in September, 1916, after these "patriots" had harassed its advertisers into submission.

Order #3 immediately halted the teaching of the German language in Montana schools, both public and private. The order listed a series of "pro-German" books to be removed from the shelves of all school libraries and public libraries. In Lewistown, Brockway, and at the State University of Montana in Missoula, "suspect" books were burned in public bonfires. The librarian at Hilger, a community northeast of Lewistown, wrote to the State Council (*RS 19*, Box 4, folder 19, Mrs. Emil Peterson to Council, May 14, 1918, MHSA):

> Last month we weeded out all german [sic] texts that were in our school library, clipped out all german songs in our books of national songs, blotted out the coat of arms and the german flags in the dictionaries, and urged that every home should destroy the german-text and [banned] library books that they possess. We also spell "germany" without a capital letter.
>
> A few days ago, we burned all of our *West's Ancient Worlds* [one of the texts on the Council's banned list], and I have the permission of our school trustees to destroy any texts found to contain german propaganda.

Order #3 also banned the use of German from the pulpit. This decision—from which the State Council never wavered—devastated a number of German-language congregations in eastern Montana, particularly Lutheran, Congregational, Mennonite, and Hutterite groups.

In heart-wrenching letters to the State Council, ministers pleaded for some modification of Order #3. For example, Lutheran pastor H. E. Vomhof of Laurel in 1918 wrote to Council Secretary Greenfield (*RS 19*, Box 3, folder 11, letter of September 8, 1918, MHSA):

> I am coming to you in the interest of my congregation. It consists of Russians of the Volga district. Many of them, especially the old people, are not able to speak a word of English, and they understand very little. Of a sermon preached in English, the majority understand nothing but the words "God," "Jesus," and "amen," or the names of the Apostles when mentioned....

Now my desire is that you ask the Council to allow us to have our communion services—also the funeral services—in German. To partake of the Lord's Supper without understanding what is said would be sinful. Hence we cannot celebrate the Lord's Supper—although that celebration is allowed and guaranteed us by the Constitution of the United States....

Remember, I do not desire to have all services in German. I do not ask for more than the above mentioned, although I believe that the worshiping of the people in any language should be left free—war or no war.

When some congregations began to meet in private homes, rather than in churches, to worship in German, the State Council specifically banned that practice. Even after the war was over (November 11, 1918), the Council punitively held fast to its ban forbidding German in Montana churches.

Order #3 also produced some unexpected results. For instance, there were about 700 families of Mennonites whom the Great Northern Railway had settled, early in the 1910s, on the Fort Peck Indian Reservation and near Chinook. Because of the State Council's hard-line enforcement of Order #3, more than 500 of these families relocated to British Columbia in 1918.

Perhaps most frightening about the actions of the high-handed state, county, and community councils is that they practiced their peculiar brand of "100% Americanism" on their own neighbors! Friend turned on friend; family turned on family; communities were shredded by suspicion, and threats, and bizarre actions—all in the name of "patriotism."

Because it was so strongly emotional, there simply was no way to stop this white-hot hysteria on Armistice Day (November 11, 1918). So the ethnic hatred and divisiveness continued, well into the early 1920s. For most Montanans, the hysteria finally played out then. But some of the hard-core purveyors of intolerance moved into the Montana Realm of the Ku Klux Klan, officially founded in 1923.

Interestingly the 1918 enabling legislation for the Montana Council of Defense required it to dissolve three months after the signing of a treaty. But problems developed among State Council members in interpreting what constituted a "treaty signing." So the Council existed, at least on paper, until Governor Joseph M. Dixon finally killed it on August 24, 1921.

But by then the damage to Montana society had been done. World War I's patriotic madness had poisoned an entire generation of Montanans. It certainly affected the state's German-descent victims. But it also changed the anti-German fanatics, who either attacked their neighbors or said nothing when those attacks were made.

All of this home-front violence and "delimitation of Constitutional liberties" falls at the feet of the Montana Council of Defense. This agency acted as a parallel state government in Montana for almost two years—some of this time in a completely extra-legal capacity.

The State Council organized the hatred and the hysteria, and it fed the hatred and the hysteria. It set the pattern for county councils and community councils. And it generally condoned—even justified—the extreme actions of those subordinates. In an attempt to support the war effort to bring liberty and democracy to Europe, the Montana Council of Defense destroyed the liberty and democracy of Montanans at home.

Is the story of the Montana Council of Defense anything more than a case study—a distant piece of the past? Does it have anything to teach us today? The response obviously is "yes." That is one of the reasons that we study history!

Given the right circumstances, similar violations of our civil rights could occur again. We need to be watchful, and we need to be vocal. The actions of the Montana Council of Defense constitute one of the very darkest chapters in the Montana story. That this travesty happened here once is more than enough.

The vigilance of Montanans is required to prevent its recurrence.

This rabid editorial excerpt appeared in the Helena Daily Independent, *written by editor William A. Campbell—also a key member of the Montana Council of Defense. Campbell is commenting on the hanging of Industrial Workers of the World (IWW) organizer Frank Little in Butte on the previous day, August 1, 1917.*

"3-7-77"

Good work! Let them continue to hang every IWW in the state....

The *Independent* is convinced that unless the courts and the military authorities take a hand now and end the IWW in the West, there will be more night visits, more tugs at the rope, and more IWW tongues will wag for the last time when the noose tightens about the traitors' throats....

The time has come. The *Independent* cannot comprehend why the United States government has not, long ago, established prison camps and interned there the enemies of the American government. It is beyond the comprehension of the average citizen why the War Department has not ordered certain leaders arrested and shot....

The American plan should be to arrest all of the disloyal, strip them of their Constitutional rights, confiscate their property, place them in internment camps, and deport them to Germany once we win the war....

It sort of quickens the blood in the veins of some of the pioneers of Helena to see once again, hanging from Frank Little's body, the fatal fig-ures "3-7-77."

The words of German Lutheran theologian Martin Niemoller—in the context of World War II and Adolf Hitler's Nazis—speak to that need for vigilance:

In Germany they came first for the Communists, and I didn't speak up because I wasn't a Communist. Then they came for the Jews, and I didn't speak up because I wasn't a Jew. Then they came for the trade unionists, and I didn't speak up because I wasn't a trade unionist. Then they came for the Catholics, and I didn't speak up because I was a Protestant. Then they came for me, and by that time no one was left to speak up.

SOME ORDERS OF THE
MONTANA COUNCIL OF DEFENSE, 1918

1. No parade or public demonstration will be held without the written permission of the Governor (March 15, 1918).

2. All persons not working in useful and legitimate jobs for at least 5 days per week will be considered "vagrants" and must register with local authorities (April 22, 1918).

3. The German language will not be permitted in any Montana schools or churches; specified books (and other books deemed pro-German) will be removed from libraries (April 22, 1918)

5. No intoxicating liquors will be served to any member of the United States armed forces (May 27, 1918).

6. County Councils of Defense are empowered to create and enforce herd districts (May 27, 1918).

7. The State Council will investigate and hear all matters involving "public safety," exercising subpoena power and the power to enforce its decisions (May 28, 1918).

8. The State Council, in its hearings, will conform to accepted rules of subpoena, examination, and transcription; a witness is entitled to counsel (May 28, 1918).

9. All burning will be prohibited during the months of June, July, August, and September (June 24, 1918).

10. During August and September, businessmen will make only one delivery each day, thereby freeing their employees for harvest work on local farms (June 24, 1918).

12. No new newspaper will be created in the state; weekly newspapers are prohibited from becoming dailies (August 12, 1918).

17. No dance or benefit will be held without the permission of the County Council of Defense (October 7, 1918).

SOURCES

The core source for this chapter is the extensive collection of papers: Record Series 19: Montana Council of Defense, 1916-1921, Montana Historical Society Archives, Helena. This material can be supplemented with the pertinent state *Laws and Resolutions* passed by the 1917 legislature in regular and extraordinary sessions, and by the state document: *Proceedings of the Court for the Trial of Impeachment: the People of the State of Montana…v. Charles L. Crum…* (Helena: State Publishing, 1919).

Periodical pieces that apply include: O. A. Hilton, "Public Opinion and Civil Liberties in Wartime, 1917-1919," *Southwestern Social Science Quarterly,* 28 (1955), 32-48; Benjamin Rader, "The Montana Lumber Strike of 1917," *Pacific Historical Review,* 36 (May, 1967),189-207; Hugh T. Lovin, "World War Vigilantes in Idaho, 1917-1918," *Idaho Yesterdays,* 18, #3 (Fall, 1974), 2-11; and Anna Zellick, "Patriots on the Rampage: Mob Action in Lewistown, 1917-1918," *Montana: The Magazine of Western History,* 31, #1 (Winter, 1981), 30-43. See especially: Arnon Gutfeld, *Montana's Agony: Years of War and Hysteria,* 1917-1921 (Gainesville: University Presses of Florida, 1973).

Much work in this field remains buried in honors papers and theses. See particularly: Charles S. Johnson, "Two Montana Newspapers—the *Butte Bulletin* and the *Helena Independent*—and the Montana Council of Defense, 1917-1921," B.A. Honors Paper, University of Montana, 1970; Johnson, "An Editor and a War: Will A. Campbell and the *Helena Independent,* 1914-1921," M.A. thesis, University of Montana, 1977; Kurt Wetzel, "The Making of an American Radical: Bill Dunne in Butte," M.A. thesis, University of Montana, 1970; Timothy C. McDonald, "The Montana Press and American Neutrality in the First World War," M.A. seminar paper, University of Montana, 1975; Mark Mackin, "The Council for Defense: Autocracy in Montana, 1917-1918," B.A. Honors Paper, Carroll College, 1976; Arnon Gutfeld, "The Butte Labor Strikes and Company Retaliation during World War I," M.A. thesis, University of Montana, 1967. See especially: Nancy Rice Fritz, "The Montana Council of Defense," M.A. thesis, University of Montana, 1966.

The other rich source of color for this chapter is Montana's statewide array of newspapers—but particularly the *Butte Daily Bulletin* and the *Helena Independent.*

CHAPTER 11

THE RHYTHMS OF LIFE IN "NEXT-YEAR COUNTRY"

I loved the prairie, even while I feared it.
"God's country," the old-timers called it.
There is something about it which gets a
man—or a woman. I feared its relentless-
ness, its silence, and its sameness, even as
I loved the tawny spread of its sun-
drenched ridges, its shimmering waves
of desert air, its terrific sweep of the
untrammeled wind, and its burning
stars in a midnight sky.
Still in my dreams I can feel the
force of that wind, and hear its
mournful wail around my shack in
the lonely hours of the night.
Pearl Price Robertson,
"Homestead Days in Montana,"
The Frontier, *1933*

Montana led the nation in homesteading. Hopeful claimants filed on more "free" public land here than in any other state—in excess of 32,000,000 acres! Most of this activity fell between 1912 and 1918 and involved 320-acre dryland claims in semi-arid central and eastern Montana.

Unlike earlier frontiers, the Montana homestead boom involved significant numbers of women. However, very much like earlier Montana boom-and-bust frontiers, the honyockers' dreams ended in failure—this time dashed by drought.

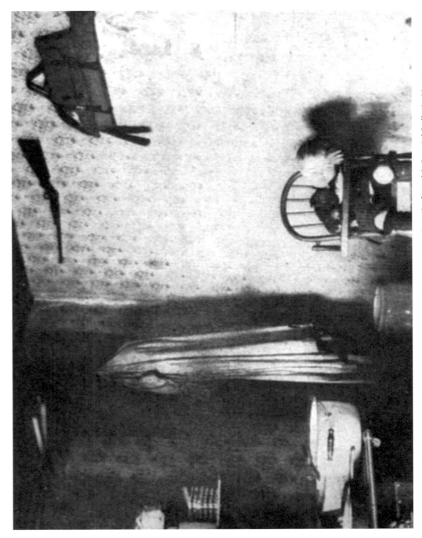

A homestead child was pictured in the Montana State Board of Health Special Bulletin No. 4.
Photo courtesy of Montana State University, Bozeman

The state's homestead movement troubles Montana historians. First, it is a phenomenon tough to quantify, particularly in terms of the number of people involved. Montana's 1910 census recorded 376,056 persons, and its 1920 count reached 548,889—an increase of 69 percent.

Yet the peak of the homestead boom rests between these two surveys—probably in 1917-1918. An official state promotional publication claimed that Montana's population in 1918 had increased to 769,590 (a figure not matched until the 1970s!). More realistic analysts conclude that the Montana homestead boom (1912-1918) drew about 75,000 settlers, almost 60,000 of whom had abandoned their claims and the state before 1922!

By 1919, "to take the cure" had become a popular Montana dryland phrase. It meant the act of simply walking away from a failed homestead—abandoning its buildings, fields, equipment, livestock, and accumulated debt. It meant abandoning one's dreams.

Montana historians from Joseph Kinsey Howard to Michael P. Malone to Harry Fritz have agreed that the homestead frontier was a devastating tragedy of both the land and the people. They cite multiple factors that combined to produce this euphoric boom frontier.

These factors include: liberalized federal homestead legislation that encouraged settlement; lavish promotional campaigns by transcontinental railroads, by the state of Montana, and by local booster groups; the popularization of dry-farming methods; a wartime economy that increased markets and raised market prices; a wet cycle (1910-1916) that produced abnormally bountiful harvests. Herein also lay the seeds of the inevitable bust.

Moreover, the Montana high-plains homestead frontier only reluctantly has revealed its secrets. For the most part, the voices of the 60,000 "leavers" remain silent. Reminiscences of the male "stickers" tend to pivot between melancholy and bravado. So, primarily through the more prevalent writings and interviews of homestead women have historians peered into life on the dryland homestead.

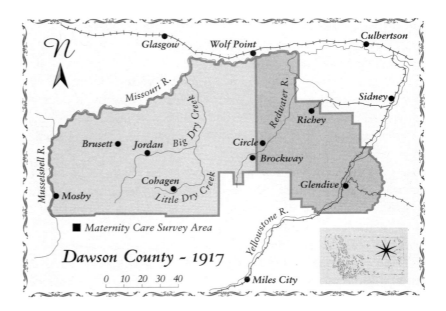

Some common homestead-life themes emerge from these women's stories. The cramped quarters of the homestead house—whether a 14-by-20 tarpaper shack, or a dark, dank sodhouse, or a log dugout—produced serious overcrowding and a lack of privacy. The dull yellow light of the kerosene lamp limited evening activities.

The need for a constant, clean water supply plagued most dry-land homesteaders, as did protection from disease-carrying flies. Bedbugs remained a problem in homes built of unpeeled logs. And, for settlers without a cat, mice became bothersome. They carved holes large enough for a rattlesnake to slither into the house.

A homestead mother was responsible for the housework and child care, as well as for stocking and preparing food. Washing the family's clothes proved her most arduous task, because it involved hauling and heating water, prior to back-breaking work on the scrub board. Other chores frequently included milking, churning, gardening, gathering coal or chopping wood, keeping chickens, feeding pigs, and caring for large stock. In season, most women also helped with the field work and cooked for lambing or harvest crews.

Few generalizations legitimately can be made about the reaction of the dryland-homestead woman to Montana's prairie life. Faced with long periods of isolation and few women living nearby, the female homesteader certainly suffered from loneliness. But wide individual differences existed in the effects of that loneliness—from welcomed relief to insanity. If homesteading meant new, harsh, overwhelming experiences to some women, it offered welcome challenges to others, especially those who preferred farm work to domestic chores.

Most women agreed, however, that the isolation of the dryland claim contributed directly to their two greatest fears: childhood diseases and childbirth. Removed from even the most basic medical assistance, many a homestead mother lived in terror that such communicable diseases as typhoid fever, cholera, diphtheria, scarlet fever, pneumonia, or smallpox would attack her family. Next she feared the complications of childbirth far from conventional medical help. She feared for the life of her newborn. She feared for herself.

On all counts, the dryland mother's fears were warranted. Small, prairie burial plots and homestead ghost-town cemeteries record the high rate of infant, child, and adolescent deaths. The high risk of homestead childbirth was more precisely recorded.

In the summer of 1917—right in the midst of World War I—representatives of the Children's Bureau of the U.S. Department of Labor arrived in eastern Montana. For six months, two teams of women, under the direction of Viola Paradise, surveyed homestead mothers within a 5,500-square-mile area in western Dawson County—an expanse larger than the state of Connecticut! (After 1919 this region comprised all of Garfield County and the western portion of McCone County: that land from Brockway west to the Musselshell River, and from the Little Dry north to the Missouri River.)

The Children's Bureau recently had completed similar maternity studies in North Carolina, Wisconsin, and Kansas. But its agents had never seen country like the lower Musselshell Valley, the Missouri River Breaks, and the Big Dry. This vast sweep of semi-arid prairie, coulees, and breaks mightily impressed the surveyors (Viola I. Paradise, *Maternity Care and the Welfare of Young Children in a Homesteading County in Montana* [Washington, D.C.: Government Printing Office, 1919], 15):

> The country varies greatly in appearance, but always there are tremendous, almost incredible distances. The great, wild, rugged, sweeping plains—broken by buttes of many shapes and by sudden gray cut banks—were, at the end of a cruelly dry season, burnt dun and brown and yellow....
>
> The country, except for a few river-bottom cottonwoods and except in the breaks, is treeless. An occasional little tar-paper shack, or the "soddie" of some homesteader, or a log house, or a sheep herder's white covered wagon on these sweeping plains and hills merely accents the wild vastness of earth and sky.

The area's stark isolation most impressed the federal researchers. No resident lived closer to the county seat (Glendive) than 50 miles; some resided almost 150 miles from it. No organized telephone communication existed, the area was inaccessible by railroad, and wagon/auto roads were primitive at best and always seasonal. The weather frequently proved extreme and hostile.

Although this land supported scores of fourth-class post offices, its only real community was Jordan (200 population; 250 in winter), with Circle (250-300 population) lying just outside the survey boundary. Not a single hospital or medical specialist (trained nurse or licensed midwife) operated in the entire area, 105 miles by 85 miles. Three physicians registered by the state of Montana lived in the west end of Dawson County, but two of these doctors said that they had chosen the area to homestead, not to practice medicine.

Field agents for the federal survey visited 463 mothers in all—an ethnically diverse sample that included women of Dutch, Russian, Irish, Scotch, German, French Basque, and Norwegian descent.

NURSING IN PHILLIPS COUNTY

Mary Miller

In 1914 my son George was bitten by the pioneer bug, and we left Iowa to come to Montana. We homesteaded near Walsh, in [what would become] Phillips County [southeast of Whitewater and about 15 miles north of Saco]. We built our shacks close together on our claims, bought a few head of cattle, and began farming.

I was frequently called out by the neighbors who were sick, for they soon found out I would accept no money and that caring for sick people was a duty of my faith.

One March morning [in 1917] I was busy with my housework when I saw a tiny boy struggling through the snow drifts. I knew it was a neighbor's child, Billy, who was about six years old. His family lived about two miles below us. The snow was too deep for a car, and the drifts were pretty bad for a sleigh. It was early March, and we had had a terrible winter on the bench.

The little fellow came in, played around for a while, ate his dinner, and stood around talking to me while I made cookies. Suddenly he said, "We got a little baby at our house."

"No," I said. "When did it come?"

"Last night," he said. "The kids were asleep. I helped Mother. I carried the little baby upstairs and helped Mother upstairs too."

"Where is your Daddy," I asked.

"Oh, he went to town the other day. He got a job. I helped Mother myself."

I ran to the door and called to George, "Come quick! Billy says they've got a new baby, his father is gone, and his mother and the little children are all alone. We have to go down there. Get the car."

"We can't get a car down there," George said. "I'll have to hitch up a team." So George went out on foot, down to the big pasture and got a team.

It was nearly dark when we reached the little house on the flat. The fires were out and the two little ones were crying. They were too small to get themselves anything to eat. I ran up the stairs, but to my surprise the mother was quite well, and the poor new baby was resting quietly.

I had called a doctor and a nurse, and I called the recreant father, and I brought food. Soon we had fires, a light, and the house was put in order. By the time the doctor and the nurse arrived, things were pretty ship-shape.

Many women would have died under such an ordeal, but both baby and mother came through in fine shape. Some folks say that we women are getting too soft. This girl, though, was pioneer stuff, if there ever was.

—*Interview with Mary Miller in: Works Projects Administration, Montana Federal Writers Project, "Livestock History: Phillips County— Experiences of Practical Nurses among Homesteaders," Microfilm #250, Reel 28, Montana Historical Society Library, Helena.*

They focused on a five-year survey period (1912 to 1917), and they began to gather statistics and stories. What they quickly discovered was that most women simply worked childbirth around their usual homestead chores (Paradise, 58-59):

One mother reported that, besides her housework, her usual tasks were milking, churning, the care of chickens, gardening, and carrying water from a well over 300 feet from the house. She continued all her work up to the day before confinement, and she did a large washing on that day.

Later in the day, she walked 2 miles to a neighbor's house, where labor suddenly began—all this in spite of the fact that she had not been well during pregnancy and that the membranes had ruptured 5 days before parturition. The father was away "freighting" at the time of confinement. Consequently he could not relieve the mother of her work.

The mother remained at the neighbor's house for confinement and for 6 days following. The day she reached her home, her husband (who had returned) did her work for her. But beginning the next day—that is, one week following confinement—she resumed her chores, housework, and washing, in addition to the added care of the new baby, who was not very strong.

When the baby was 4 months old, the mother had to cook for 3 harvesters for one week, and a month later for 6 thrashers for one day.

The findings of the Dawson County survey document the fears of homestead women concerning childbirth. The inaccessibility of medical care during confinement was the most striking finding of the inquiry. As a result, 104 mothers (22 percent) in the 463-member sample simply left the area to obtain adequate medical care either in larger Montana communities or out of state.

Virtually all mothers said that they would have preferred to leave, but such a choice was expensive—even if one spent her confinement with relatives. Other mothers planned to leave but misjudged the time of birth (Paradise, 47-48):

One family started out in a sleigh at 7:00 in the morning on a 60-mile ride to the hospital [in Circle]. Toward evening the mother began having labor pains. They had gone too far to return home and, deciding that it would be best to try to get to the hospital, they drove all night.

The next morning at 10 o'clock the baby was born, in the snow, 10 miles from town. The father was the mother's only attendant, and he cut and tied the cord. They then borrowed a more comfortable vehicle from a family that lived near the road and continued their trip to the hospital, the mother carrying the baby in her lap.

Another experience illustrates the complications that harsh weather, long prairie distances, and primitive roads brought to childbirth (Paradise, 48):

This woman left the homestead with her husband in November, two weeks before confinement. After a 65-mile auto ride to the railroad [at Glendive], they went over 70 miles farther by train to get to a hospital [in Miles City].

They started back before the baby was one month old, in some of the worst winter weather. They knew that this was unwise, but the mother was so worried about the other children at home alone—who would have no way to get help if any of them should become sick—that she was unwilling to wait any longer.

The 65-mile journey from the railroad took four days. One night they drove till 10 o'clock before finding a place to sleep. They also spent one whole day covering the four miles between two post offices, because the road, though fairly level, was so deep with snow that their car could hardly get through.

Of the 359 mothers who stayed in the survey area, 129 (36 percent) were attended by a physician. In almost one-half of these cases, however, the physician arrived at the homestead after the birth of the baby. Those women not attended by a physician most frequently received care from other women (181; 50 percent) or were attended by their husbands (46; 13 percent). Three women (1 percent) delivered their babies entirely alone (Paradise, 28):

> One young mother, whose confinement came before she expected it, found herself absolutely alone at childbirth and for two days thereafter. The father, who had gone on business to the railroad a few days earlier, had arranged for a neighbor to stay with his wife.
>
> At the last minute, the neighbor was unable to come, and the mother—having no one to help her, to give nursing care, or to do her housework—had to cut and tie the cord, care for herself and the baby, and get what little food she ate for two days. At the end of this time, the husband returned and summoned a neighbor. This experience, which would have been terrifying at any time, was especially hard because the mother, who was only 19 years old, was having her first baby. Fortunately she suffered no permanent ill effects. But she was weak for about six months after childbirth and did practically no work during that time.

Viola Paradise's report also speaks candidly about the role played by fathers during childbirth on the Montana homestead (Paradise, 31).

> Most of the fathers who had to deliver their wives felt that the danger of

such lack of care was too great to be risked again, if in any way it could be avoided. One father said that he would never attend a confinement again. In fact, he would start to the hospital with his wife six months before confinement was expected. He now feels that no price is too high to pay for adequate confinement care.

The Children's Bureau study reveals that more than three-quarters of the area's mothers had received no prenatal care at all: they saw no physician; they had neither physical examination, nor measurements, nor urinalysis. For prenatal and birth information and supplies, some relied on printed material obtained through the mail.

Other expectant mothers purchased mail-order patent medicines advertised in local newspapers. These panaceas included "Easy Childbirth Tablets" ordered from Illinois and "Mother's Little Helper" pills provided by a Texas doctor. Still other women sought assistance in home remedies—usually comprising olive oil, milk of magnesia, whiskey, or simple cathartics.

The Paradise report was unable to determine the infant mortality rate during the five-year study period. However, one of its most disturbing findings involves the maternal death rate. During the five-year survey, 628 live births occurred in the area, and eight mothers died from diseases of pregnancy or confinement. Thus the survey's mortality rate was 12.7 deaths per 1,000 births.

This figure stands in stark contrast to the rate in Italy of 2.4, to the Kansas figure of 2.9, to the Wisconsin rate of 6.0, and even to the national average (1915) of 6.6. Montana was, indeed, a dangerous place to give birth. The report concluded that, because of their isolation, rural Montana women frequently received health care inferior to that obtained by America's urban poor.

In the fall of 1917, to mitigate this high death rate among mothers, the Children's Bureau and the Montana Board of Health's Child Welfare Division ran four children's health conferences in western Dawson County. At each five-day gathering, the attendant

THE RANCH IN THE COULEE

He built the ranch house down a little draw,
So that he should have wood and water near.
The bluffs rose all around. She never saw
The arching sky, the mountains lifting clear;
But to the west the close hills fell away
And she could glimpse a few feet of the road.
The stage to Roundup went by every day,
Sometimes a rancher town-bound with his load,
An auto swirling dusty through the heat,
Or children trudging home on tired feet.

At first she watched it as she did her work,
A horseman pounding by gave her a thrill,
But then within her brain began to lurk
The fear that if she lingered from the sill
Someone might pass unseen. So she began
To keep the highroad always within sight,
And when she found it empty long she ran
And beat upon the pane and cried with fright.
The winter was the worst. When snow would fall
He found it hard to quiet her at all.

> —*Gwendolen Haste,*
> *"Montana Wives—I," in:* Young Land,
> *New York: Coward-McCann, 1930.*

nurses emphasized the values of breast-feeding and well-child exams, as well as arranging for every mother to consult with a government physician about her children's health problems.

The response among local homestead mothers was overwhelming. More than 75 mothers attended the sessions, and nurses examined 130 children, most of them under 6 years of age. Some families drove more than 30 miles in wagons to attend a conference, and

THE COMPLICATIONS OF
HOMESTEAD CHILDBIRTH

Harsh weather, swollen rivers and creeks, impassable roads—all of which made it difficult or impossible to secure a physician at certain times of the year—also complicated obtaining less-skilled care, such as that of a midwife or a practical nurse. This Dawson County family's experience illustrates several of the problems encountered while procuring care of even marginal quality.

* * * * * *

The parents knew that it would be impossible to secure a physician, because the nearest one was 40 miles away and across the Missouri River, which at that time was not navigable because of the ice. So the mother had engaged a neighbor who was looked upon in the community as a midwife.

However, labor set in at midnight a few days before the confinement was expected. The father, afraid to leave the mother, sent his oldest son (then a boy of 13 years) out into the blizzard for the midwife. The boy took a wagon and team. He then stopped to get a neighbor's boy of the same age, to help him find the way. Together these two children set out. They soon were lost in the storm.

Meanwhile, the mother was growing very anxious about the boys.

"I was more worried about them than about my confinement," she said, in telling of her experience.

After a long while, the father stepped outside and heard someone shouting near the house.

The two boys, after going a little distance, had become lost in the bad lands. They climbed out of the wagon to see if they could find a road, but the snow had covered every familiar landmark. They felt about for a while in the pitch dark and then could not find even the team and the wagon. After wandering around for a long time, by great good luck they happened to stray near home.

The next day, when they went out to look for the team, wagon tracks and their footprints were found on the edge of a 30-foot cut bank.

"They escaped it by a miracle," said the father.

"If we had been in the country longer, we would have known better than to send them out on such a night. But our boy had always had such a good sense of direction, and he thought he knew the way."

Meanwhile the father, who knew nothing about the care of a woman in confinement, delivered his wife—although with fear and trepidation. (Her previous confinements had all been attended by a physician.)

"Altogether it was a terrifying time," he said.

The next day the midwife was sent for to see if the mother was in good condition.

—*Viola I. Paradise*, Maternity Care and the
Welfare of Young Children in a Homesteading County in Montana
(*Washington, D.C.: Government Printing Office, 1919), 30-31.*

many rode more than 15 miles to the meeting sites. As pilot projects, these four conferences demonstrated the value of an aggressive maternity-care program on the Montana prairies.

The Paradise study also concluded with specific recommendations on maternity care in Dawson County. These wide-ranging proposals advocated the institution of a telephone network, the improvement of county roads and bridges, and the establishment of inexpensive "cottage maternity" hospitals in area towns.

The report's primary recommendation, however, urged the hiring of public-health nurses for every Montana county. In addition to teaching residents about sanitation and first aid, these nurses would provide reliable literature on prenatal care, childbirth, and newborn care. By working through the county schools, they could perform well-child examinations even in such remote areas as the Missouri Breaks and the Big Dry. They also could continue the children's health conferences run so successfully by the Children's Bureau in 1917.

The federal agency promised that Montana's outrageous maternal death rate could be cut significantly by these county-based public-health nurses. The 1917 Montana legislature had agreed. It created a separate Child Welfare Division within the State Board of Health and authorized the hiring of nurses by county governments. With

MOTHERING ON THE HOMESTEAD

At the time of World War I (1917-1918), obstetricians normally prescribed nine or ten days of bed rest for the new mother—and complete rest for at least two weeks. They recommended that the woman perform no heavy work for one month following the birth, or she would risk her future health.

Those might have been workable guidelines for Eastern women and for upper-class mothers. However, a woman's life on the Montana homestead kept her from following this prescription.

* * * * * *

We interviewed one mother who had six children, of whom the oldest was 12 and the youngest was 3. During the last three months of her pregnancy, her husband was herding sheep over 5 miles away, so she rode to see him once a week.

She had made this long trip on horseback just two days before the baby was born. The next day she did a large washing, though she had no washing machine or wringer. On the morning of the day that her baby was born, she moved a heavy piece of furniture down into the cellar.

Besides her housework, this mother had continued all her chores up to the day of confinement. These included caring for the garden and the chickens, milking, looking after the stock, and carrying water from the well, which was 60 feet deep and a quarter of a mile away. The only aid she had during her pregnancy was from her two older children—a boy of 12 and a girl of 11.

Her new baby was born prematurely and was very small. A neighbor came and did the housework for 4 days after the baby was born. The mother stayed in bed only 5 days and, at the end of the week, she was doing all her housework except washing. At the end of two weeks, she had resumed her washing and chores.

—Viola I. Paradise, Maternity Care and the
Welfare of Young Children in a Homesteading County in Montana
(Washington, D.C. Government Printing Office, 1919), 59.

assistance by county home-demonstration agents, information and advice regarding maternity care rapidly spread to Montana homestead mothers—at least to those who remained on the Montana plains after the "bust" of 1918-1922.

These "stickers" and their homestead children formed the core of Montana's twentieth-century agricultural sector. Their common character was one of strength, resilience, and realism. They passed their determination and optimism to their Montana descendants—now faced with equally dire economic circumstances in agri-business.

Best to remember the words of a homestead woman, Pearl Price Robertson—the mother of nine children, six of whom were born in Montana. Pearl and her husband Alec had arrived from New York and homesteaded in northern Chouteau County in 1910 ("Homestead Days in Montana," *The Frontier*, XIII, #3, March, 1933, 225):

> We have no regrets. Life is fuller and sweeter through lessons learned in privation. And around our homestead days some of life's fondest memories still cling....
>
> I feel that creating a home and rearing a family in Montana has been a grand success. And my cup seems filled to overflowing with the sweetness and joy of living....We are of Montana, now and always—boosters still!

SOURCES

General Great Plains background for the topic of homestead maternity should include the following works: Elinor P. Stewart, *Letters of a Woman Homesteader* (Lincoln: University of Nebraska, 1961); Sandra L. Myres, *Westering Women and the Frontier Experience, 1800-1915* (Albuquerque: University of New Mexico, 1982); Mary W. M. Hargreaves, "Homesteading and Homemaking on the Plains: A Review," *Agricultural History*, 47 (April, 1973), 156-163; Hargreaves, "Women in the Agricultural Settlement of the Northern Plains," *Agricultural History*, 50 (January, 1976), 179-189.

A sampling of Montana homestead pieces should include: Milton Shatraw, *Thrashin' Time: Memories of a Montana Boyhood* (Palo Alto: American West Publishing, 1970); T. Eugene Barrows, *Homestead Days* (Chicago: Brownstone Books,

1981); Belvina Williamson Bertino, *The Scissorbills* (New York: Vantage, 1976), Hughie Call, *Golden Fleece* (Lincoln: University of Nebraska, 1942/1981); Maggie Gorman Davis, *The Montana Years, 1910-1916* (Owensboro, Kentucky: McDowell Publications, 1980); Lillie Hall Hollingshead, *The Years of No Return* (Havre: Bear Paw Printers, 1974); Cora Pickens, *A Honyock Family* (Ekalaka, n.p., 1967).

Specific contextual pieces include: Pearl Price Robertson, "Homestead Days in Montana" in H. G. Merriam, ed., *Way Out West* (Norman: University of Oklahoma, 1969), 221-242; Anna Zellick, "Immigrant Homesteader in Montana, Anna Pipinich," *Environmental Review*, 4 (1977), 2-16; Rex C. Myers, "Homestead on the Range: the Emergence of Community in Eastern Montana, 1900-1925," *Great Plains Quarterly*, 10, #4 (Fall, 1990), 218-227; various historical pieces that appear in *The Frontier* (later *The Frontier and Midland*), the literary magazine published by the University of Montana from 1920 to 1939; and any of the scores of Montana local/county history volumes.

Montana: The Magazine of Western History provides a wealth of Montana homestead accounts. See: Mabel Lux, "The Honyockers of Harlem," 13, #4 (Fall, 1963), 2-14; William E. Kilgour, "The Nester," 15, #1 (Winter, 1965), 37-51; Marie Snedecor, "The Homesteaders: Their Dreams Held No Shadows," 19, #2 (Spring, 1969), 10-27; Mary Knoble Young, "The Wind in Floyd Knoble's Barn," 23, #1 (Winter, 1973), 76-81; Ruth E. Dixon Cameron, "Homestead Fun," 31, #2 (Spring, 1981), 68-69; Dorothy Kimball, "'Alone on That Prairie...' The Homestead Narrative of Nellie Rogney," 33, #4 (Fall, 1983), 52-62.

From the same publication, see also: Jean E. Dryden and Sandra L. Myres, "Homesteading on the Canadian Prairies: the Letters of Barbara Alice Slater, 1909-1918," 37, #1 (Winter, 1987), 14-33; Ellie Arguimbau, "Pearl Danniel: Homesteader in Big Dry Country," 46, #3 (Summer, 1994), 62-70.

Specific to the issue of maternity, see particularly Mary Melcher, "Women's Matters: Birth Control, Prenatal Care, and Childbirth in Rural Montana, 1910-1940," *Montana: The Magazine of Western History*, 41, #2 (Spring, 1991), 47-56. For homestead poetry, see: Gwendolen Haste, *Young Land* (New York: Coward-McCann, 1930).

The concept document for this chapter is: Viola Paradise, *Maternity Care and the Welfare of Young Children in a Homesteading County in Montana*. U.S. Department of Labor, Children's Bureau (Washington, D.C.: Government Printing Office, 1919), passim.

CHAPTER TWELVE

RED WHEAT
MONTANA'S PRAIRIE RADICALS, 1918-1937

TO THE FARMERS AND WORKERS
OF SHERIDAN COUNTY
GREETINGS
The Communist Party, U.S.A., of
the State of Montana and the
county of Sheridan, by the Section
Committee of the Communist
Party, Section Sheridan County, of
District No. 11, C.P.U.S.A., sends
greetings to the farmers and work-
ers of Sheridan County, Montana.
The Communist vote cast in the
county at the recent election is
very gratifying and in itself
is a splendid victory.
There are 577 farmers and workers
in Sheridan County who voted for
[Communist Party Presidential
candidate William Z.] Foster and
[Vice-presidential candidate James
W.] Ford. There are 577 who are
thru [sic] with capitalism and the
capitalist parties, who are not concerned with whether [President
Herbert] Hoover was defeated and
[President-elect Franklin D.]
Roosevelt elected. 577 [voters]

> have definitely committed them-
> selves to the overthrow of the capi-
> talist system of production and dis-
> tribution and the substitution of
> the Communist system in its place.
> And Comrades: That is a revolu-
> tionary victory! A greater victory
> than most of us comprehend....
> There are nearly 1,000
> Communists or near-Communists
> in Sheridan County.
> That is a showing to be proud of.
> *(Plentywood)* Producers News,
> *November 11, 1932*

When the Union of Soviet Socialist Republics (U.S.S.R.) collapsed in 1991, you could almost hear the sigh of relief rise from
northeastern Montana. For, with the dissolution of the Soviet
Union, many old-time residents of Daniels and Sheridan
counties—and particularly Plentywood—felt that a lifelong stigma
had been lifted. No longer would they be derisively labeled—however wrongly—"Socialists," "Commies," "Pinkos," and "Reds."

Now, perhaps, these northeastern Montanans can look objective-
ly at the unusual events that evolved between World War I and
World War II. For the entire radical interlude on the northern
Great Plains is an intriguing historical phenomenon. Scores of
Montana communities would kill to incorporate Plentywood's
story in their heritage! Can you imagine what the people of Butte
would do if they owned Plentywood's story?

Count on Montana's own Ivan Doig to research the Plentywood
radical story and to weave it into gloriously tight fiction. Doig's novel
Bucking the Sun (1996) transposes time and character just a bit.

Charles "Red Flag" Taylor stands to the right of these protesters' sign.
Photo originally published in Montana: the Magazine of Western History, courtesy Mary Ingerson

SHERIDAN COUNTY FARMERS
AND AUTHORITIES CLASH

Plentywood. May 2—Guns were roaring and fire hoses were brought into action by a small army of deputy sheriffs and gun thugs when Sheriff Hans Madsen of Sheridan County forced through the sale of a farmer's combine here today.

From 250 to 300 farmers had gathered behind the county jail, called on short notice by the United Farmers League and the Farm[ers] Holiday Association to back up Pete Andersen, farmer of Dagmar and owner of the combine, in his demand for either the combine or mortgage papers.

Armed to the teeth with shotguns, rifles, revolvers, and sawed-off shotguns, and with fire engines in readiness, the sheriff and his band of 25 went to work to rob the farmer of a piece of machinery....

The first one to start shooting was [J. Frank] Murray, the under-sheriff. Shaking and trembling all over, he pressed the trigger of his sawed-off shotgun, shooting over the heads of the crowd. When he saw that the shot did not have the effect he evidently had expected, he maddened and hit the fellow next to him, Simon Swanson, in the face with the gun....

Several shots rang out. One went off in the sheriff's office, where a nervous deputy pulled the trigger by mistake, when Sheriff Madsen and his aides climbed on top of the combine. At this time, with the help of several Plentywood business firms, the fire hoses were turned on the farmers.

And the farmers were not only to be drenched with water. Sulphuric [sic] acid and by-carbonate [sic] soda mixed with water was used to disperse the crowd. However, the pressure of the water lasted only a short while. Suddenly, in several places, the hoses sprang leaks, and deputies, firemen, and some spectators got equally drenched with chemicals and water....

Most outstanding, his gun leveled against the farmers, was His Honor the Mayor of the City of Plentywood, Percy Neville, chairman of the relief committee and agent for the International Harvester Company. Bob Robke, chief of police, was swinging a blackjack....

The struggle around the combine brought into evidence a perfect line-up of the classes that are struggling in Sheridan County—and, for that matter, in every capitalist county in the world. Ex-bankers, implement dealers, businessmen, officials, and lumpen-proletarians [sic], elements who can be bought for anything cheaply, were fighting the farmers. The fascist forces of a fast-decaying system were fighting the men and women who will bring about a new and better society—the workers and tillers of the soil.

—*(Plentywood)* Producers News, *May 4, 1934*

Yet—to his great credit as a historian—Doig offers tantalizing glimpses of a fantastic, virtually untold chapter in the story of eastern Montana. Now, just as school children begin to grasp "honyockers," with their deep accents and overalls, they need to understand an even more complex subject. For those farmers were immersed thoroughly in international labor and reform politics.

Plentywood's story is as remarkable as it is compelling. In brief: radicalism swept across the northern Great Plains on the heels of poor markets, drought, and massive agrarian failures. Through a series of increasingly radical organizations and political parties, farmers in northeastern Montana, North and South Dakota, and Minnesota sought relief from this devastation.

Finally, in the 1920s and the 1930s in Sheridan County, citizens elected a Communist sheriff, supported other Communist candidates, and saw one of their local newspapers—the (Plentywood) *Producers News*—become a national voice for the Communist Party of the United States (CPUSA). It is, indeed, a most unusual story.

That frustrated farmers would seek nonconformist answers to their plight is not surprising. Even in the bonanza years prior to 1916, they battled railroad freight-rate monopolies, fluctuating international market prices, and unresponsive political parties. In addition, the large Scandinavian immigration to the Dakotas and northeastern Montana transplanted there a tradition of social experimentation and cooperation. For example, Danish cooperatives in Dagmar had proven especially effective prior to World War I.

The earliest form of prairie radicalism extended beyond

CHARLEY TAYLOR DOES THE ELGIN CAFÉ

For a considerable time, Jim Popesku, the proprietor of the Elgin Café in Plentywood, had advertised in Charley Taylor's weekly Producers News. *In mid-August, 1927, he pulled his ad because he disagreed with Taylor's politics. An infuriated "Red Flag" Taylor countered in his next edition (August 19, 1927) with the following "news story."*

Cockroaches in Soup at Elgin

A patron of the Elgin Café, a local restaurant, left the establishment, run by Jim Popesku, a few days ago, reporting that there were cockroaches in his soup. He stated that he would bring the matter to the attention of the State Department of Health and ask for an inspection of the kitchen of the establishment mentioned.

He further claims that it has spoiled his appetite for soup because every time he orders or sees soup it has a tendency to affect his stomach and cause him to vomit. Swallowing a cockroach in a spoonful of soup is not a pleasant operation, this man says, because the legs of the insect tickle the throat and might cause the ejection of the soup already half digested, to the disgust and inconvenience of other patrons in the place.

It is expected that Mr. Popesku will use some insecticide for the eradication of any cockroaches around his kitchen sinks, and thereby make it unnecessary for the officers of the Health Department to make a trip to Plentywood to inspect his place. He realizes that the vomiting of a guest on his tables would empty his place of business and cause many farmers who have hitherto patronized his restaurant to look elsewhere for a pleasant place to eat.

When Mr. Popesku refused to return his advertising business to the News, *Taylor ran a series of front-page columns concerning the café-owner's proclivity to overwork his waitresses, to recycle food from plates, and to battle his cockroaches. Simultaneously the editor prominently featured sizable ads for Popesku's competition, the City Café.*

Shortly thereafter, a newcomer to Plentywood—reputedly an Industrial

Workers of the World (IWW) agent sent by Taylor—visited the Elgin Café at noon. Once served, he pulled a well-cooked mouse from his soup bowl, to the revulsion of two dozen other patrons. Popesku quickly emerged from the kitchen and chased the diner from his establishment. Taylor, however, ran references to "the mouse in the soup" in the Producers News *for almost two years.*

Progressivism and involved the Socialist Party. Eugene V. Debs ran for President as a Socialist on four occasions, and polled 10,885 Montana votes (13.6 percent) in 1912. The widespread appeal of Socialism prompted the electors of Butte to choose a Socialist mayor and administration in 1911. The voters of Sheridan County, created in 1913, supported Socialist candidates on the county, state, and national levels.

Socialism in northeastern Montana primarily laid the groundwork for subsequent left-wing movements. In 1915 agrarian reform on the northern Plains gained greater focus with the formation of the Nonpartisan League (NPL) in North Dakota. Rather than float its own political party, the NPL endorsed sympathetic candidates in the Democrat and Republican primaries and then supported them fully in the general election.

The NPL moved into eastern Montana in 1917, in the midst of another year of severe drought and crop failures. As homesteaders abandoned the country in droves, many of the survivors looked to nonconformist politics for solutions—or, at least, for relief. The Nonpartisan League capitalized on the general popularity of Progressivism to push reform even further. NPL leaders advocated the state ownership of grain elevators and flour mills, the abolition of taxes on farm improvements, state-funded hail insurance, and the strict regulation of railroad freighting. In 1918 Montanans sent 21 NPL legislators to Helena.

The NPL deftly handled agrarian rallies and mass meetings. For example, organizers widely publicized the July 3, 1920, appearance of dynamic NPL stump orator Arthur C. Townley at Medicine Lake—via that revolutionary means of transport, the "aeroplane." A huge crowd of holiday celebrants assembled to see the flying machine!—and stayed to hear Townley's radical message. The *Producers News* recounted (July 9, 1920):

> A.C. Townley, president of the National Nonpartisan League, arrived in a bombing plane and addressed the largest audience ever congregated in northeastern Montana—the crowd estimated at from seven to ten thousand people. Mr. Townley spoke in his usual straight-from-the-shoulder manner, much to the discomfort of the enemies of the farmers and the hypocrites who claim that they believe in the League, but not in its leaders. As he made his points and drove them home, he was wildly cheered by the huge audience.

By 1919 the League boasted 20,000 dues-paying members on the northern Great Plains. Despite this degree of success, rural radicalism in eastern Montana might have withered and quietly died— except for one Charles E. Taylor.

In 1918 the Nonpartisan League sent 34-year-old Taylor to Plentywood to create a newspaper that would become a loud voice for rural reform. They selected the name *Producers News* to emphasize the distinction between workers/farmers (the "producers") and businessmen (the "managers"). By selling shares in the People's Publishing Company to local farmers and ranchers, the *News* transformed its readers into its owners.

Taylor proved the perfect choice to carry the reform message to a desperate audience besieged by hardship. During the next twenty years, he would shape the *Producers News* into an outrageous publication that attacked: other local newspapers, traditional political parties, the Anaconda Company ("the enemy of popular government"), and any other perceived enemy of the Great Plains farmer. He became a lightning rod for all opposition to reform, and his enemies labeled him "red" (meaning "radical") well before he embraced the Communist Party.

Charley Taylor was a brash, robust, and highly intelligent journalist. Born in Wisconsin (1884) and raised in Minnesota, he worked on the *Aitkin Age* as a youngster and graduated from Hamline University in St. Paul. He then taught school in both Minnesota and Wyoming. When the U.S. entered World War I, he and his brother dissolved their farming partnership in Minnesota, and Charley offered his services to the Nonpartisan League. Before the war was over, he and his recent bride, Agda Lundren, had settled in Plentywood—a town of nearly one thousand residents.

Taylor immediately established strong ties with his agrarian readership. His paper offered a compelling mixture of "Local News" columns, fiery editorials, a strong reform message, and international reports of left-wing activities. The mixture proved magical, and the News quickly built a subscription list that embarrassed the other dozen weekly papers in Sheridan County. Some of Charley's nervy demeanor was revealed when the Producers New, still in its first year, pronounced him "Sheridan County's most distinguished citizen!"

From its inception, the *News* brazenly attacked national candidates, county Republicans, businessmen (whom Taylor derisively called "Mainstreeters"), and other editors. The paper invariably revealed the editor's imaginative sense of humor. Charley once vilified rival editor Joe Dolin and his Plentywood *Pioneer Press* with these words (*Producers News*, November 17, 1922):

> There is an old saying about the stuck pig being the pig that squeals. And it is a fact that it is possible to gauge the hurt of a hog by the volume and tone of the squeal emitted by the swine. Be that as it may, we reprint the following from that nauseous rag that emits itself once a week from its sty down the street....

In a journalistic era that knew no libel, Taylor repeatedly assailed Burley Bowler. In 1924 Bowler was the editor of the "Scobey Poker Chip"—really the (Scobey) *Daniels County Leader*—(*Producers News*, September 19, 1924):

Take Burley, for instance. In Plentywood and Antelope and Flaxville, where he has operated, he is known as a cheap, a saloon rounder, a bum, and a tinhorn gambler. He lived in each of these towns as long as he could make a living, [until] he had to get out. No one believes a word he says about anything. He is known by all as a willful and wanton liar, a gambler, and a libertine. [Every] dreg of the gutter has more prestige than he has.

Bowler responded by consistently referring to Taylor as "that impractical, ridiculous editor of the 'Producers Noose.'"

When Plentywood resident Lawrence S. Olson—initially a vocal supporter of Taylor—defected to the competing newspaper, the editor turned spiteful. Taylor first referred to the broad-hipped turncoat as "L.S." Olsen. Then he transformed the initials into the blatant nickname "Lard S." *News* readers gleefully joined in the derisive game, and Mr. Olson took this nickname to his grave.

Charley Taylor's charismatic personality and his ability to communicate with local farmers created widespread support for the *Producers News* in northeastern Montana. The paper's obvious left-wing perspective well served the purposes of the Nonpartisan League. And the League proved immediately successful. In 1918 in Sheridan County, the NPL elected every official on the county ballot except one state senator and the superintendent of schools! The same year, Taylor estimated that, in Sheridan County alone, the NPL counted 4,000 members out of a total population of 13,000. And remember that women were voting in Montana by that time—showing that the NAP was appealing to more factions than drought-affected farmers.

As the drought deepened and the rural economy faltered, Sheridan County radicals solidified their control of the county government. In 1922 they also sent the handsome, six-foot Taylor—by this time nicknamed "Red Flag" Taylor by his enemies—to the Montana Senate.

During the early 1920s, Taylor had joined the Communist cause, although he did not reveal this association to his readers. The

THE DEPRESSION IN
NORTHEASTERN MONTANA

*Cal Peterson, the mayor of Plentywood from 1931 to 1933, reflected on
the desperate economic climate of the times:*

"It was during the Depression period. We were paying our bills
with Registered Warrants. About the only tax revenue was from
the Great Northern [Railway Company], and they were paying
under protest. The city police was the only office on salary and
that was a small one. It was only by the strictest cuts in city
expenses that we were able to come through these distressing conditions and times."

—*from* Plentywood, the Golden Years, 1912-1962

Producers News simply became more radical, while calling itself "the
voice of the beleaguered farmer." In 1922 Sheridan County voters
elected Taylor's close friend Rodney Salisbury as county sheriff.
Salisbury was an avowed Communist. He held the office until
1928—despite constant criticism that he condoned all forms of
bootlegging during this period of Prohibition.

In 1923 Sheridan County radicals again changed their political
cape. Just as the Socialist Party mutated into the Nonpartisan
League, the League transformed into the Farmer-Labor Party
(FLP). Taylor had been elected as a Republican in 1922, but then
ran successfully on the Farmer-Labor ticket in 1926.

During the mid-1920s, local voters filled the Sheridan County
courthouse with Farmer-Labor officials. In 1922, 1924, and 1926,
they sent Farmer-Labor representatives to the state legislature. The
most visible evidence of the radical party's success was the building
of the Farmer-Labor Temple—a massive meeting hall (now the
Mar-Chan Apartments)—in Plentywood in 1924.

Both 1927 and 1928 brought bountiful grain harvests to northeastern Montana, and the radicals' program suffered proportionately. Yet when drought and devastation returned in 1929, subscription figures at the *Producers News* regained former heights. In 1930 "Red Flag" Taylor's popularity boosted him into the race for Montana's U.S. Senate seat on the Farmer-Labor ticket. By this time, however, Harry E. Polk had purchased the competing Plentywood *Herald* and turned it into a solid vehicle to unite the opposition to the left-wingers.

Taylor welcomed Polk to the heated political fray in northeastern Montana (*Producers News*, October 19, 1928):

> We don't believe that a man who quit teaching school in Bowbells, North Dakota, because of alleged intimate relations with young and tender school girls, a man who was compelled to return money to the teachers' employment fund of North Dakota that he had taken, and who was caught teaching on a fake certificate—and whose certificate to teach was finally annulled by Miss Minnie J. Nielsen, Superintendent of Public Instruction of North Dakota, for low, indecent and immoral conduct in the high schools at Williston—and a man who was kicked out of the Masonic Lodge at Bowbells because of his questionable conduct, is just the man to come to Plentywood and commence to make changes here.

In 1931 Sheridan County radicals again converted themselves, this time from the Farmer-Labor Party into the United Farmers League (UFL). This organization was a thinly-veiled front for the Communist Party of the United States. The UFL unsuccessfully sought to convert the economic crash, droughts, dust storms, insect infestations, and falling grain prices into the overthrow of the capitalistic system.

During this phase, the *Producers News* carried headlines that implored readers to

SUPPORT THE UFL!

DEFEND THE SOVIET UNION!

Its original slogan of "A paper of the people, for the people, by the people!" became "An Official Organ of the United Farmers League."

The election of 1932 created a watershed. For the first time, the Sheridan County radicals ran openly on the Communist Party ticket. Conservative opponents, led by *Herald* editor Harry Polk, formed a "Fusion Party" of Democrats and Republicans. The Fusionists vowed to battle the "reds" without mercy. In 1932 the Fusion slate won decisively, despite the *Producers News* claim that 577 citizens in the county had voted a straight Communist ticket.

The dwindling strength of the radical movement focused on subverting farm evictions, foreclosure sales, and farm-machinery repossessions in the county. In this campaign, during the early 1930s, the local Communists proved remarkably successful.

Sheridan County radicalism, however, suffered a severe blow when charismatic Comrade Taylor was "removed" from the *Producers News* in 1930. After the defeat of most of the Farmer-Labor candidates in 1928 and Charley's own loss in the U.S. Senate race in 1930, the CPUSA replaced "Red Flag" with Erik Bert, of New York City. Under the new editor, the *News* published much less local material and included many more reports of national Communist activities. Thus coverage of the senior-class play at Plentywood High School was replaced by a report on a class-struggle, worker-management confrontation in North Carolina.

As a result, the *Producers News* gradually lost subscribers. Dwindling income forced it to reduce its usual eight-or-more pages to a four-page edition. Quickly the CPUSA began directly to subsidize publication of the *News*. In return, the CPUSA demanded that the weekly deliver a tougher Communist line. Thus, from 1931 to 1934, the People's Publishing Company printed two editions each week: a "county edition" for local distribution; a "national edition," which was the official organ of the United Farmers League.

Farmer-owners of the *Producers News* forced the reinstatement of Taylor as editor in 1933, but his rapport with the general agrarian population of northeastern Montana had diminished greatly. In 1934 he again was "reassigned." This time editor Alfred Miller replaced him. The *News* immediately became even more stridently Communist.

When Miller faced federal deportation proceedings in 1935, "Red Flag" Taylor returned to run the *Producers News* for the third and last time. He pledged that the paper would return to handling Sheridan County news and (*Producers News*, July 26, 1935):

> Politically it will support the idea of a mass labor party built upon the immediate needs of the farmers and workers, as opposed to the interest of their exploiters.

After a heavy dose of Communist Party extravagance, the "new" Charley Taylor seemed a breath of fresh air.

But it was too late. Despite the renunciation of his Communist ties, Taylor could not rekindle the locals' radical flame—even in the depths of the Depression. Editor Polk of the *Herald* crowed (September 13, 1934): "Two is company; three is a crowd; and four is a Communist mass meeting."

From 1935 to 1937, the *Producers News* did serve as the official organ of the Farmers Holiday Association, affiliated with the leftist Farmers Union. This organization dedicated itself to preventing farm seizures and evictions. Yet the rhetoric of the *News* rang hollow. Taylor printed the final issue of the *Producers News* on March 5, 1937, and he removed to Seattle.

In retrospect, two incidents sorely damaged the radical cause in northeastern Montana: the 1926 robbery of the Sheridan County Courthouse; the 1932 funeral of Janis Salisbury. These two events directly reduced popular support for the *Producers News*. And Taylor's "reassignments" in 1930 and 1934 sealed the deal.

On November 30, 1926—at the height of the Farmer-Labor control of Sheridan County politics—a daring robbery occurred. Since that was the final day for the payment without penalty of property taxes in that term, County Treasurer Eng Torstenson and Deputy Treasurer Anna Hovet had kept the office open an extra hour. At 5:45, when they were the only employees left in the Courthouse, two masked men burst into the Treasurer's office and locked them in the vault. The robbers departed with approximately $60,000 in bonds and $45,000 in cash. Unsubstantiated reports described a large, swift touring car that sped into North Dakota.

No one ever solved the Sheridan County Courthouse robbery. The National Surety Company investigated the crime for three years. Finally it paid off the county's claim for reimbursement. Widespread local opinion called this heist of public funds "an inside job." Many residents speculated that the Taylor-Salisbury alliance was responsible. This allegation hurt the radical cause, although no one ever filed charges against either the editor-senator or the sheriff.

Similar damage to radicalism in northeastern Montana resulted from the funeral of Rodney Salisbury's 14-year-old daughter, Janis, on March 5, 1932. For years the *Producers News* had ducked the question of religion. Rather, it muted the standard Community Party atheism to avoid offending its traditionally devout readership. However, Salisbury—then the state organizer for the Communist-backed United Farmers League—organized and directed a Bolshevik service and burial for his daughter.

The funeral was held in the Farmer-Labor Temple in Plentywood, attended by more than 450 standing-room-only friends. A red flag covered the coffin, surrounded by banks of flowers donated by the Young Pioneers, the United Farmers League, the *Producers News*, and the Communist Party.

Red-and-black draperies that displayed the hammer-and-sickle covered the hall's windows and stage. The uniformed Young Pioneers led the audience in singing "The International"—"the hymn of the toiling masses throughout the world"—and Janis's favorite song, "The Red Flag."

A procession of mourners then followed the Young Pioneers,

carrying the Communist flag, to the Salisbury farm, where Janis was buried. At the gravesite, her friends delivered the Bolshevik farewell, the Pioneer Pledge:

> Stand ready for the cause of the working class.
> Are you ready?
> Always ready!
> I pledge allegiance to the workers' red flag and to the cause for which it stands. One aim throughout our lives: Freedom for the working class.

Harry Polk of the Plentywood *Herald* released an account of this event to the *Great Falls Tribune* and to the wire services. Quickly Janis's funeral became a national item. Many Sheridan County residents marked this overt display of Communist conventions as the beginning of their disaffection with radicalism.

The demise of the radical movement in eastern Montana occurred quietly during the 1930s. Despite continued economic depression and agricultural failure, Sheridan County farmers returned to more traditional politics. New Deal programs that slowly infiltrated the area offered some tangible solutions for decades of suffering. Ultimately these farmers abandoned the mutating Communist agenda—carried first by the Socialists, then by the Nonpartisan League, then by the Farmer-Labor Party, then by the United Farmers League, then by the Communist Party of the United States, and finally by the Farmers Holiday Association.

The evolution of radicalism in northeastern Montana depended on devastating economic and agricultural conditions. The enigmatic Charley "Red Flag" Taylor then became the catalyst, and his farmer-owned *Producers News* focused the dissent. Both the Sheridan County Courthouse robbery (1926) and the funeral of Janis Salisbury (1932) precipitated the downfall of the movement. Yet the two dismissals of Taylor from the *News* proved every bit as significant.

In 1917 Nonpartisan League minister S. R. Maxwell had parodied the Twenty-third Psalm to portray the frustration of many farmers on the northern Great Plains (Robert L. Morlan, *Political Prairie Fire*, 1955, p. 21):

> The politician is my shepherd,
> I shall not want;
> Previous to election day, he filleth my pocket with cigars
> And my present glory runneth over.
>
> But although he causeth me to vote for him on election day,
> Suddenly, after election, he knoweth me no more.
> He eateth rich plums of political patronage behind closed doors,
> And me he cannot remember;
>
> Surely the wool hath been pulled over my eyes
> All the days of my life,
> And I shall dwell in political obscurity forever.

Yet the radicals of northeastern Montana did not succumb to this fate. In the face of incredible conditions, they fought for their farms, their beliefs, their way of life, and their future.

From 1918 to 1928, Montana radicalism thrived in Sheridan County—with Plentywood at center stage. Almost another decade passed before the movement bottomed out. What an incredible episode in the continuum of Montana politics! What an illustration of Montana diversity and political experimentation!

It is more than time for us all to follow the lead of author Ivan Doig—to probe, to discuss, and to understand this phenomenon. The residents of northeastern Montana carry an admirable legacy. With the 1991 collapse of the Soviet Union, they now can honor and enjoy it fully.

SOURCES

For general background information on radicalism in America, see: Robert M. Morlan, *Political Prairie Fire: The Nonpartisan League, 1915-1922* (Minneapolis: University of Minnesota, 1955/1968/1985); Lowell K. Dyson, *Red Harvest: The Communist Party and American Farmers* (Lincoln: University of Nebraska, 1982); William Preston, Jr., *Aliens and Dissenters: The Federal Suppression of Radicals, 1903-1933* (Urbana: University of Illinois, 1964/1994).

To view radicalism in the context of the northern Great Plains and Montana, see: Jerry W. Calvert, *The Gibraltar: Socialism and Labor in Butte, Montana, 1895-1920* (Helena: Montana Historical Society, 1988).

William C. Pratt's several pieces also apply to this category: "Radicals, Farmers, and Historians: Some Recent Scholarship about Agrarian Radicalism in the Upper Midwest," *North Dakota History*, 52 (Fall, 1985), 12-24; "Socialism on the Northern Plains, 1900-1924," *South Dakota History*, 18 (Spring/Summer, 1988), 1-35; "Farmers, Communists, and the FBI in the Upper Midwest," *Agricultural History*, 63, #3 (Summer, 1989), 61-80; "Rural Radicalism on the Northern Plains, 1912-1950," *Montana: The Magazine of Western History*, 42, #1 (Winter, 1992), 42-55; "Workers, Unions, and Historians on the Northern Plains," *Great Plains Quarterly*, 16, #4 (Fall, 1996), 229-250.

For area history concerning Plentywood and Sheridan County, see: Magnus Aasheim, comp., *Sheridan's Daybreak: A Story of Sheridan County and Its Pioneers* (Great Falls: Blue Print and Letter, 1970); Aasheim, comp., *Sheridan's Daybreak II* (Aberdeen, S.D.: North Plains Press, 1984); *Plentywood—the Golden Years, 1912-1962* (Plentywood: Herald Printers, 1962); *Plentywood Portrait: Toil, Soil, Oil* (Plentywood: Herald Printers, 1987).

To look at radicalism in the context of northeastern Montana, see: Charles Vindex, "Radical Rule in Montana," *Montana: The Magazine of Western History*, 18, #1 (January, 1968), 2-18; Gerald Zahavi, " 'Who's Going to Dance with Somebody Who Calls You a Mainstreeter?': Communism, Culture and Community in Sheridan County, Montana, 1918-1934," *Great Plains Quarterly*, 16, #4 (Fall, 1996), 251-286; Verlaine Stoner McDonald, "Red Waves of Grain: An Analysis of Radical Farm Movement Rhetoric in Montana, 1918-1937," Ph.D. diss., University of Southern California, 1994.

A treasure trove of first-hand information is contained in two sets of oral-history interviews held by the Montana Historical Society Archives in Helena. Four interviews done by Laurie Mercier in the early 1980s for the "Montanans at Work" project include:

OH 402: Charles Carbone

OH 404: Andrew L. Michels

OH 408: Roy Rue and Helen Dahl Rue

OH 409: Lillian Nelson Kitzenberg

Additional information is contained in a set of interviews done by Jackie Day in the mid-1980s for the "Small Town Montana" project:

OH 869: Arthur Gabrielson

OH 870: Fay Chandler and Violet Cybulski Chandler

OH 871: Bernadine Prader Logan

OH 873: Louise Kavon

OH 875: Chester "Chet" Holje

OH 876: Clifford Peterson

OH 879: Irvin "Shorty" Timmerman

OH 881: Harold DeSilva

Finally, local newspapers provide a wealth of colorful material for this topic—featuring "Red Flag" Taylor's (Plentywood) *Producers News.* See also: the *Plentywood Herald;* the (Plentywood) *Pioneer Press;* the *Medicine Lake Wave;* the (Scobey) *Daniels County Leader.* The Montana Historical Society Library holds all of these papers on microfilm, and they are available through Inter-Library Loan.

Heavy-handed symbolism tells the I.W.W.'s message.
From One Big Union Monthly, *July 1920,*
courtesy Montana Historical Society, Helena

CHAPTER 13

WHO KILLED TOM MANNING?
IN A COMPANY TOWN, COMPANY JUSTICE

The foreman of the Coroner's Jury
rose, paused a moment, and then
spoke to a hushed, standing-
room-only crowd.
"In the matter of the inquest held
in Silver Bow County, Montana,
from April 29 to May 13, 1920,
we find the following verdict:
"Thomas Manning died on April
25, 1920, at St. James Hospital in
Butte, from the effects of a wound
caused by a .32-caliber bullet fired
from a pistol in the hands of some
person to this jury unknown."

By 1920 labor strife had racked Butte for six years. In 1914 the Butte Miners' Union Hall had been dynamited, the Montana National Guard had occupied the city, and Butte's Socialist government had collapsed. Rising copper prices during World War I (1914-1918) accelerated labor conflict, as miners fought for better working conditions underground and higher wages above ground. Walkouts and strikes occurred with greater frequency—some triggered by such tragedies as the Speculator Mine Disaster (June 8, 1917), in which 164 miners lost their lives.

Throughout this six-year period, the radical Industrial Workers of the World (IWW) gained strength among Butte wage-earners.

The "Wobblies" advocated the overthrow of the capitalist system through the "direct action" of a working-class revolution. The IWW cause advanced considerably when, early on the morning of August 1, 1917, six masked men hustled IWW organizer Frank Little from his boarding house on North Wyoming Street, dragged him behind their auto to the outskirts of town, beat him severely, and hanged him from a Milwaukee Road trestle. No one ever was indicted for Little's murder, although local opinion identified the killers as men associated with Butte's primary employer, the Anaconda Copper Mining Company—simply known as "the Company." World War I also fostered rampant jingoism and the repression of both thought and action considered "un-American," Bolshevik, or revolutionary. The Montana Council of Defense led a statewide campaign against dissent, including an attempt to shut down Bill Dunne's *Butte Daily Bulletin*—the radical voice of Butte labor and the major alternative to the Anaconda Company's "captive press."

To expose sedition and treason, the federal government operated a national program of political surveillance—with its U.S. Justice Department Bureau of Investigation and its Military Intelligence agents spread throughout the Butte mining community. Other infiltrators among the miners represented the private-detective firms contracted by the Company. One undercover informant noted (Jerry W. Calvert, *The Gibraltar: Socialism and Labor in Butte, Montana, 1895-1920*, Helena: Montana Historical Society, 1988, p. 124):

> If they [the Wobblies] only knew who the "stools" were and how many of them there were, they would sure be a dismayed bunch. To think that so many of their supposed best men were paid agents makes me laugh every time I think of it.

Government agents in Butte routinely shared surveillance information on "radicals" with Anaconda Company officials, and gradually the Company refined its "rustling card" employment system to deter identifiable IWW members from working in the mines. U.S. Post Office authorities regularly intercepted the mail of IWW leaders and delivered it to the Bureau of Investigation office in Butte. When federal troops occupied the city under a martial-law declaration (August 17, 1919), they demonstrably sided with the mining companies against the "seditious," striking workers.

During the 1914-1920 period, democratic rights and Constitutionally guaranteed civil liberties became subordinated to an enforced intolerance against dissent and to the increased production of copper ore. The slogan "Get the rock in the box!" epitomized the Company's policy.

Following an unsuccessful miners' strike in 1917, IWW strength in Butte grew and was channeled through the Metal Mine Workers' Industrial Union #800. The IWW organized a two-week miners' strike in September 1918, and it directed another strike that began on February 7, 1919, when the Anaconda Company declared a $1-per-day wage cut. Large groups of strikers picketed the mines and shut down operations on the Hill. Approximately 8,000 workers ultimately joined the walkout.

Governor Samuel V. Stewart requested additional federal troops; three companies of infantry reached Butte on February 9. The next day, these soldiers moved against the pickets with fixed bayonets (wounding nine strikers) and raided the IWW headquarters in Finlander Hall on North Wyoming Street (bayoneting John Kinari in the stomach). This strike was resolved on February 17, after the troops pulled back to guard mining-company property and the strikers abandoned mass picketing.

Immediately following the 1919 strike, IWW organizers began planning an even more comprehensive strike. From their many operatives within the union, both the Federal Bureau of Investigation and the Anaconda Company learned of growing miner sentiment for a general strike. The Company countered by hiring more armed guards (often non-Montanans secured through national detective agencies) and by stationing them on mine property. When the IWW local voted to call a strike for April 19, 1920, the news surprised none of the parties involved. At the time of this strike, the Montana Department of Labor and Industry estimated that more than 8,000 men worked in the Butte mines, with 6,000 of them employed by the Anaconda Copper Mining Company.

IWW circulars flooded Butte and listed the strikers' demands:

1. A work day of six hours, from collar to collar.
2. A minimum daily wage scale of $7.
3. The abolition of the "rustling card" system.
4. The end of the contract-and the bonus-mining systems.
5. At least two men working on all machines.
6. At least two men working together on all mine jobs.
7. The release of all political and industrial prisoners in the United States.

Although these demands focused on shorter hours, increased wages, and better working conditions, Demand #7 revealed the influence of the IWW. As "Wobbly" leaders C. W. Sellars and A. S. "Sam" Embree noted,

> Our attitude and ultimate aim is to secure control of the mines, to take over all properties in the interests of the workers, in the interests of humanity.

But the short-term objectives of the strikers depended on closing down the mines. Early on Monday morning, April 19, hundreds of pickets grouped on North Main Street, on the Anaconda Road, and on other thoroughfares leading to the mines. They stopped miners who were walking and riding the streetcars to work and turned them away from the mine gates.

Although claims arose that the strikers handled some recalcitrant miners roughly, Sheriff John K. O'Rourke and his deputies neither arrested any of the pickets nor moved to protect any of the non-strikers. IWW efforts proved so successful that practically the entire labor force failed to report to work, and mining operations on the Hill ceased.

Hundreds of pickets swarmed over the Hill again on Tuesday, April 20, enforcing the strike. That morning the *Butte Daily Bulletin* published an editorial that purported to quote Roy Alley— an ACM Company attorney who was the personal secretary of John D. Ryan, the president of ACM. The popular belief among Butte residents was that Alley commanded the Company's private army of security guards (the IWW called them "the gunmen").

ALLEY OPENLY URGES MURDER

"The Wobblies have got us tied up again. It wouldn't be so bad if they only quit themselves, but they are interfering with our own loyal men. We need some more killings and hangings here. And, if there were any red-blooded Americans in this camp, it would be done."

—Roy Alley, in the Thornton Hotel barber shop at 9:30 yesterday morning.

To this threat, the *Bulletin* quickly responded:

So Roy Alley wants to hang someone again!

He wants more killings and hangings! "We need some more killings!"

Whom does Roy Alley mean by "we"? What does he want by "more"?

After dark on Tuesday, a large group of IWW strikers, calling themselves the "dry squad," visited saloons, hotels, pool halls, and cigar stores, demanding that the prohibition and gambling laws be enforced during the miners' strike. (Interestingly, Montana had instituted prohibition on January 1, 1919, and the federal prohibition amendment had become effective on January 16, 1920.) Finally, about midnight, the city police dispersed this group, arresting six small boys for curfew violations.

On Wednesday, April 21, 1920, events in Butte turned ugly. Sheriff O'Rourke declared that he no longer could control the situation, and he commissioned all of the ACM Company's armed guards as deputy sheriffs. The Montana Department of Labor and Industry reported:

> Many clashes occurred between mine guards and picketers at various properties during the day. According to all reports, the mine guards were unusually active, as many picketers were badly beaten, some of them quite seriously. In several places the fight was bitter, but in every instance the mine guards got the better of the encounter.

By 4:30 on Wednesday afternoon, a group of 300 to 400 unarmed strikers had assembled in front of the gates to the Neversweat Mine, located on the southeast side of the Anaconda Road (so-called because miners daily trudged up this road, which began near the intersection of East Copper and North Wyoming and ran up through Dublin Gulch, to reach the Anaconda Mine and such other major mines as the Neversweat, the Diamond, and the High Ore). On the uphill slope, behind the Neversweat gates, ranged a squad of 40 to 50 guards, armed with rifles, sawed-off shotguns, revolvers, clubs, and blackjacks. The pickets hurled profane jeers at the Company guards, and the squad returned them in kind. Into this explosive situation drove Sheriff O'Rourke and three of his deputies.

Once out of the auto, the sheriff confronted Sam Embree and the other strike leaders and tried to persuade them to move down the hill. The pickets argued that they were not standing on Company property, but were lawfully assembled on a public road. Several men produced road-tax receipts to demonstrate that they had paid for maintenance on this county road. When some miners identified specific guards who had attacked and beaten them earlier in the day, O'Rourke replied,

> All right! You stay right here! I'll investigate this! We're here to give protection to everybody!

According to Embree, O'Rourke then turned and walked to a small group of men that included Roy Alley and D'Gay Stivers—the latter another ACMA attorney who reputedly was Alley's boss and supervised the Company's security and intelligence-gathering forces. By this time the squad of guards had come down the embankment and passed through the gates of the Neversweat. Suddenly the command rang out, "Go Get 'em, Boys! Give the Sons of Bitches Hell!" Immediately a single shot was fired, reportedly by a short, stout man, wearing glasses, a dark overcoat, and a fedora. The single shot was followed by a barrage. Into the tightly packed crowd charged the Company men, pounding strikers with their rifle butts and clubs and firing their shotguns at close range.

Tom Manning and the other protesters panicked, broke ranks, and scattered downhill, pursued by the guards, who continued shooting. Sam Embree described the melee:

> I was knocked down, with my face to the ground. I had heard a shot fired from behind me (the direction from which the gunmen were coming), and then I heard a fusillade of shots. I managed to rise and began running with the other fleeing pickets down the hill. But the ground was rough, and the bullets were whistling around me and striking the ground in front of me. I saw several of my companions fall, shot in the back.
>
> I ran down to Granite Street and then went west to Wyoming and back up to Industrial Hall [Finlander Hall]. Soon some of the wounded, including Tom Manning, reached the hall, so I telephoned for doctors and an ambulance.

In all, 16 pickets were wounded in the attack—every one of them shot from behind as he fled. Dozens of other men carried bruises from clubs, blackjacks, and rifle butts. Undeniably these wounds had been inflicted by the Anaconda Company's armed guards—"the gunmen"—while serving as deputy sheriffs of Silver Bow County. Reports also would surface that members of both the city police force and the sheriff's office fired into the fleeing demonstrators. The *Butte Bulletin* speculated sarcastically (April 22, 1920):

> Sheriff O'Rourke states that his deputies did no shooting. The city police state that they did no shooting. The question occurs, "Did the 16 miners shoot themselves?" The answer to this question is: The miners were shot by the gunmen of the Anaconda Mining Company.

The *Butte Miner* (a William A. Clark newspaper tied closely to the Company) countered in an editorial (April 24, 1920):

> Those supporters of the Soviet in this community never were good sports, as is shown by the abject manner in which they squealed when they had administered to them a little of their own medicine last Wednesday afternoon.

To Tom Manning, a 25-year-old Irish miner who lived at 20 West Quartz and had worked at the Badger Mine prior to the strike, support for Soviet revolution was secondary to fighting for his life. Manning had been hit in the back by a .32-caliber, steel-jacketed, soft-nosed slug that perforated his large bowel once, ripped a hole in his stomach, and put four holes in his small bowel. The bullet remained in his body. Although doctors operated on Saturday, April 24, Manning died of peritonitis shortly after midnight on April 25.

Tom Manning left a father, a young wife, and a small son in Ireland. He had worked in Butte for three years— having followed his cousin, Jack Boyle, from the Old Country to the mines. He told Boyle that he had saved enough of his wages to bring his family to Montana in the fall of 1920. Rather than reaching these modest goals, however, Manning became a martyr to the cause of organized labor in his adopted land.

For two days, Tom Manning's body lay in state at the home of IWW sympathizer Thomas Scanlon, 316 North Idaho Street, where thousands of Butte miners and their families filed past the casket. At 9:30 on the morning of April 28, requiem mass was held at St. Patrick's Catholic Church, and approximately 3,000 mourners followed the cortege to Holy Cross Cemetery, where Manning was buried. The majority of miners in the procession wore the red arm band of the IWW.

On April 22 (the day after the attack on the Anaconda Road) almost 200 federal troops reached Butte from Fort Wright and Camp Lewis, near Spokane, Washington. On April 24 another company of reinforcements arrived. The soldiers were billeted at the Florence Hotel on East Broadway, an ACM Company building known as "The Ship." With the soldiers occupying the city, the IWW called its pickets off the Butte thoroughfares, but few miners returned to work and the strike effectively continued.

For several tense days, the confrontation between the Company and the strikers was fought in the pages of "the copper press" (particularly the *Butte Miner*, the *Butte Daily Post*, and the *Anaconda Standard*) and the union paper (the *Butte Daily Bulletin*). Butte's attention then focused on the coroner's inquest into who was responsible for the death of Tom Manning, which commenced in the Silver Bow County Courthouse on April 29.

From the outset, it appeared that truth and justice would suffer severely at the hearing. Although the inquest consumed eleven days, and 101 witnesses testified, the company orchestrated the formal presentations and manipulated the evidence. First, Silver Bow County Coroner Dan Holland claimed a sudden illness and withdrew from the case. He was replaced by Justice of the Peace John Doran, who had been elected in 1918 with Company support. Throughout the inquest, Doran's ruling on the admissibility of evidence demonstrated his allegiances.

According to the Bulletin, the six-member coroner's jury appeared equally suspect. Foreman George Hagerman was a city politician with campaign support from the Company; Tom Driscoll recently was involved in several mine-property transactions with the

Company; Mike Dougherty was a former employee of Hennessy's, the "company store"; Tom Fletcher was the brother of a Company-endorsed city alderman; Richard Dwyer was the uncle of ex-District Judge John V. Dwyer, who appeared as an attorney for the Company at the inquest; Mark Ezekiel was a local politician whose daughter had been linked to Company attorney D'Gay Stivers. Although some of these alleged relationships probably would not bear scrutiny, the coroner's jury did not project an image of impartiality.

At one courtroom table sat Tim Nolan and Lou Donovan, the two attorneys appointed on behalf of Tom Manning. The other table often provided inadequate seating for the legal trust assembled. Attorneys Nick Rotering and George Bourquin, Jr., represented the Silver Bow County Attorney's Office; Dan Kelly and D'Gay Stivers appeared for the Anaconda Company, employer of the Neversweat's security guards; Company lawyers Frank Walker and John V. Dwyer represented both the sheriff's office and the city police department.

Hearing spectators soon realized that the full resources of the ACM Company's legal division (located on the sixth floor of the Hennessy Building) would be applied to the case. The appearance of D'Gay Stivers at the attorney's table proved perhaps the greatest surprise, since he had been a participant in the incident on the Anaconda Road and surely would be called as a witness.

For the first four days of the inquest, only law-enforcement officers and witnesses sympathetic to the Company and its security forces testified. Through cross-examination, it was revealed that many of these witnesses had attended meetings in the office of attorney Dwyer in the Daly Building on April 24 to standardize their accounts of the events on the Anaconda Road.

Their story maintained that a single shot had been fired at the armed guards from an upstairs window in Simmons Boarding House, across the Anaconda Road from the Neversweat's gates. Witnesses from the boarding house later convincingly proved this story false. On the other hand, from the testimony of scores of

IWW pickets, a scenario developed that pointed accusatory fingers at both Roy Alley and D'Gay Stivers as on-site leaders of "the gunmen." Stivers admitted that he had increased his guard force at the Neversweat after a phone call from Sheriff O'Rourke at three o'clock on the afternoon of the incident. He also indicated the nature of the deputy-sheriff commissions conferred on his guards. Attorney Tim Nolan pursued this issue:

Nolan: "How did George V. Vivian [an ACM Company armed guard] secure his commission as a special deputy sheriff?"

Stivers: "I don't know."

Nolan: "Didn't Sheriff O'Rourke swear him in?"

Stivers: "I don't know. Although the sheriff was at my office at about 2 o'clock."

Nolan: "Wasn't the sheriff also in your office about 4 o'clock?"

Stivers: "I don't know."

Nolan: "Isn't it true that Sheriff O'Rourke leaves with the Anaconda Copper Mining Company a lot of blank commissions with the sheriff's name signed to them and a blank space for you to place in the names of whoever you should choose?"

Stivers: "I don't know."

Nolan: "Will you say that the sheriff does not furnish you blank commissions with his name signed to them?"

Stivers: "All I can say is that I don't know."

Nolan: "Will you say that he does not?"

Stivers: "No. I don't know. I cannot say whether he does or does not."

Testimony at the coroner's inquest did identify a number of law-enforcement officers and security guards who shot at the fleeing pickets. In instances where the accusers were IWW members, Company attorneys attempted to discredit their statements by showing that they were newly immigrated aliens. This rationale focused on "the proper kind of Americanism," rather than on the pickets' Constitutional rights. That attitude extended to the report of the hearing published by the Montana Department of Labor and Industry:

The mob that defied the sheriff on April 21 was in large part composed of aliens. The testimony at the inquest brought out the fact that 13 of the 16 men shot were foreign-born and that more than half of them were not citizens of this country.

In the end, the killer of Tom Manning could not be identified positively by the miners, since they had been rushing downhill to save their own lives. Given the composition of the jury, the court-room machinations of the Company, and Justice Doran's ruling on admissible evidence, the jury's verdict was anticipated by most of the participants. This assumption was epitomized by Mike Ostorvitch, one of the wounded miners, during the hearing.

> When asked by Attorney Nolan to look about the courtroom and see if he could identify any of the gunmen, [Ostorvitch] gazed long and earnest-ly at the members of the jury, but finally shook his head negatively.

The Butte Daily Bulletin peevishly noted that all the jury could conclude was that "TOM MANNING DEAD, ACCORDING TO VERDICT RENDERED BY CORONER'S JURY."

The Company's newspaper chain smugly reported that the jury simply could not determine Manning's killer and speculated that Manning might even have been shot at some location other than on the Anaconda Road.

Other newspapers in Montana ran stories about the strike and the inquest from the Associated Press wire. For reasons exposed by the *Bulletin* (April 27, 1920), all of these accounts shaded facts to benefit the Company:

> The Associated Press has two correspondents in Butte. One of them is an editor of the *Butte Miner*—the paper owned by ex-Senator [William A.] Clark. The other correspondent is the assistant editor of the *Butte Post*— owned by the Anaconda Mining Company. The Anaconda correspondent

of the Associated Press is one of the editors of the *Anaconda Standard* [a wholly-owned Company paper].

The inconclusive verdict of the coroner's jury in the murder of Tom Manning signaled the end of six years of labor unrest in Butte. For it demonstrated that the Anaconda Company controlled all facets of mining life in Butte: from miners' wages to their working conditions; from union activity to Constitutional rights; from legal recourse to physical violence. It would be almost fifteen years before another significant miners' strike occurred in Butte. On May 12 (the day before the end of the Manning hearing), the Anaconda Company had posted notices at its mines stating "NO MEMBER OF THE I.W.W. WILL BE EMPLOYED AT THIS PROPERTY." Calling this policy "The American Plan," it also added three questions to is "rustling card" application:

> "Are you a member of the I.W.W.?"
> "Do you believe in and support the principles and
>   purposes of the I.W.W.?"
> "Are you in sympathy with the aims and objectives
>   of the I.W.W.?"

But the Company's move to ban IWW miners was really unnecessary.

The radical union lost its power once the Manning inquest demonstrated the extensive, diverse strength of the Company. Within hours of the verdict, the Metal Mine Workers' Industrial Union #800 called off the strike, exhorting its members to apply a face-saving, slowdown, "strike on the job" tactic. This alternative proved ineffective. Federal troops withdrew from the Butte district in January, 1921.

Quite rapidly the influence of the IWW declined in Butte. No strong union rose to replace it. The *Butte Bulletin* ceased publication in January 1924. Tom Manning's murder remains officially unsolved—although the answers are as clear today as they were on that bloody April afternoon in 1920, on the Anaconda Road.

Shortly after the Manning inquest concluded, IWW essayist, poet, and songwriter Ralph Chaplin penned the thoughts of many of Butte's residents. As biased as is Chaplin's perspective, his words stand as testimony to the life and death of Tom Manning:

> The overlords of Butte will not permit their right to exploit to be challenged. Drunk with unbridled power and the countless millions profiteered during the War, with lying phrases of "law and order" on their lips, the blood of workingmen dripping from their hands, and the gold of the government bursting their coffers, they face the nation unreprimanded and unashamed— reaction militant, capitalism at its worst. ›
>
> The copper trust can murder its slaves in broad daylight on any occasion and under any pretext. There is no law to call a halt. In the confines of this greed-ruled city, the gunman has replaced the Constitution. Butte is a law unto itself.

SOURCES

For general background on the Industrial Workers of the World (IWW), see especially: Melvyn Dubofsky, *We Shall Be All: A History of the IWW* (Chicago: Quadrangle Books, 1969); Joyce L. Kornbluh, ed., *Rebel Voices: An IWW Anthology* (Ann Arbor: University of Michigan, 1964).

Context for the Tom Manning story can be gained from several sources: Jerry W. Calvert, *The Gibraltar: Socialism and Labor in Butte, Montana, 1895-1920* (Helena: Montana Historical Society, 1988); Michael P. Malone, *The Battle for Butte: Mining and Politics on the Northern Frontier, 1864-1906* (Seattle: University of Washington, 1981); David M. Emmons, *The Butte Irish: Class and Ethnicity in an American Mining Town, 1875-1925* (Urbana: University of Illinois, 1989); Burton K. Wheeler, *Yankee from the West* (Garden City, N.Y.: Doubleday, 1962); and Don James, *Butte's Memory Book* (Caldwell, Id.: Caxton, 1975).

Ancillary materials that proved helpful to this topic are: *Fourth Biennial Report of the Montana Department of Labor and Industry, 1919-1920* (Helena: Independent Printers, 1921); Sanborn Fire Insurance Company Maps and "birdseye" maps of Butte, Montana Historical Society Library, Helena; Manuscript Collection 35: Montana Governors' Papers, Montana Historical Society Archives, Helena.

A court case brought by one of the miner victims in the riot, *McCarthy* v. *Anaconda Copper Mining Company* (in which by the Montana Supreme Court found for the defendant), contains a good deal of information regarding the activities of April 21, 1920. See Microfilm S-5423, Montana Historical Society Library, Helena.

Finally, the richest source for information on the Manning story is the following array of contemporary Montana newspapers: the *Butte Daily Bulletin* (William Dunne's radical labor paper); the *Butte Miner* (a W. A. Clark paper, pro-ACM); the *Anaconda Standard* (the flagship of the ACM chain); the *Butte Daily Post* (an ACM paper); the (Hamilton) *Western News* (Miles Romney's anti-ACM weekly).

CHAPTER FOURTEEN

"BIG MEDICINE"
A TALISMAN FOR ALL MONTANANS

This is one of the great historic and
rare items of Americana.
Michael Kennedy,
Director, Montana Historical Society
November 29, 1960

It is simply human nature to cherish what is rare or particularly unusual. Such is the case with the American bison.

This national symbol once roamed from Pennsylvania to Oregon and from Mexico to the Great Slave Lake in Canada. About the time that Meriwether Lewis and William Clark trekked through Montana (1805-1806), an estimated 60 million American bison grazed the Great Plains. Understandably any variation in the bison's normally brown, curly coat elicited comment. An albino or a white buffalo brought amazement and prestige.

An albino calf appears in about one of 5 million bison births. White buffalo calves—varying in shades from yellowish fawn to dappled gray to dark cream—occur more frequently, but are still extremely rare. Preeminent bison expert William T. Hornaday noted (1887):

> I have met many old buffalo hunters, who had killed thousands and seen scores of thousands of buffaloes, yet had never seen a white one. From all accounts, it appears that not over ten or eleven white buffaloes, or white buffalo skins, were ever seen by white men.

Big Medicine.
Photo courtesy of Montana Historical Society, Helena

In the 1800s, the genetic lines needed to produce a white buffalo seemed stronger on the northern Great Plains than in the southern Plains herds. For example, writer/ethnologist George Bird Grinnell interviewed (*Forest and Stream,* December 21, 1901) the famous southern Plains hide-trader George Bent. Bent lived among the Southern Cheyennes and the Arapahos, traveling widely on the Plains during the 1860s and 1870s. Among the tens of thousands of buffalo hides he handled, he reported seeing only five unusually colored ones in his lifetime—of which only one was white.

On the northern Great Plains, the white strain is documented early. In 1754 Hudson's Bay Company trader Anthony Hendry visited a Blackfoot camp in the lower Battle River area of west-central Saskatchewan. Here he found a white buffalo-skin used as a seat or a "cushion" for a respected headman.

Similarly, in 1875, hunter/hide-buyer "A. L. O." joined a party of two hundred lodges of Teton Sioux to hunt buffalo in southwestern Saskatchewan, on Frenchman's Creek. The natives discovered and killed a four-year-old milky-white cow, which "A. L. O." called (*Northwest Magazine,* August, 1885): "the most beautiful and singular animal I have ever seen on the prairie." The whites subsequently secured the sacred hide through trickery.

In 1879 Grinnell encountered a pied buffalo skin that had been sold by some Cree hunters to a Fort Benton trader.

> It was white on the head, legs, and belly, with a wide band of white bordering the normal dark brown coloring—just beautiful. If I recollect aright, this particular hide was sold on the [Missouri] river to an Englishman for $500 (David Dary, *The Buffalo Book,* 208).

An 1888 item in the *Helena Daily Herald* noted (April 19):

> A white buffalo robe is a rare possession. O. W. Jackson, the music man, has just brought one from Fort Benton....The robe is from the cabinet

collection of Indian curiosities and fine furs and robes of John J. Healy, formerly of Fort Benton.

> The robe—really more of a bright cream color than pure white—was bought from an Indian hunter more than 20 years ago. It was evidently from the back of a yearling, being small compared to the size of the usual robe. Get a look at it, that you may swear you have, of a verity, seen a white buffalo robe.

Obviously the white buffalo carried exceptional monetary value to Euro-Americans, who coveted it as a curiosity.

However, Plains tribes long had depended on the bison for their very survival. Hence they revered the bison and imbued the hunt, the butchering, and the use of bison parts with intense spirituality. Most—but not all—of these Indian bands celebrated the white buffalo as a powerful symbol of special favor, a sacred blessing. A white robe also carried exceptional social status. The huntsman who killed a white buffalo brought honor not only to himself, but also to his family and to his entire band.

Some Plains groups did not credit the white buffalo with special powers. These natives included the Cree, the Assiniboine, the Northern Cheyenne, and individual bands of Sioux and Blackfeet. Such Indians were eager to trade a white hide, because of its exceptional value, with bands who prized the token.

In the 1860s, the Mandans offered a Canadian trader 60 brown robes in exchange for his hide of a white cow, tanned with hoofs, snout, and tail intact. A Gros Ventre band once bartered 15 horses laden with guns, cloth, blankets, brown robes, and other treasures to some Assiniboines for a white robe.

The white hide also could be given as a special gift by non-worshiping natives. The Missouri River traveler Prince Alexander Philip Maximilian of Wied-Neuwied noted on his 1833-1834 trip (Reuben G. Thwaites, *Early Western Travels*, vol. 22):

> The Yanktonans [Sioux] showed us a beautiful skin of a young, white

female buffalo, which they intended as a present for the Mandans, by whom such skins are highly valued. They had already sent them a white buffalo calf....

Besides the Mandans and the Gros Ventres, other Plains natives (and seasonal Plains visitors) venerated the white buffalo: the Southern Cheyennes; the Arikaras; the Pawnee; some Sioux bands, like the Lakota; the Fox; the Salish; the Piegans; and the Sarcee. Among these peoples, the icon appeared in such names of honor as "the White Buffalo," "White Buffalo Calf," "the White Cow," "White Buffalo Robe," and "White Bull."

Grinnell remarked of the Southern Cheyenne (*Forest and Stream*, 1901):

> [They] regard a white buffalo as something sacred....They believe that the white buffalo belongs far to the north, that it comes from where— according to tradition—the buffalo originally came out of the ground. They regard it as the chief of the buffalo.

Most northern Plains believers linked the white buffalo to the recurring legend of the White Buffalo Calf Woman (please see the sidebar). Thus the talisman signified hope, the return of plenty and power, and the unity of all peoples. On occasion, a leader would wear a white robe into battle, for extra protection. In some cases, medicine men would use a white robe as a cover-wrap for the medicine bundle or in ceremonies to cure illness.

Some Plains natives, like the Piegans, believed that a white buffalo was the property of the Sun God. After carefully tanning the robe, medicine men ceremoniously raised it on a pole as a consecrated, community offering. It remained there, protecting the celebrants, until it disintegrated in the elements. These tribes never consumed the meat, as it was sacred.

Raymond J. DeMallie, director of the American Indian Studies

Research Institute at the University of Indiana, explains another variation (*Baltimore Sun*, September 19, 1994):

> Traditionally, when the Sioux found a white buffalo, they killed it. They left the meat for wild animals to eat. They carefully skinned and decorated the hide, and then burned it, to give it back to the spirits. If you pray for something, you're going to sacrifice the most valuable thing you have. And the most precious thing you can sacrifice is this [white hide], because it is so rare.

From an estimated peak of 60 million animals in 1800, the American bison was hunted almost to extinction by 1885. The "kill off" of the massive northern Great Plains herd took only 12 years (1871-1883). In 1890 a mere 1,100 bison survived in the whole United States. With this eradication disappeared all Native American hope of seeing another white buffalo calf.

Those odds only magnified the joy that swept through the national Indian community in the spring of 1933. For, on May 3, range-rider John A. McDonald discovered a white buffalo calf born to a common brown cow on the Department of the Interior's National Bison Range in western Montana, near Moiese. Within days, local Salish leaders held a ceremony of celebration. Arriving in the depths of the Great Depression—just as brand-new President Franklin D. Roosevelt was creating New Deal solutions to ease the country's economic and social woes—the symbolism of the remarkable birth was lost on neither native nor Euro-American Montanans.

Congress had established the Moiese Bison Range in 1909—from expropriated lands within the Flathead Indian Reservation—in an attempt to save the devastated species. The campaign for the reserve's creation originated with William Hornaday and the American Bison Society, but then gained the support of famed University of Montana biologist Morton J. Elrod and the national endorsement of President Teddy Roosevelt. Today the 18,500-acre reserve is run by the U. S. Fish and Wildlife Service and carries from 350 to 500 bison, depending upon the season. It also supports populations of elk, deer, bighorn sheep, and pronghorn antelope.

The core bison herd of 44 head at Moiese included 13 bulls and 24 cows purchased in 1908 by the American Bison Society from the estate of Kalispell entrepreneur Charles E. Conrad. These animals could trace their blood lines to the Flathead Valley's original Walking Coyote quartet (1873) and the Pablo-Allard herd of the 1880s-1890s. To this 37-head Conrad bunch, authorities added 7 donated animals: 2 from Montana; 2 from Texas; 3 from New Hampshire. Obviously, somewhere in this 44-head gene pool nestled the white-buffalo strain.

In May 1933, Range workers dubbed the wobbly calf "Whitey," although a few lobbied for "Little New Deal." Within two years he had evolved into "Old Whitey." Then officially he became "Big Medicine," in deference to the spiritual symbolism he carried for many Native Americans.

The white calf was not an albino, for he sported bluish-gray (rather than pink) eyes and tan (rather than white) hooves. In addition, he carried a wooly knob of natural brown hair atop his head—a mahogany topknot between his horns that most resembled an Eton cap.

This deviation from albinism made the young bull even more special and certainly contributed to his longevity. Although his coat annually became lightly tinged with cream or beige just after the spring molt, it bleached to an almost pure white by autumn. That color pattern lasted throughout his 26-year lifetime.

Once they stumbled on the white strain in Big Medicine's mother, Bison Range officials decided to exploit it. In 1936 they bred the three-year-old bull to his mother—a union that provided the necessary matched set of recessive albino genes. Indeed, in 1937, this union produced an albino calf named "Little Medicine."

A true albino with pink eyes, white hooves, and a pure-white coat, the young bull also was blind and deaf. When his mother rejected her disabled offspring, managers paired Little Medicine with his unidentical twin brother "Brownie" and recruited a Jersey cow to wet-nurse them both. At six months, they shipped both calves to the National Zoological Gardens in Washington, D.C. Here Little Medicine grew into a fine adult and lived for 12 years. In 1949 officials created a mannequin mount and since then have displayed Little Medicine at the National Zoo.

Within four years, Big Medicine grew into a magnificent, statuesque animal: 1,900 pounds, 6 feet tall at the hump, and 12 feet from the tip of his nose to the end of his tail. At first allowed to roam the range with the refuge herd much of the year, he spent summers with a small herd in the exhibition pasture, near the headquarters building. As a young adult, he battled other bulls for control of cows and ultimately sired scores of offspring. He ruled the exhibition-pasture herd until 1947, when he was deposed by a younger bull.

Despite the Great Depression (1929-1941) and World War II (1941-1945), Big Medicine built a solid reputation as a visitor attraction, both among Native Americans and whites. The idea of this majestic white animal—whether a spiritual icon or a remarkable curiosity—captured the imagination of a nation struggling to survive the day-to-day problems of a collapsed national economy. Individuals, families, and small groups arrived at Moiese on pilgrimages simply to look at Big Medicine and be inspired. Soon managers assigned him permanently to the exhibition pasture, both to improve his diet and to make him available to visitors.

This public interest absolutely exploded in the post-war years, as Americans abandoned gas rationing, and tourism boomed in the West. Between 1946 and 1956, Big Medicine reigned as a media king. Magazine articles, color brochures, newsreel footage, and newspaper features broadcast the story of the white monarch.

What school child in western Montana did not make a field trip

THE LEGEND OF THE
WHITE BUFFALO CALF WOMAN

One summer, long ago, the seven sacred council fires of the Lakota Sioux came together and camped. Every day they sent scouts to look for game, but the scouts found nothing, and the people were starving.

Two young men were sent out from the camp in search of buffalo. In their wanderings, they spied a beautiful young woman. She was more fair to look upon than any of the Sioux maidens. One of the young men was wise and good. His heart was brave and strong. The other was foolish.

The foolish one said, "Here is a beautiful young girl on the prairie alone. Let us capture her."

The young man with sense said, "No, that would be wrong. This is a holy woman."

They were as yet some little distance from her, and she had attracted their attention by singing. After they made signs to her, she approached and, knowing the conversation which had passed between the two young men, she said, "I am alone and in your power."

In spite of the protests of his companion, the foolish young man accosted her. Then a great mist suddenly arose and enveloped them and spread over the prairie. The air was filled with terrible hissing sounds. As suddenly as it came, the fog lifted, and it seemed to take with it numberless rattlesnakes.

Then the wise young man saw the young woman standing near him. Between her and himself, he saw the ghastly bones of his companion from which the flesh had been entirely consumed by the rattlesnakes.

The woman said, "You are wise and brave and good. I have taken pity on you and your people. Go and tell them that I know they are poor and hungry and that I will take pity on them."

The young man returned to the camp and told of what he had seen and heard. A large lodge was pitched in the center of the camp. The beautiful woman had followed the young man and, as she approached the village, she was met by the medicine man and carried on a blanket. She carried a large bundle and a fan of sage leaves, lifting them toward the sun.

A large fire was built in the tepee. Circle after circle of men, women, and children formed outside, and a great circle of fires also was formed about the lodge. All eyes were on the beautiful woman.

She opened her bundle and said, "I have taken pity on you and have brought you four things which will be good for you—tobacco, a red robe, a white shield, and a war bonnet of eagle feathers. And I have also brought you this sacred pipe which will tell you when the bison are near and plentiful by its increased weight."

She then presented the pipe to the chief medicine man of the Sioux, accompanied by much good advice. Before she left, she told the people that she would come back to them, appearing in every generation cycle.

The beautiful young woman walked across the prairie, away from the camp, and was silhouetted against the red ball of the setting sun. Suddenly she stopped and rolled over four times. The first time she turned into a black buffalo; the second time into a brown one; the third time into a red one. The fourth time she rolled over, she turned into a white buffalo calf. And a white buffalo is the most sacred living thing you could ever encounter.

The White Buffalo Calf Woman disappeared over the horizon. As soon as she had vanished, buffalo in great herds appeared, allowing themselves to be killed so that the people might survive. After that day, the Lakota honored her pipe, and buffalo were always plentiful.

> —*John G. Carter, consultant for the Smithsonian Institution, in the Washington (D.C.)* Evening Post, *November 7, 1938.*

to see Big Medicine? Montanans began calling him "the most photographed bison in America," and no one challenged their claim. Visits to the National Bison Range and the sale of Big Medicine postcards increased annually. Although the white bull never left the federal reserve, his fame spread worldwide.

In the midst of this relative media frenzy, one Montanan looked to the future. On December 8, 1953, Montana historian Ross Toole, then director of the Montana Historical Society in Helena, wrote to the superintendent of the Bison Range, John E. Schwartz. He said (Director's General Correspondence: BA-BR—"Big Medicine," 1953-1974, Montana Historical Society Archives, Helena):

> I would like to put in the bid of the Historical Society of Montana for
> the white buffalo...after the buffalo dies. It is the intent of the Historical
> Society to mount this very rare specimen and display him in a permanent
> place in the new State Historical Museum in Helena.

Subsequent correspondence between the two public servants
shows that Toole's intent was to preserve Big Medicine as an icon
for all Montanans, for all races. Superintendent Schwartz then
responded on January 22, 1954:

> ...We have received authorization from our Washington Office to
> donate the head and hide of this white buffalo to the Montana Historical
> Society upon the death of this animal...with the understanding that the
> Historical Society will bear any expenses involved in the handling and
> preparation of the specimen for display purposes....We shall plan to make
> this animal available to you as soon as it dies.

Almost immediately Toole's foresight proved fortuitous for
Montanans. During the summer of 1954, C. A. Reynolds,
Chairman of the Board of the H. D. Lee Company (as in "Lee western wear") of Kansas City, worked through high-level Department
of the Interior channels to secure Big Medicine's hide for the
planned Cowboy Hall of Fame (now National Cowboy & Western
Heritage Museum) in Oklahoma City, Oklahoma. When he was
rebuffed, he tried political sources close to fellow-Republican
President Dwight D. Eisenhower, but that avenue also failed. In the
end, the Bison Range had committed to the Montana Historical
Society, and Secretary of the Interior Douglas McKay would not
bow to pressure applied by influential Republican contributors.

In November, 1957, Ross Toole concluded a deal by which noted
Browning sculptor/taxidermist Robert Scriver agreed to prepare the
Big Medicine mount. As the white monarch's health was deterio-
rating, Scriver believed it important to prepare before the bison's

death. He wrote (Director's General Correspondence, November 5, 1957, Montana Historical Society Archives):

> I should do some advance study of the animal while it is still alive....I will start a study of his characteristics and attitude, and do some sketches and photographs by making a trip to Moiese....Also, in the event of the sudden death of the animal, I will be ready to start work immediately, day or night.

In 1954 Superintendent Schwartz suggested that Big Medicine might be killed while still in prime condition, thus producing an excellent mount. His Department of the Interior superiors, however, vetoed that plan, citing obvious public-relations problems.

The dilemma was that, by 1956, the 23-year-old Big Medicine had worn most of his teeth to the gums and could not graze. As a result, he was dropping weight quickly. So, to prolong his life, Range workers began hand-feeding the white bull in the exhibition pasture. For the last three years of his life, Big Medicine survived on a diet of steamed barley soaked in molasses, high-protein rabbit pellets, and tender, third-cut alfalfa. Nevertheless his health continued to fail.

Then, on August 25, 1959, Big Medicine died in the exhibition pasture. Radio stations in western Montana interrupted their regular programming to announce the death. The official Bison Range log read:

> On August 25, Big Medicine was noticed lying in the pasture, unable to get up. He died on the spot. "Old Whitey" had been on the Bison Range for 26 years and 3 months and was our biggest tourist attraction....He had progressively grown weaker, and his death was no surprise. He was stone deaf and nearly blind....The hide was skinned out for a full-size mount.

At the time of his death—in the heat of summer—Big Medicine had dropped to less than 1,100 pounds and his coat was in extremely poor condition. Nevertheless, Range personnel shipped the

125-pound hide to the respected Jonas Brothers processors in Denver, with instructions to hand-tan the specimen.

After skinning the animal, Range Manager C. J. Henry offered Big Medicine's meat to local Salish leaders. They refused, however, stating that it was sacred meat and not to be consumed. With no takers, the meat spoiled; workers dumped it in "Gut Gulch"—along with the carcass—on Bison Range land. When informed of Big Medicine's death on August 28, Bob Scriver and a Blackfeet assistant drove to Moiese to retrieve the carcass, to use for measurements.

Scriver described the experience at "Gut Gulch" as "plenty stinko." He continued,

> We put clothes pins on our noses and dug in among the flies and maggots to pick up as much of the body as we could salvage. In spite of maggots several inches deep, we loaded the two halves of the carcass in my truck and drove back to Browning.

During the winter of 1959-1960, Scriver finished the mannequin and awaited the tanned hide. When it arrived from Denver in July, 1960, the artist found that it had lost even more hair in the processing. Scriver requested brown buffalo hair from the Bison Range and sent it to a friend in Hollywood, California. This expert bleached the hair to match Big Medicine. Scriver used this substitute hair to patch bare spots on the hide.

Finally, in early July, 1961, the finished mount was trucked from Browning to Helena. On July 13, in elaborate ceremonies reminiscent of "the King is dead; long live the King," Montana Governor Donald Nutter officially dedicated Big Medicine. More than 250 people, both Native Americans and non-Indians, attended the celebration. The stately animal immediately became a part of the Society's permanent museum exhibit and an instant hit among visitors.

Since this dedication, the Society has presented Big Medicine as a sacred/spiritual exhibit—a treasure for all Montanans. When museum workers temporarily removed the mount in 1969 for area renovations, the reaction among visitors was immediate and heated. Since Big Medicine's return to public view in 1970, he has been visited by more than 90,000 people annually.

And, really, he survives for these admirers because of one man. Had K. Ross Toole postponed writing his letter to the Bison Range in 1953, Montanans today would be traveling to the National Cowboy & Western Heritage Museum in Oklahoma City to see their magnificent white buffalo.

Those of us who are accustomed to taking Big Medicine for granted need again to look at the odds against his birth. Through perceptive management, the white bull became a gift to all Montanans—a talisman of good fortune, harmony, and hope. But especially he became a gift to those Montana Indians whose ancestors revered the white buffalo of the Great Plains.

Since 1933 Big Medicine has reigned as a "Montana treasure"— one of a kind—and thus he will remain.

SOURCES

General texts that place the white buffalo in the context of the American bison include: William T. Hornaday, *The Extermination of the American Bison, with a Sketch of Its Discovery and Life History* (Washington, D.C.: General Printing Office, 1889); David A. Dary, *The Buffalo Book: The Full Saga of the American Animal* (Chicago: Sage, 1974); Tom McHugh, *The Time of the Buffalo* (New York: Knopf, 1972); F. G. Roe, *The North American Buffalo: a Critical Study of the Species in its Wild State* (Toronto: University of Toronto Press, 1951); Larry Barsness, *Heads, Hides and Horns: The Compleat Buffalo Book* (Fort Worth: Texas Christian University Press, 1985); Barsness, *The Bison in Art: A Graphic Chronicle of the American Bison* (Flagstaff: Northland Press, 1977).

Pieces addressing the white buffalo as a phenomenon are: George Bird Grinnell, "The White Buffalo," *Forest and Stream,* December 21, 1901; A. L. O., "The White Buffalo," *The Northwest* (August, 1885), 36; F. G. Roe, "White Buffalo," *Transactions of the Royal Society of Canada,* 3rd Series, Vol. 38 (May 1944), 155-173; Harold McCracken, "The Sacred White Buffalo," *Natural History Magazine*

(September, 1946), 304-309, 341; and Paul Fugleberg, *Buffalo Savers: The Story of the Allard-Pablo Herd* (Polson: Treasure State Publishing, 1991).

Big Medicine is the focus of a number of specific pieces: Geneva E. Wright, "Big Medicine: Heap Good Magic," *Farms Illustrated* (September, 1946), 12-14; G. E. Eichhorn, "Big Medicine Rates as Top Attraction at Bison Range," *Great Falls Tribune,* June 21, 1959; Paul Fugleberg, "Big Medicine, Famous Albino Buffalo, Attracts Worldwide Fame Without Leaving Home Pastures," (Polson) *Flathead Courier-Beacon,* June, 1961; Carl D. Hansen, "White Buffalo: the Facts and Legends—Big Medicine," *Kalispell Weekly News,* July 5, 1978; Fugleberg, "Rare Albino Buffalo Still on Display in Helena Museum," *Great Falls Tribune,* April 10, 1983. Myriad other Montana newspaper articles have addressed Big Medicine through the years.

CHAPTER FIFTEEN

REBEL WITH A CAUSE
JEANNETTE RANKIN'S SECOND "NO" VOTE IN 1941

On Sunday morning, December 7, 1941, Montana Congress-woman Jeannette Rankin bustled about her modest apartment in Washington, D.C. During that afternoon, fragmentary reports about the Japanese attack on Pearl Harbor crackled sporadically over her radio. Nevertheless, Jeannette and her sister Edna packed an overnight bag for the politician's trip to Detroit. For, on December 8, Jeannette was scheduled to deliver a speech on "international peace and nonintervention."

Although she caught the train to Detroit, Rankin rode it only as far as Pittsburgh. There she learned that President Franklin D. Roosevelt would seek a declaration of war from Congress on Monday. The representative immediately boarded another train back to the capital, arriving in the pre-dawn hours, in plenty of time for the vote.

Jeannette spent Monday morning alone, driving the streets of Washington. She had used this tactic before: it allowed her privacy, to contemplate a problem without interruption. On the issue of committing the United States to another world war, however, the Montana politician was resolute. Others might have believed her vote in doubt, but Rankin entertained no indecision. She saw only one choice—although she knew that her vote would dumbfound, frustrate, even enrage many of her Montana constituents.

Had Montanans considered carefully the history and development of their 61-year-old representative, however, they easily could have predicted her December 8 decision. For Jeannette's career always had been one of consistency and commitment.

Jeannette Rankin was born on June 11, 1880, at the family's Grant Creek Ranch, six miles outside Missoula, Montana Territory. She was the first of John and Olive Rankin's seven children—six girls and a boy. John Rankin was a successful rancher and businessman in western Montana, and Olive had worked as a schoolteacher before their marriage. All six of the surviving children (one had died in infancy) graduated from the University of Montana, and many of them enjoyed public-service careers.

After Jeannette graduated in 1902, with a degree in biology, she taught school near Missoula and in Whitehall. By 1908 she had enrolled at the New York School of Philanthropy, working in social welfare. Later she attended the University of Washington, where she became involved in the Washington State suffrage campaign.

Particularly this experience proved valuable, for she returned to Montana and became an organizer of the Montana suffrage movement after 1911. She stumped the state for the woman's vote and became Montana's most visible suffrage leader—young, vivacious, well-spoken, unafraid, the personification of the "new voting woman."

Jeannette's philosophy embraced mainstream Progressivism, as did that of her politically-active brother, Wellington D. Rankin. Both rejoiced when the Montana electorate passed woman suffrage in 1914.

Given the strength of Progressivism in the state, Wellington then advised Jeannette to run for national office—and he served as her campaign manager. She was successful in the 1916 election and became one of Montana's two at-large representatives. At a time when most women in the nation were denied the right to vote, Rankin had become the first woman to sit in the U.S. Congress.

Rankin in a publicity photograph for her second Congressional campaign, 1940.
Photo courtesy Montana Historical Society Helena

The 36-year-old representative's very first vote (April 6, 1917) addressed the emotional issue of U.S. entry into World War I. With 55 Congressmen, Jeannette opposed American involvement, stating: "I wish to stand by my country, but I cannot vote for war. I vote 'No!'" She subsequently remarked,

> I have always felt that there was significance in the fact that the first woman who was ever asked in Congress what she thought about war, said "No!"

Miss Rankin would reflect that this vote constituted the single most important act of her life, because of the way that it crystallized her thinking from that point forward. In August 1917, she noted:

> I tried to let Montana people know that, whenever a question arose on which I had received no definite instructions, I would vote in accordance with my highest ideals.

And more and more those ideals were being shaped by the concept of international peace. On the floor of the House, in December 1917, she spoke even more candidly:

> I believe that war is a stupid and a futile way of attempting to settle international difficulties....I believe war can be avoided and will be avoided when the people...have the controlling voice in their government.

Nevertheless, the Congresswoman's opposition to such a popular war proved critical when she sought reelection in 1918. On Wellington's advice, she ran for the U.S. Senate, but was defeated soundly in the Republican primary. She then ran in the general election as a National Party candidate, but again was defeated. During the campaigns, Jeannette argued that, as a pacifist/feminist, her ultimate goal was humanitarianism. But in the super-patriot hysteria that swept across Montana during World War I, her argument found few receptive ears.

Jeannette Rankin's lifelong commitment to peace changed form after her 1918 defeats. For the next two decades, she signed on with a series of national advocate groups as a grass-roots organizer. From the Women's International League for Peace and Freedom, to the Georgia Peace Society, to the Women's Peace Union, to the National Council for the Prevention of War, she used both Montana and her adopted home of Georgia as bases of operation.

During the 1920s and the 1930s, Rankin gradually refined a peace philosophy that supported international cooperation, but opposed American intervention in foreign situations. Although not an isolationist (as had become Montana Senator Burton K. Wheeler during the 1930s), Jeannette advocated the use of American military force only in defense of the continental United States.

The summers that Jeannette spent in Europe (1931-1937) solidified these beliefs, to which she testified before Congressional committees during the mid-1930s. Her recommendations to achieve international peace involved the removal of profit-making from war and expanding the American electorate by registering more women. But always she saw peace first as a woman's mission:

> The peace problem is a woman's problem. Disarmament will not be won without their aid. So long as they shirk…something will be radically wanting in the peace activities of the public and the state….Therefore, peace is a woman's job.

Finally, in 1939, Jeannette resolved to run again for Congress. From this most-public platform she better could broadcast her views on peace. Again with the financial help and political advice of her brother Wellington, Rankin campaigned tirelessly in Montana's First (Western) District as a Republican pacifist. Her campaign slogan revealed no evasion: "Prepare to the limit for defense; keep our men out of Europe!"

Rankin received the endorsement of Senator Wheeler, also running for reelection in 1940. Moreover she appealed to both labor and women, and she benefited from a strong peace sentiment in the district. In November 1940, Rankin defeated liberal Democrat Jerry O'Connell by more than 9,000 votes. She also became one of the few Republicans elected despite Roosevelt's national sweep to a third consecutive term.

The Congress to which Jeannette returned in the spring of 1941 was somewhat different from that of 1917—in that it included five other women in the House and two women in the Senate. No representative worked more diligently for peace during 1941 than did Rankin. She fought both the Lend-Lease Bill and legislation to implement the draft; she called for a national election to determine American opinions about entering the European war.

As 1941 progressed, however, American public opinion shifted from its firm resolve never to be drawn into foreign conflicts. Although Rankin's mail, during the summer of 1941, ran as high as 95 percent against going to war, national sentiment differed greatly. By early December, national polls showed that almost 75 percent of the American public supported the country's involvement in the European war on some basis.

So now we return to Jeannette, whom we left driving alone through the streets of Washington on the morning of December 8—effectively avoiding phone calls and dodging visitors who wished to influence her vote.

As in 1917, she consulted Wellington by phone. As in 1917, Wellington advised her to vote for war. (His precise words in 1917 were: "Vote a man's vote!") Still, anyone who had followed the career of "the lady from Montana" knew what she would do—if she had the courage to do it.

President Roosevelt arrived at the Capitol shortly after noon on Monday and requested a declaration of war against Japan. In the House a motion was made to suspend the rules and pass the resolution on a voice vote, but Miss Rankin objected and killed the motion. Although she tried to force a floor debate on the issue, she was shouted down. The roll-call vote proceeded.

From the back of the chamber, when her name was called, Rankin cast a firm "No!" She then violated protocol by commenting on her vote: "As a woman I cannot go to war, and I refuse to send anyone else."

A chorus of hisses and boos rose from the floor and the packed galleries and cascaded down on her. Although colleagues rushed to her desk to persuade her to change her mind, Jeannette remained obdurate. By 1:30 p.m., Congress had passed a declaration of war, with only a single dissenting vote: 82-0 in the Senate, and 388-1 in the House.

Upon leaving the safety of the House chamber, Rankin was accosted by boisterous, outraged citizens who demanded that she change her vote. To avoid their pushing, shouting, and obscenities, she ducked into a phone booth and called Capitol police for protection. Within minutes they were escorting her to her office, where two officers remained through the afternoon.

Jeannette's staff shielded her from reporters and critics by locking the office door and deflecting all incoming calls. She made a single call, to Wellington in Helena, who huffed unsympathetically, "Montana is 110 percent against you!" She then began to draft a letter to her constituents explaining her vote. That evening, safe in her small apartment, Jeannette remarked to her sister Edna, "I have nothing left now, except my integrity."

Public reaction to Congresswoman Rankin's vote proved both swift and hostile. Vilified by national radio commentators and newspaper columnists, Rankin also received hundreds of letters of condemnation. A sampling:

> Why in hell don't you leave that job. You disgrace the office you hold. Damn you!

You are the only living argument against giving unmarried women the vote.

You are an old fossil. Never should you have been an official of any kind—rather an undertaker's assistant, for women only.

Did the Nazis promise you a husband for your vote?

Over the course of several months, letters from Montana slightly would favor her vote—and mail from throughout the Western Hemisphere ran 10-to-1 supporting her stand on the war. However, the immediate, vocal reaction was overwhelmingly antagonistic.

Particularly the reaction of Montanans to their Congresswoman's vote was quick and dirty—especially among Republicans. Into the breach jumped prominent Montana Republican (former president of the Montana Republican Central Committee and Republican National Committeeman) Dan Whetstone, longtime editor/publisher of the (Cut Bank) *Pioneer Press.* On December 8, just hours after the Congressional vote, Whetstone fired off a telegram to Representative Rankin and then put its text on the Associated Press wire:

> Messages from all parts of Montana indicate disappointment over your attitude in failing to support the war decision. I urge and beseech you to redeem Montana's honor and loyalty by changing your vote as early as possible.

Other Montana groups also moved quickly to distance themselves from the maverick Republican representative. For example, the executive committee of the Montana American Legion, through its departmental commander James T. Annin of Columbus, resolved:

> …Congresswoman Rankin's vote is not representative of the attitude and sentiment of her constituents—and we do emphatically declare that such vote is deplored and regretted by the entire membership of the American Legion of Montana.

The committee stopped just short of demanding Jeannette's immediate resignation from Congress.

Similarly, Fred L. Hill of Great Falls, the vice-chairman of the Young Republican Clubs of Montana, wired Rankin's office:

> Your vote [is] a terrible disappointment to the Republican Party, the State of Montana, and the United States. No consideration can excuse it. It was not representative of the Young Republicans of this state and it should be changed.

And, in a clearly sexist manner, the Young Republican Club of Harlem, Montana, snarled:

> You made an ass out of yourself, trying to be like a man. Now come home like a lady.

In the days immediately following the surprise attack on Pearl Harbor, the entire nation suffered a chaotic rush of changing emotions: surprise, shock; dismay, confusion, anger, determination. With this sequence working at different levels, in different parts of the country, whenever the "anger" emotion was reached, Jeannette Rankin became the easiest target for that emotion.

Perhaps most surprising and dismaying to Rankin was her unexpected repudiation by small women's groups across the state. For instance, the Missoula Woman's Club challenged Jeannette's integrity (*Daily Missoulian*, December 13, 1941):

> At a meeting of the Woman's Club in Orchard Homes [during the 1940 campaign], you promised not to vote for war except in case of aggression. The United States was maliciously attacked by Japan. Your vote does not represent the women of this club, who helped to put you in office.

Similar responses came from such disparate organizations as the Missoula chapter of the American Association of University

Women, the Women's Auxiliary of the Dawson Post of the American Legion in Glendive, the Hinsdale Woman's Club, and the Business and Professional Women's Club of Ekalaka.

Less painful should have been the almost ridiculous, anachronistic telegram received by Rankin from the Cowpokes Union of Deer Lodge, Montana:

> In view of the bad storms in the offing and the way you botched up the last branding, we would like to have you saddle up your bronc, tie your bedroll on behind, and just ride home—as we have decided it best to let the rest of our critters run as mavericks until we have a chance to send a new rep after the next election.

During December, 1941, "the lady from Montana" graphically was reminded what loneliness the combination of pacifism and dissent could produce. Among the quickest of critics appeared Neil D. Healy of Columbus, chairman of the Montana Young Republicans Club. On December 8 he wired to Representative Rankin:

> Your vote on the Japanese war issue is unquestionably contrary to the belief of the great majority of Montana Young Republicans. On their behalf an explanation of your vote is urgently requested.

Jeannette, however, already had penned a draft of her rationale when she received Healy's wire. Although Rankin's staff sent airmail copies of this explanation to all of the newspapers in Montana's Western District, it appeared in only a few publications. Her statement was printed most prominently in the (Deer Lodge) *Silver State Post*, the (Plains) *Plainsman*, the *Daily Missoulian*, the (Libby) *Western News*, and the (Helena) *People's Voice*. In her public release, Jeannette reasoned:

> December 8, 1941—When I cast the only vote against war, I remembered

the promise I had made during my campaign for election to do everything possible to keep this country out of war. I was thinking of the pledges I had made to the mothers and fathers of Montana that I would do all in my power to prevent their sons from being slaughtered on foreign battlefields.

…But now we are sending American men and boys into a war to "protect" the United States, and doing it based only on a few brief, incomplete radio reports, which do not pretend to give the entire story.

It may be that it is right for us to enter the conflict with Japan. If so, it is my belief that all the facts surrounding the present situation should be brought into the open and given to the Congress and the American people.

So in casting my vote today, I voted my convictions and redeemed my campaign pledges. I feel I voted as the mothers would have had me vote.

Editorial response to the Congresswoman's statement varied little. Typical were two comments:

> As far as we are concerned, her explanation is totally unsatisfactory
> —Whitefish Pilot, *December 16, 1941*
>
> It is not convincing
> —Kalispell Times, *December 11, 1941*

In this context, noted editor Tom Stout, of the Lewistown *Democrat-News* (December 15, 1941), proved the most loquacious:

> Our firm determination to maintain an uncritical attitude toward Congresswoman Jeannette Rankin…was sadly weakened when we…read her explanation of her vote. Had Miss Rankin simply stood on her record as a sincere pacifist who believes that war is never justifiable under any circumstances, we would have been entirely willing to let the matter stand (as we intend to do anyway), but her utterly silly explanation strains that resolution to the breaking point.

More and more obviously, the Montana representative could not recapture the support of her constituency through reason—given the national fervor for waging war.

The extent to which Congresswoman Rankin had isolated herself in the House was demonstrated on Thursday, December 11, when Congress voted on separate resolutions declaring war on Germany and Italy. In the Senate, the two resolutions passed 88-0 and 90-0, respectively; in the House the vote ran 393-0 and 399-0, respectively. In this situation, Rankin again violated protocol by simply voting "present" in each roll call—in effect casting a somewhat softer "No" vote than she had cast on Monday.

Meanwhile, adverse reaction to Jeannette's votes mushroomed in Montana. Editorial pages across the state criticized her initial "No" vote, employing either outrage or sarcasm or condescension. For example, J. C. Hallack of the *Glasgow Messenger* (December 11, 1941) commented:

> Only one voice registered a negative vote. This single negative vote was cast by a fanatical woman who failed to see beyond the confines of her own warped perspective. It is regrettable that she is from Montana, because she certainly is not representing Montana's feeling or desires.

Harry Billings, editor of the *Camas Hot Springs Exchange*, developed this sentiment further (December 11, 1941):

> We can't condemn Miss Rankin for being a traitor to America, because we don't believe she is. But we do pity her ignorance, stupidity, and blindness.
>
> America being a free country precludes the possibility of recalling Miss Rankin from Washington, unless she commits a felony. However, we lend our voice to that of Dan Whetstone and thousands of other Montanans that Miss Rankin either change her vote and "remove the stain from Montana" or else resign!

Interestingly the Anaconda Copper Mining Company's newspaper chain adopted a relatively non-controversial, condescending editorial position—as illustrated by the chain's flagship paper, the (Butte) *Montana Standard* (December 10, 1941):

> Miss Rankin, of course, has her own conscience to answer to. Her courage is admirable. But we Montanans regret her judgment....

Other Montana newspapers, however, commented with disgust and hatred. For example, the Miles City *Daily Star* commented:

> ...Being from Montana, Miss Rankin should have remembered that, in the days of the Vigilantes, lawlessness was cleaned up now and then by a good public hanging. That is the method that has to be applied to Japan, and no one should have known that better than Miss Rankin.
>
> All we can do now is offer our humble and respectful apologies to the rest of the states of the United States—and see to it that Jeannette Rankin is gracefully retired from representing us in the halls of Congress at the end of her term next year.

Other editors reached deeper into the emotional bag and mixed cute with crude. "Bing," the owner of the *Grass Range Review*, remarked:

> Congresswoman Jeanette [sic] Rankin had another swooning spell and was the only member of the House to vote against war with Japan. The Japs taught us a dear lesson, and Jeanette did the same for the voters of the First District of Montana.

With an editorial entitled "Bye, Bye, Jeannette," the *Harlowton Press* joined a growing group of Republican papers that attacked Rankin (December 13, 1941):

> Montana has little to be proud of in its Western District representative to Congress. Jeannette Rankin's lone vote in support of Japan's ruthless military

regime may be her own personal conviction, but it certainly is in accord with the views of Hitler, Benito, Hirohito and Company. We trust she will call on these gentlemen for her December check and further wages....We think western Montana should recall Miss Rankin from Washington.

And the editor of the Choteau *Acantha* devised an even more graphic punishment (December 22, 1941):

> For Jeannette Rankin—an order that she be publicly spanked on the floor of the House. That an old-fashioned hairbrush be used, as per the good old days. And be it specifically stipulated that there be no silk, rayon, or any other fabric between the backside of the hairbrush and the point of contact with Jeannette's anatomy.

Although editorial comment ran overwhelmingly against the Congresswoman's action, it took Montana citizens, in vitriolic "letters to the editor" to deride Rankin with nicknames. She was variously called: "Jeannette from Georgia"; "Jap Lover"; "Bitch Rankin"; "Skunk"; "Fuzzy-thinking Fanatic"; "Traitor Nazi"; "Pig Rankin." Writing in the (Libby) *Western News* (December 18, 1941), "A Mother" suggested that Jeannette "will evermore be known as 'Montana's Shame.'" And a contributor to the *Great Falls Tribune* (December 14, 1941) commented that, hereafter, we should "refer to our Montana congressman as 'Japanette Rankin.'"

Yet these same "letters to the editor" columns (although much less popular forums than they are today) carried what little public support existed for Rankin. For example, Joan Wheeler, a Missoula County High School junior, reasoned in the *Daily Missoulian* (December 17, 1941):

> ...Whether we agree with that woman or not, she had the God-given right to stand up and claim her right of free speech, without a mob of panic-stricken people forgetting what democracy means, and demanding her job.

The people must agree that, when this woman was elected, everyone knew her platform. Hats off to this woman who has the strength of her convictions.

In a commendable act of courage, the (Red Lodge) *Carbon County News* ran a lengthy front-page editorial (December 19, 1941) defending Rankin's actions. But it was left to H. S. Bruce, managing editor of the (Helena) *People's Voice* to pen the most supportive observations, under the title "388-to-1."

> Republican Representative Jeannette Rankin of Montana was booed in the House of Representatives Monday. Americans should instead thank God that they have before them her splendid example of courage and conviction….That lone "one," linked with the "388," should remind us of the devotion of our purpose….Now, and even more when the going gets tough, the sight of the figures "388-1" should make us buck up and fight with renewed courage and conviction.
>
> Had the vote been "389-0," we should have no prominent reminder, no simple expression of the values for which we fight. Miss Rankin, in doing her duty to her country as she saw fit, has truly made a great contribution to America and the cause upon which we embark.

Such complimentary remarks on Rankin's stand remained infrequent through December 1941, and into the next year. Rather, apocryphal stories developed (as they had in 1917) that Jeannette wept openly prior to and/or during her war vote. Another wire-service story dismissed Rankin with an overtly sexist description (Lewistown *Democrat-News,* December 12, 1941):

> It had been a terrible week for Miss Rankin—and she showed it. Her fluffy, gray, bobbed hair was not as neatly coiffured as on Monday. The part was a bit irregular. Instead of forming a halo accenting her dark, vivacious eyes and clear skin, her hair was a bit limp.
>
> She had on a sapphire-blue wool frock and around her neck she wore a

long silver chain with a large silver medallion. On her left arm was a match-
ing bracelet. She had on her horn-rimmed glasses....

As the clerk's voice droned through the alphabet, nearer and nearer to
"R," Miss Rankin nervously clasped and unclasped her handbag....

Almost incredibly, not a single Montana editor, in his annual
Christmas editorial for 1941, chose to comment on Representative
Rankin's December 8 vote in the context of the traditional "Peace
on earth; good will to men" message.

Jeannette Rankin's "No" vote in 1941 so isolated her from the
Congressional mainstream that she proved relatively ineffective for
the remainder of her term. She participated in few floor debates and
concentrated on ways to mitigate the effects of war on her constituents—for example, by strengthening draft deferments. Given
the national preoccupation with the war effort, however, Rankin
was simply forgotten.

Jeannette's primary project during her last year in Congress was
to conduct an investigation of possible collusion between President
Roosevelt and British Prime Minister Winston Churchill to draw
the United States into World War II. She also dealt with the possi-
bility that the surprise attack on Pearl Harbor might have been
known to President Roosevelt and could have been avoided.

Rankin printed her findings in the *Congressional Record* on
December 8, 1942—the anniversary of her "No" vote. Scholarly
research in this field continues to support Rankin's conclusions and
only confirms the clarity of her thought. It ties Roosevelt to Churchill
in just such a plan to draw the U.S. into the European war. And it supports the position that Roosevelt knew something about the Japanese
targeting Pearl Harbor before the surprise attack occurred.

After her second term, Jeannette never again ran for public office.
She returned to her Georgia home, with frequent visits to Montana,
and immersed herself again in the cause of international peace. She
traveled to India seven times between 1946 and 1971 to study the

pacifist methods of Mohandas Gandhi and Jawaharlal Nehru. She also investigated pacifism in such diverse cultures as those in South America, Africa, Indonesia, Russia, Turkey, Ireland, and Czechoslovakia during this 25-year period.

Rankin's last public prominence appeared in the late 1960s, when anti-Vietnam War protesters organized the "Jeannette Rankin Brigade." And she marched at the head of the brigade in Washington, D.C., on January 15, 1968, leading thousands of women in an anti-war protest. The resultant publicity returned Rankin to the public eye—speaking to a third generation of Americans on the topic of peace as an alternative to war.

And therein lies Jeannette Rankin's influence on American life, on American politics, and on American thought. She developed her philosophy and remained true to it throughout her life—regardless of public opinion and political consequences. That philosophy coincided with popular American thought only cyclically—immediately prior to World War I, just before World War II, and during the Vietnam War.

What is enduring about Montana Representative Rankin is her courage. She remained principled and committed throughout her life, regardless of political repercussions. She remained firm in her beliefs, regardless of popular opinion.

It is that courage which was praised by the eminent editor William Allen White in his *Emporia* (Kansas) *Gazette* shortly after Rankin's December 8 "No" vote:

> When, in a hundred years from now, courage—sheer courage based upon moral indignation—is celebrated in this country, the name of Jeannette Rankin, who stood firm in folly for her faith, will be written in monumental bronze—not for what she did, but for the way that she did it.
>
> Probably a hundred men in Congress would have liked to do what she did. Not one of them had the courage to do it. The *Gazette* entirely disagrees with the wisdom of her position. But, Lord, it was a brave thing she did!

Now, more than fifty years after that second "No" vote, that is why Montanans recognize and revere Jeannette Rankin. And they do recognize and revere her. In 1980 Ms. Terry Mimnaugh's life-size statue of Jeannette was placed on the first-floor landing of the Montana State Capitol. In 1985 a duplicate of the Mimnaugh statue filled Montana's second spot in Statuary Hall in the national Capitol in Washington, D.C.—where she joined Charlie Russell.

Finally, Montanans have come to recognize and revere Jeannette Rankin for her remarkable career. She has proven to be, truly, "a rebel with a cause."

SOURCES

Important biographical works on Jeannette Rankin include: Kevin S. Giles, *Flight of the Dove: The Story of Jeannette Rankin* (Beaverton, Oregon: Touchstone Press, 1980); Hannah Josephson, *Jeannette Rankin: First Lady in Congress, A Biography* (New York: Bobbs-Merrill, 1974); Mary Barmeyer O'Brien, *Jeannette Rankin, 1880-1973: Bright Star in the Big Sky* (Helena: Falcon Press, 1995)—juvenile.

Other solid background sources, more difficult to obtain, are: John C. Board, "The Lady from Montana: Jeannette Rankin," M.A. thesis, University of Wyoming-Laramie, 1964; Ted C. Harris, "Jeannette Rankin: Suffragist, First Woman Elected to Congress, and Pacifist," Ph.D. dissertation, University of Georgia, 1972; Ronald Schaeffer, "Jeannette Rankin: Progressive Isolationist," Ph.D. dissertation, Princeton University, 1959; Doris Buck Ward, "The Winning of Woman Suffrage in Montana," M.A. thesis, Montana State University-Bozeman, 1974.

Periodical pieces tend to concentrate on specific aspects of Rankin's life: Harriet Hyman Alonzo, "Jeannette Rankin and the Women's Peace Union," *Montana: The Magazine of Western History*, 39, #2 (Spring, 1989), 34-49; John C. Board, "Jeannette Rankin: the Lady from Montana," *Montana: The Magazine of Western History*, 17, #3 (Summer, 1967), 2-17; Mackey Brown, "Montana's First Woman Politician—A Recollection of Jeannette Rankin Campaigning," *Montana Business Quarterly*, 9, #4 (Autumn, 1971), 23-26; T. A. Larson, "Montana Women and the Battle for the Ballot: Woman Suffrage in the Treasure State," *Montana: The Magazine of Western History*, 23, #1 (Winter, 1973), 24-31.

See also: Joan Hoff Wilson, "'Peace Is a Woman's Job...'—Jeannette Rankin and American Foreign Policy: the Origins of Her Pacifism," *Montana: The Magazine of Western History,* 30, #1 (Winter, 1980), 28-41; Wilson, "'Peace Is a Woman's Job…'—Jeannette Rankin and American Foreign Policy: Her Lifework as a Pacifist," *Montana: The Magazine of Western History,* 30, #2 (Spring, 1980), 38-53; Ted C. Harris, "Jeannette Rankin in Georgia," *Georgia Historical Quarterly,* 58, #1 (Spring, 1974), 55-77.

This chapter's survey of Montanans' reactions to Rankin's second "No" vote depends heavily on the wealth of Montana daily and weekly newspapers—all of which were perused for the month of December 1941.

INDEX